Settler Memory

KEVIN BRUYNEEL

Settler Memory

The Disavowal of Indigeneity and the
Politics of Race in the United States

The University of North Carolina Press Chapel Hill

This book was published with the assistance of the Anniversary Fund of the University of North Carolina Press.

Set in Arno Pro by Westchester Publishing Services
Manufactured in the United States of America

The University of North Carolina Press has been a member of the
Green Press Initiative since 2003.

Library of Congress Cataloging-in-Publication Data
Names: Bruyneel, Kevin, author.
Title: Settler memory : the disavowal of indigeneity and the politics of race
    in the United States / Kevin Bruyneel.
Other titles: Critical indigeneities.
Description: Chapel Hill : University of North Carolina Press, [2021] |
    Series: Critical indigeneities | Includes bibliographical references and index.
Identifiers: LCCN 2021007916 | ISBN 9781469665221 (cloth) |
    ISBN 9781469665238 (paperback) | ISBN 9781469665245 (ebook)
Subjects: LCSH: Whites—United States—Relations with Indians. | Indians of North America—
    Social conditions. | Racism—United States. | Imperialism. | United States—Race relations.
Classification: LCC E98.S67 B78 2021 | DDC 305.800973—dc23
LC record available at https://lccn.loc.gov/2021007916

Cover illustration: Plains of Johnson County, Wyoming. Photograph by Carol M. Highsmith,
courtesy of the Gates Frontiers Fund Wyoming Collection within the Carol M. Highsmith
Archive, Library of Congress, Prints and Photograph Division (LCCN 2017884700).

To Pagan

Contents

Illustration

Preface

In the words of Lee Maracle, memory is "tricky," "slippery," and "powerful."[1] Memory is never seamlessly bound nor concretely sure-footed. It is subject to new stimuli, waning importance, conflicting interests, and colliding memories. Memory is also fundamental to individual and collective identities in and through time. For Maracle's part, she is speaking about how memory "serves" her community, the Stó:lō Nation ("people of the river") of the Coast Salish peoples, and for Indigenous peoples more generally. As she notes, for Stó:lō people, "our memories stretch back for thousands of years, but we don't think about them until the condition for the use of memory ripens and calls us to remember."[2] By contrast, "when settlers ask us to 'forget the past,' they are asking us to remain powerless. . . . They are also asking us to be stupid."[3] Maracle contrasts Indigenous peoples' process of collective remembrance as a mode of renewal and redetermination to settler efforts to ward off the power of memory, specifically that of conquest, colonialism, settlement, and Indigenous persistence and resistance. *Settler Memory* takes up this matter of the collective and political relationship to memory not primarily as it concerns what Indigenous peoples remember or forget but rather as it relates to how and what settler societies remember, forget, and disavow regarding colonialism and Indigenous peoples.

Maracle speaks to the dynamics of her and other Indigenous peoples' collective memories in a way that I cannot. I am not of an Indigenous nation, formally or informally. I do share with Maracle a certain ancestral, geographic history, but not via Indigeneity. My ancestry is that of white settlers to Canada, specifically to the unceded traditional territories of the Coast Salish peoples of the Musqueam, Squamish, and Tsleil-Waututh Nations, in the area also known as Greater Vancouver. Constructing my ancestry in this way invokes both colonialism and settlement as producing my subject position historically and to this day. It is, if a small step, a refusal to disavow the tricky, slippery, and powerful political role that memory serves for us all, in contested and complicated ways. While my focus of study is different from that pursued by Maracle, I find her insights generative for fashioning collective memories that offer alternative political and social imaginaries to those that predominate in settler colonial contexts. Thus, I return to Maracle every so often for conceptual and lyrical provocation and inspiration for how to "pull the moments of our story together, search for its possibilities, imagine how this story, these moments can contribute to the good life and create a picture from them."[4]

While the narrative of the preface thus far concerns the Canadian settler colonial context, this book's focus is the United States, where I have resided for many years. I moved to the other side of the settler colonial border when I was twenty-five to attend graduate school and have lived here ever since, now in Somerville, Massachusetts, the traditional territories of the Massachusett people. During that time, I have grappled with what it means to be, in the least, white and settler in a U.S. context in which the racial identity of whiteness is increasingly up for some measurable, though still insufficient, political and scholarly attention through concepts such as *white privilege*.[5] By contrast, the settler aspect of my and millions of other white people's social, political, and economic standing remains virtually absent from public and scholarly discourse. This is not to say Canada is much better in this regard. For Canada is, as I am inclined to say to those who dare to celebrate it, the world's most overrated country, often lauded for its multiculturalism and seeming niceness when in fact it was founded as and continues to be a white supremacist settler colonial state.[6] Still, it is in the United States context where I find the inattention to settler colonialism and Indigeneity to be striking and even more concerning given U.S. imperial influence in the world. This is a matter of particular urgency for me to account for and offer ways to address given that, while most of my published work is in the fields of Indigenous studies and settler colonialism, my disciplines of training and other fields of study and teaching are U.S. politics, political theory, critical race studies, and whiteness studies. Except for Indigenous studies and settler colonial studies, these fields often reproduce, habitually more than intentionally, the constitutive absences of Indigeneity and settler colonialism that persist in general U.S. discourse, politics, and popular culture. This is something I came to realize even more as I sought to research and teach directly at the intersection of race and Indigenous studies.

For over twenty years, I have taught political theory, U.S. politics, Indigenous studies, and critical race studies, all in the United States. In so doing, I persistently faced—and more often than not failed!—the challenge of how to incorporate and connect Indigenous politics and settler colonialism to the topics of U.S. politics, political theory, and race studies, especially the structures and practices of white supremacy and Black radical politics. The problem was not a lack of worthwhile and engaging materials but rather the presence of settler colonial assumptions that even some of the most influential frameworks, narratives, and writers do not attend to, or do so intermittently, even hesitantly. This I discovered to be evidence of the work of settler memory, reflective rarely of the intentionality or even necessarily subject position of the writers themselves but rather of a formative, if never seamless and often contested, collective memory of the politics of race in the United States.

Settler memory refers to the way in which a settler society habitually reproduces memories of Indigenous people's history and of settler colonial violence and dispossession and in the same moment undercuts the political relevance of this memory by disavowing the presence of Indigenous people as contemporary agents and of settler colonialism as a persistent shaping force.[7] What I call the *work of settler memory* refers to a process of remembering and disavowing Indigenous political agency, colonialist dispossession, and violence toward Indigenous peoples. In the U.S. context, one can locate settler memory at work in place names (numerous states, cities, streets, and other topographical markers, including Wall Street, initially built as a wall to protect Dutch settlers from Indigenous people);[8] sports team names past and present (e.g., Washington Redsk*ns, Kansas City Chiefs); holidays and holiday rituals (e.g., Thanksgiving and Columbus Day); consumer products (e.g., Jeep Cherokee, Pontiac); literary, film, and television stories (e.g., *Pocahontas*, *The Last of the Mohicans*, and the many cowboy-and-Indian-themed shows); U.S. military nomenclature (e.g., Black Hawk and Apache helicopters); and the myths and narratives (e.g., manifest destiny) that have a shaping force on the story of the nation that calls itself America. These are examples of what I refer to as *mnemonic* devices that prompt and reproduce settler memory. The reach and range of this list indicates that the mnemonic reminders of the history of Indigenous peoples and colonialism on these lands are ubiquitous, just as is the accompanying disavowal of the social and political relevance of Indigenous people's politics and of settler colonialism.

I attend to collective memory—and will expand on it more in the book's introduction —because it is an important cultural and political function and process for defining and situating a people in and through time, in relationship to other people, and often in relationship to territory. For this reason, memory is a fundamental component of our political and collective lives. The terms and meanings of collective memories are contested political realms, never wholly encompassing nor singular. Collective memories are variously constructed, reaffirmed, argued over, colliding, and refashioned through such means as elite narratives, popular culture, historical teachings, national and communal myths, social and political movements, mainstream politics, and public memorials. In June 2020, we saw this play out publicly as statues of Confederate generals and Christopher Columbus, among others, were top-pled and even beheaded by activists.[9] People who defend these statues often accuse those who take them down of seeking to "erase history."[10] However, when activists seek to remove a statue they engage in the politics of memory not to deny or forget the past but to actively remember and make consequen-tial the past's meaning and legacy for the present. As P. J. Brendese notes: "The phrase *politics of memory* refers to the power relations that shape what is available to be remembered, who is permitted to remember, and the practices, occasions, and timing of remembering and forgetting."[11] I would adjust this definition slightly to focus not only on the *what* of remembrance but the *how* of it, attending to the forms that memories take—often contested forms over the same topic, the same *what*—as defining the heart of a politics of memory. In this regard, then, efforts to topple or decapitate such statues as that of Con-federate leaders and Columbus do not deny the history of slavery and colonial conquest but rather seek to place the violence and horror that these statues represent at the center of our understanding of their relevance for our time. These efforts often collide with those who articulate collective memories that defend these memorials by disavowing their relationship to racial and colo-nial meaning either in the past itself or as it regards the past's impact on the present. To speak of colliding forces of memory is to refuse the idea of memo-ries as engaged in what Michael Rothberg aptly critiques as a "zero-sum game" that does not account for how such collisions or contests "produce not less memory but more, even if the field of public memory remains unequal."[12]

This book examines the colliding forces in the politics of memory by tak-ing account of the role of settler memory in the stories passed on by some of the influential scholarly narratives, frameworks, and writers that attend to the history, meaning, and lessons of the political life of race in the United States. By the political life of race, I mean the function of this concept in the creation and maintenance of white supremacy in its political, economic, and sociocul-tural practices and structures. A number of the narratives, frameworks, and authors I discuss, such as that concerning Bacon's Rebellion in the seventeenth century, the Reconstruction era of the nineteenth century, and the work of James Baldwin, have proven vital for those of us seeking to understand the history of U.S. white supremacy, the political meaning of whiteness, the inter-relationship of race and class, the dynamics of structural oppression, and the theory and politics of antiracist resistance. I count myself among those in-debted to them and many others I will discuss, as they taught me how to criti-cally analyze and make sense of U.S. racial history and politics. Still, it became increasingly clear to me that even some of the formative frameworks on race politics and history in political theory, critical race studies, and whiteness studies habitually replicate the settler memory of Indigenous people and settler colonialism, reproducing rather than refusing a process that occurs in the wider U.S. political culture. This study, then, is an intervention in and a reimagining of the popular memories of race politics in order to draw out the "tricky" and "slippery" ways in which the constitutive relationships of, in particular, white supremacy to colonialism, enslavement to dispossession, labor to land, Blackness to Indigeneity, and whiteness to settlerness are elided. I believe this effort is particularly urgent for white settlers, especially those students and scholars writing on white supremacy, colonialism, enslavement, dispossession, labor, land, Blackness, Indigeneity, and whiteness, as we must engage with how the meaning of our whiteness is intertwined with the history and present of conquest and settlement. To this end, in the book I set out settler memory as a powerful function of memory in settler colonial societies, consider the implication for the politics of race as we commonly know and understand it, and then offer ways to see what the refusal of settler memory might mean for generating or centering alternative political imaginaries and memories. The works of Indigenous and Black writers and activists who engage the fraught relationship of the past in the present have consistently provoked me to refuse the comfort of settler memory in my scholarship, teaching, and political commitments, in particular as it concerns the relationship between abolitionist and decolonization politics.

For example, I read a resistance to and a refusal of the workings of settler memory in Oglala Lakota poet Layli Long Soldier's poem *Whereas*, which is a word used exactly twenty times in the Native American apology resolution signed by President Barack Obama on December 19, 2009. This resolution is an apology for the harm done to Indigenous peoples, but the resolution expressly does not commit the United States to any sort of tangible form of action to address the damage done. Long Soldier thus posits the oft used word "whereas" in the resolution as emblematic of a settler poetics that gestures toward and then away from material and political accountability for the past and present of colonialism in the United States. Long Soldier draws out how the settler "whereas" of Obama's apology disavows the political accountability and collective responsibility of the United States for the violent actions and territorial dispossessions for which Obama ostensibly apologized.[13] I will return to Long Soldier's poem in the book's conclusion, but among the points she makes here is that settler colonialism's past is not really of the past for Indigenous peoples nor for the settler society; the damage continues as does resistance to it. In a similar vein, Black studies and literature scholar Christina Sharpe proposes thinking of Black being as existing "*in* the wake," which is "to occupy and be occupied by the continuous and changing present of slavery's as yet unresolved unfolding."[14] Here, I link Long Soldier and Sharpe for the distinctive ways in which they speak to how, in Sharpe's words, the "past that is not past reappears, always, to rupture the present."[15] To address these persistent ruptures of the past upon the present, Sharpe suggests the power of *wake work*, which is "a mode of inhabiting *and* rupturing this episteme with our known lived and un/imaginable lives. With that analytic we might imagine otherwise from what we know now in the wake of slavery."[16] During a February 2017 panel on her book, *In the Wake*, Sharpe described wake work as "a reading practice, a critical practice, a practice of care, a practice of thinking, and of attempting to see and look . . . [and] community response work as a type of wake work."[17] I am especially taken by the idea of wake work as a community response built upon critical practices of care and thinking, as the basis for organizing, mutual aid, and collective engagement in political struggles that seek to abolish white supremacy and capitalism and decolonize settler claims to land and life.

Whether it is their intention or not, Long Soldier and Sharpe also provide generative interventions and lessons for potential collaborators in abolitionist and decolonization politics who are neither Black nor Indigenous, and in particular, but not exclusively, I mean white settlers who may see ourselves as collaborators. To be a collaborator via the mode of wake work cannot and should not mean claiming the experience of Black and Indigenous peoples as reflective of one's own, or ventriloquizing as such. Rather, we—and I mean we as in white settler subjects—have to be accountable to the long story of white settler nation and state building. This means constructing our commitments based upon engaging in the critical practices of thinking, care, and action that acknowledge "the past that is not past." To acknowledge means more than knowing this history, as important as that is. It means challenging and colliding against the collective memories that narrow the possibilities for radical transformation. Capitalism, climate change, mass incarceration, state surveillance, militarism, violence, and heteropatriarchy are among the major forces of domination that are a problem for us all in some way, and settler colonialism and white supremacy serve and are served by them all. In addressing and opposing these structural forces, those of us who are white settlers cannot and should not claim to be *in the wake* of slavery and settler colonialism or participate in the discourse of the "whereas." In colloquial terms, the "whereas" is the formal version of white settler-splaining deflections such as "on the other hand," "well, actually," or "just to play the devil's advocate." More often than not, white settlers utilize these forms of deflection strategies as a way to disavow our implication in white settler colonial rule and thus also the urgency to be part of the opposition to it. This opposition requires defined commitments to abolish and decolonize the white settler state as an outcome that is best for anyone who seeks to live in a world free from environmental and human degradation, suffering, and exploitation and thereby free to pursue radical, nonoppressive forms of individual and collective existence. This requires critical engagement with and resistance against other white settlers as a core principle and practice of our fight for and pursuit of a better world. This struggle and set of commitments must be understood and acted upon by the settler population as our problem; not our problem *too*, but our problem, full stop. In this spirit, this book critically rereads and rethinks the memory politics embedded in those scholarly and popular narratives that explain the political life of race in a manner that lodges white settler status, Indigeneity, and settler colonialism into the background of U.S. race politics. Dislodging them from their background location may allow for the fashioning, renewal, or centering of memories in the service of scholarly and political discourses that seek to address the crises of our time and imagine and create a better world. The hope is that this book can do its small part to help facilitate this dislodging.

Acknowledgments

After *The Third Space of Sovereignty*, I had a few ideas of what to do next, but nothing took hold for a while. It was a meandering path, leading to some sleepless nights and incoherent responses when faced with that devilish question "So, what are you working on?" Thus, I was, and remain, very fortunate to have the support of so many people along the way to completing *Settler Memory*.

From its earliest form to its final stages, this project benefited immeasurably from feedback from colleagues when I presented at conferences of the American and Western Political Science Associations, the American Studies Association, and the Native American and Indigenous Studies Association (NAISA). In particular, it was upon the invitation of the ever-so-generous Audra Simpson that I first presented at a NAISA conference and met and built friendships and collegial relationships with fantastic scholars and people in Indigenous studies. I also presented different portions of this work at Columbia University; the University of St. Andrews; Queen's University; the University of Oregon; Cornell University; the New School; Tufts University; the University of British Colombia; New York University; Williams College; and the University of Massachusetts Amherst. I thank all who invited me for the vital and edifying forums for discussion, critique, and engagement.

It is impossible to keep track of all the conversations and exchanges I had with so many colleagues along the way who played a role in how I formulated, refined, and shaped the argument and direction of the book. In this process, I am grateful for the wise words and insights of Libby Anker, Joanne Barker, Cristina Beltrán, Gerry Berk, Nick Brown, Jodi Byrd, Jessica Cattelino, Bruno Cornellier, Glen Coulthard, Adam Dahl, Rita Dhamoon, Jaskiran Dhillon, Vince Diaz, Elizabeth Ellis, Nick Estes, Jennifer Gaboury, Mishuana Goeman, Alyosha Goldstein, Jane Gordon, Laura Grattan, Mike Griffiths, Lisa Kahaleole Hall, James Ingram, Maria John, Kim Johnson, Sheryl Lightfoot, Lisa Lowe, Johnny Mack, Annie Menzel, Scott Lauria Morgensen, Dory Nason, Eli Nelson, Rob Nichols, Anne Norton, the late Joel Olson, K-Sue Park, Shiri Pasternak, Aziz Rana, Neil Roberts, Michael Rothberg, Heike Schotten, Audra Simpson, Jakeet Singh, Heidi Kiiwetinepinesiik Stark, Kim TallBear, Coll Thrush, Phil Triadafilopoulos, Dale Turner, Robert Warrior, and the late Patrick Wolfe. As well, I thank my comrades on the collective of *Abolition: A Journal of Insurgent Politics*, from whom I continue to learn much about abolitionist commitments and collective liberation.

Many friends and comrades took time out of their busy schedules to read one or more chapters and provide detailed notes and thoughts. In so doing, each person offered both support and much-needed, constructive direction. For their work and care, I thank Lawrie Balfour, Edmund Fong, Victoria Hattam, Joe Lowndes, Daniel Martinez HoSang, George Shulman, Nancy Wadsworth, and Priscilla Yamin. Notably, Sandy Grande read drafts of multiple chapters, some of which were, let's face it, a bit of a hot mess. Sandy provided rigorous readings, timely suggestions, and even a subtle kick in the pants on a matter or two. I only hope to return the favor one day and earn a few Rez girl points! Mark Rifkin's amazing peer review of the book was so precise, helpful, and clear, I swear it could have been its own publishable article. Thank you to Mark and to the anonymous reviewer for your insights and direction.

You cannot do better than to have Jean O'Brien and J. Kēhaulani Kauanui as series editors. I was eager to have my book in the Critical Indigeneities series because of my respect for their scholarship, their brilliance, and their thoughtfulness. Over our numerous video-conference meetings to discuss chapter drafts, their advice, kindness, and enthusiastic support were invaluable. Mark Simpson-Vos, executive editor of the University of North Carolina (UNC) Press, is always there for whatever one might need, leading with wisdom, humanity, and care. Huge thank you to the entire UNC Press team for their work on and support for the book.

We need friends to keep us afloat, centered, and laughing even in the best of times, and these have not been the best of times. Thus, I am lucky to have in my life such friends, including many of the wonderful people I have already mentioned along with, in particular, Jon Dietrick, Brian Seitz, Marjorie Feld, Stephen Deets, Sophia Chang, Craig Robertson, Diana Greiner, Greta Schwerner, Samara Smith, Liza Sutton, Cat Celebrezze, Liz Canner, Alex Barnett, John Ewing, Zara Cooper, Meredith Levy, Ben Stumpf, Dave Macdougall, Innes McColl, Scott Harding, Heesok Chang, Bud Schmeling, Steve Palmer, and the Highland Kitchen crew. I am thankful for the support I have received from Babson College in the research and writing of the book, and for having great faculty and staff colleagues and friends across campus. In many ways, the impetus for this book emerged through teaching many iterations of my Critical Race and Indigenous Studies course at Babson College. I learned a lot from my students across many semesters as we turned our classroom at a business college into a place for radical critique of white supremacy, settler colonialism, racial capitalism, and heteropatriarchy. In my time at Babson, no group of people can really compare to the scholars of Babson Posse 11 who I mentored. They may have made my hair a little grayer and thinner, but they also made life that much richer, and better seasoned, with love, laughter, and honesty. BP Lit/Posse love and thanks to eleven of my favorite people: Jery Almonte, Stefanie Cañete, Patrice Henry, Stephanie Herrera, James Jackson, Lisa Liu, Omari Ross, Rashawn Russell, Gurparshad Singh, Fatoumata Sow, and Ashley Walters.

As with most families, 2020 was a tough year and continues to be on in to 2021. My love and hopes for the best possible health go to my parents, Alan and Rosemarie; thanks so much for everything you have done to make the life I lead possible. My siblings, Kellie and Kent, and I live in three different corners of the continent and have had to use every technology and trick at our disposal to work together, brainstorm, and guide our family through some bumpy waters, under Kellie's leadership and through her considerable efforts. My love and unwavering appreciation for both of them grows with each day.

Pagan and I are nearing twenty years together. I cannot imagine my world without you; my in-house Fauci, podsplainer, writer extraordinaire, and love of my life. Thank you, for everything.

EARLIER ITERATIONS OF PORTIONS of some chapters were published as "The Trouble with Amnesia: Collective Memory and Colonial Injustice in the United States," in *Political Creativity: Reconfiguring Institutional Order and Change*, ed. Gerald Berk, Dennis Galvan, and Victoria Hattam (Philadelphia: University of Pennsylvania Press, 2013): 236–257; "Race, Colonialism, and the Politics of Indian Sports Names and Mascots: The Washington Football Team Case," *Native American and Indigenous Studies* 3, no. 2 (2016): 1–24; "Codename Geronimo: Settler Memory and the Production of American Statism," *Settler Colonial Studies* 6, no. 4 (2016): 349–364; "Creolizing Collective Memory: Refusing the Settler Memory of the Reconstruction Era," *The Journal of French and Francophone Philosophy* 25, no. 2 (2017): 36–44; and "Wake Work vs. Work of Settler Memory: Modes of Solidarity in #NoDAPL, Black Lives Matter and Anti-Trumpism," in *Standing with Standing Rock: Voices from the #NoDAPL Movement*, ed. Nick Estes and Jaskiran Dhillon (Minneapolis: University of Minnesota Press, 2019): 311–327.

Note on Terminology

Language is a fluid structure and set of practices. No approach is perfect, but here is mine for the book. I most often utilize the terms *Indigenous* and *Indigeneity* to refer to the peoples and subject position of communities who experienced or are descendants and citizens of those nations or tribes who experienced European colonization and settlement over the past five centuries. Encompassing terminology such as that of *Indigenous* exists in a dyadic, often antagonistic relationship to that of settler or colonizer, but it is not meant to homogenize or subsume the specific national and tribal identifications of peoples in relation to their own communities.[1] Other terms utilized on occasion in the book include *Native, Native American, Indian, American Indian,* or *First Nation,* depending upon the source utilized or context. *Indigenous* is more of an umbrella term that is both a political position vis-à-vis colonialism/colonists and has social, cultural, and historical substance that coheres a sense of a people, especially as it concerns the history, traditions, and practices of the hundreds of Native nations and tribes. Thus, I capitalize *Indigenous* as I do *Black,* while I do not do so with *white* or *settler,* reading these as more distinctly political than cultural identities that would lack much substance and cohesion should the structural underpinnings of their meaning, status, and benefits be abolished and decolonized.[2] When possible, I prioritize the specific identifications and terms utilized by Indigenous sources, scholars, and voices, and I follow a practice of stating the Indigenous nation or tribe of any scholar or source at first mention in the book. I base that on how that person refers to citizenship or community identification. Finally, I utilize the terms *United States* or *U.S.* to refer to the distinct, traceable history and present of the legal and political entity and set of state institutions of this geopolitical context. I use the term *American* when appropriate for referencing the dominant national identity of the United States.

Settler Memory

Introduction

Settler Memory

In 2015, Rachel Dolezal, then president of the Spokane, Washington, chapter of the National Association for the Advancement of Colored People (NAACP), became the subject of national controversy when her parents revealed that Dolezal, who openly identified as a Black person, was born of parents who self-identified as white. In the face of significant criticism that she was a racial fraud, Dolezal steadfastly maintained that she was Black. Dolezal's story set off a barrage of media and scholarly commentary and analyses on the meaning of whiteness and Blackness in contemporary American life. While Dolezal and her parents did not agree about whether or not she was Black, they did agree that she had Native American ancestry—"faint traces" of it in the words of her parents.[1] In one interview, Dolezal even claimed "she'd been born in a 'tepee' and spent parts of her childhood hunting for food with a 'bow and arrow.'"[2] Apart from people who write in the area of Indigenous studies, this part of Dolezal's self-defined biography received almost no concerted public commentary in this national discussion on the meaning and function of race in the United States.[3] It was either accepted or, if questionable, still not deemed a pressing matter for public discussion.

My concern here is not with Rachel Dolezal specifically but rather that her case exemplifies the public and political discourse regarding race in the United States and the place of Indigeneity in relation to it. The debate over Dolezal's racial identity seemed to lead nowhere, with no new insights, no change in her own stance on the matter, and no clarity about how to understand and theorize race in the United States. Like her purported ancestry, Dolezal's claim to Native American identity was but a faint trace amid the American public debate about her claimed Blackness. In comparison to Dolezal, Massachusetts Democratic senator Elizabeth Warren has made a barely substantiated claim to distant Cherokee ancestry, and it was claimed for her by Harvard University.[4] While Warren has been questioned and criticized for this claim by many, including U.S. president Donald Trump, as I will discuss in chapter 5, it has not undermined her status as a major figure in the Democratic Party, including becoming a viable candidate for its 2020 presidential nomination, although she did not win the nomination.

There are many factors at work in Warren's political status that cannot be reduced to this one claim about Indigenous ancestry, but it is worth noting the surface contrasts in the Dolezal and Warren cases. Dolezal is now persona non grata in mainstream political circles and is a generally disdained and mocked figure. By contrast, Warren is a central figure in one of the two major U.S. political parties and is generally admired and respected by those on the liberal to left side of the political spectrum. Dolezal's claims placed her beyond the pale of mainstream politics, and her purported faint traces of Indigeneity made no real impact on the debate and had nothing to do with her downfall. Warren's claim to Indigenous ancestry remains fodder for public and political debate but has not had a defining negative impact on her political fortunes.

The Dolezal/Warren comparison offers a sense of the complicated relationship of Indigeneity and settler colonialism to race studies, discourse, and politics in the United States. In this regard, Sisseton Wahpeton Oyate scholar Kim TallBear argues that so-called Indian *blood*, or ancestry, has become a "desired object. Its complete loss would be lamented, as the 'First American' is central to the country's nation-building project—to constructing moral legitimacy and a uniquely American identity."[5] TallBear's point is that Indigeneity is neither simply eliminated nor absent in U.S. social and political life but rather is absorbed mnemonically, as a constitutive ancestral memory lodged in the background of the meaning of American peoplehood, in particular for white Americans. Settler colonial societies are built on the elimination and invisibility of Indigenous peoples, which among other processes involves diluting by absorbing (and thereby eliminating) Indigeneity into whiteness in a manner that does not diminish whiteness; it strengthens it, as a fundamentally settler identity. Those who make claims such as that made by Warren thereby affirm rather than qualify their whiteness in a settler colonial context, as it serves to reinforce the settler foundation of whiteness in which Indigeneity is both there and not-there as an ancestral trace of the past. Thus, Warren and others, like Dolezal herself in this instance, are not violating the hegemonic logic of racial politics in the United States in which Indigeneity is more of a faint trace than an active presence. They are reaffirming this logic. Building on the insights of Indigenous studies scholars such as Kim TallBear, I argue that this simultaneous absence and presence of Indigeneity is inherent to the popular politics, discourse, and debates about race in the United States, and in U.S. political life in general. This complicated absent/present dynamic—as I call it, *settler memory*—not only undermines the effort to understand Indigenous people's politics and settler colonialism in the U.S. context but also stalls the effort to advance the conversation around race itself, including on some of the pressing issues of our time, such as that around racial capitalism, the violence of policing, mass incarceration, and the relationship of race to class, gender, and heteropatriarchy. Settler memory has this undermining effect by rendering Indigenous peoples and settler colonialism invisible or barely visible as active contemporary forces. As such, it also elides from public and political discussion the *settler* part of white identity and white supremacist policies, practices, and discourse. I thus put forth settler memory as an analytic that offers a way to explain how Indigeneity resides so often in the background of race and other political discussions in the United States.

The work of settler memory resonates with and helps to reproduce *colonial unknowing*. This is the valuable analytic conceived by Manu Vimalassery, Juliana Hu Pegues, and Alyosha Goldstein to refer to the way in which colonialism is, at once, "simultaneously everywhere and nowhere."[6] I argue that it is not only a colonial unknowing that settler memory produces; it also fosters racial unknowing. With respect to race and white supremacy, Moon-Kie Jung devises the phrase *symbolic perversity* to refer to the way in which those in the dominant racial group "can and do know about the suffering of their racial others, but this knowledge fails to register or matter. . . . The effect of this knowing-unknowing is the depraved racial indifference to racial inequalities— depraved for its knowingness but indifferent in usually unknowing, reflexive ways."[7] In many ways, what Jung is talking about here is less an unknowing than a disavowal, an active form of deflection from the implications and obligations to attend to what one knows.

As James Baldwin put it in his 1963 letter to his nephew James, many white people "know better, but, as you will discover, people find it very difficult to act on what they know. To act is to be committed, and to be committed is to be in danger. In this case, the danger, in the minds of most white Americans, is the loss of their identity."[8] Baldwin points to a key distinction here, which is that the problem at hand is less epistemological, a matter of knowledge, at least on its own, than political and ontological, regarding a threat white people sense will be posed to their individual and collective identities, power, and status if they act upon what they know. As political theorist George Shulman puts it regarding the white American relationship to the history of U.S. white supremacy, what we have here is a "problem of disavowal, not error or ignorance."[9] In contrast to a more liberal theoretical approach that can view the persistence of white supremacy and racial inequality as a result of a lack of education or the presence of individual biases, Shulman's theorization of disavowal draws out the fundamental role of political power, status, identifications, and interests that cannot be eliminated by greater awareness alone. Beenash Jafri elaborates on the role of disavowal in white settler societies: "A quintessential feature of white settler mythologies is, therefore, the disavowal of conquest, genocide, slavery, and the exploitation of the labour of peoples of colour. In North America, it is still the case that European conquest and colonization are often denied, largely through the fantasy that North America was peacefully settled and not colonized."[10] Jafri links the disavowal of conquest and of slavery to the productive myths and memories that secure and protect white settler standing. This linkage between the colonization of Indigenous peoples and the enslavement of Black people is important to mark out for my study, for while settler memory attends to the disavowal of Indigeneity and settler colonialism directly, it also fosters what Jung calls the "depraved racial indifference" of white Americans to U.S. white supremacy generally and anti-Blackness specifically.

In *Settler Memory*, I do not argue that one set of focal points, such as Black politics or white supremacy, is getting too much attention in the United States, while Indigenous politics and settler colonialism do not get enough, as if it is a competition, a zero-sum game. Rather, the claim here is that the work of settler memory undermines critical attention to white settler society as a whole, affecting all who live under its domination and seek its abolition. In this spirit, Justin Leroy sets out an important analytical and political concern:

> Settler colonialism is a logic of indigenous erasure that has developed and sustained itself through anti-blackness. Anti-black racism, in turn, has overcome the setbacks of emancipation and the black freedom struggle by calling upon discourses of securitization and militarized occupation with roots in colonialism. However, these mutually constitutive origins are lost in recent claims that indigenous dispossession or racial slavery must vie for exceptional status as the foundational violence of modernity. Such claims are a form of colonial unknowing; the refusal to see the full scope of slavery and settlement's interconnected history abets a colonial ontology.[11]

Leroy calls out the disavowal of the intertwined relationship between Indigenous territorial dispossession and Black enslavement that occurs when one or the other is purported to have foundational primacy.[12] My study builds upon this concern to consider how the absence and presence of Indigeneity through settler memory fuels anti-Black racism and how this coproduced anti-Blackness sustains the erasure of Indigenous people and settler colonialism in U.S. political memory. This premise exists in a degree of tension with a popular line of argument, offered especially by theorists of the Afro-pessimist tradition such as Frank Wilderson, that positions anti-Blackness as having *exceptional status* not equally coimplicated with Indigenous dispossession and elimination. As Wilderson states, "Though Blacks are indeed sentient beings, the structure of the entire world's semantic field—regardless of cultural and national discrepancies . . . is sutured by anti-Black solidarity."[13] By contrast, I take the position that we limit our grasp of anti-Blackness, enslavement, and white supremacy if we do not attend to the mutually constitutive relationship with Indigeneity, settler colonialism, and heteropatriarchy.

In his book *Red, White & Black: Cinema and the Structure of U.S. Antagonisms*, Wilderson does signal an aim to take seriously the complicated dimensions and dominations that shape the triad in the title, as early in the text he states: "Give Turtle Island back to the 'Savage.' Give life itself back to the Slave. Two simple sentences, fourteen simple words, and the structure of U.S. (and perhaps global) antagonisms would be dismantled."[14] However, it is not long before he refers to the "irreconcilable demands of Indigenism and Blackness."[15] Clearer distinctions emerge as he clarifies the oppositional terms that define the subjects of the white-Black-Red triad: "I use *White, Human, Master, Settler*, and sometimes *non-Black* interchangeably to connote a paradigmatic entity that exists ontologically as a position of life in relation to the Black or Slave, one of death. The Red, Indigenous, or 'Savage' position exists liminally as half-death and half-life between the Slave (Black) and the Human (White, or non-Black)."[16] The "Black and Human" dyad produced out of enslavement stands as the defining and fundamental antagonism to Wilderson and "supercedes the 'antagonism' between worker and capitalist in political economy, as well as the gendered 'antagonism' in libidinal economy."[17] The structure of Wilderson's non-Black/Black dyad is thus rife with elisions, and directly so concerning Indigeneity. Wilderson positions Settler with White, Human, and Master, but he places Indigeneity, the seemingly obvious antagonistic position to Settler, in a liminal zone, between life and death, between siding with Master/Settler/life or siding with Slave/Blackness/death. For Wilderson, there is no self-standing ontological and antagonistic position for Indigeneity on its own terms, as this positionality emerges only through political articulations that place the Indigenous person in a position of either anti-Black solidarity or Black solidarity. By contrast, I read anti-Blackness as, in no small part, rooted in and fueled by white settler imperatives of belonging, status, security, profit, power, and safety in relationship to these lands—lands claimed through Indigenous dispossession—and the racialized and gendered fears regarding those peoples white settlers deem or are told threaten this sense of belonging, status, economic and political security, and safety, beginning with Black and Indigenous peoples. Shona Jackson speaks to this coimplication: "To be anti-black is also to be fundamentally anti-Indigenous. It is a rejection of indigeneity (both in the New World and in Africa) as incompatible with the epistemic terrain of European modernity, its social and political structures, representative frames, and transformative processes."[18] This is not to say all peoples are *Indigenous* in a sweeping way that does not account for and can even undermine the specificities of geopolitical context and the substantiated claims of Indigenous nations to their land—to reclaiming land stolen by settler colonial states such as the United States—that have distinct and persistent bases and urgency to them. It is to say that the inability or unwillingness to address Indigeneity and settler colonialism on their own terms and in relation to Blackness and white supremacy narrows the scope of race politics, such as concerning the range of contentions and sources of anti-Blackness rooted in enslavement and exploitation that are directly implicated with Indigenous dispossession and genocide. My attention to settler memory seeks to explain why this is so.

The analytic of settler memory could apply to any settler state context, but the geopolitical focus of this study is the U.S. context. As Patrick Wolfe noted in his final work, *Traces of History: Elementary Structures of Race*, "The enslavement of Africans in the United States produced the most rigorously polarized regime of race" compared to Australia, Brazil, Israel/Palestine, and the other contexts he examines, and one should include Canada and Aotearoa/New Zealand in this list as well.[19] Wolfe's historically grounded assertion speaks to the idea that there is a decidedly hegemonic polarity in the U.S. racial regime, specifically in the form of the white-Black binary. The binary logic here is that whiteness and Blackness define one other as intrinsically cocreative and exclusively entwined together, where whiteness has its fundamental meaning in relation to, and over, that of Blackness, as we saw reproduced in Wilderson's formulation. This logic has a powerful hold in the U.S. context, but as noted this framing is troubled, at least as a binary, if one accounts for settler identity as also constitutive of whiteness, which thereby implicates a direct relationship to Indigeneity. As it concerns the white-Black binary in relation to Indigeneity, one can imagine it as similar to a three-dimensional image or picture that when viewed straight on conveys a simple two-dimensional representation but when tilted even slightly reveals another element that shifts one's sense of the entire scene. Working with this metaphor, the work of settler memory leaves settlerness and Indigeneity as, at best, faint traces in the background of the two-dimensional white-Black binary in U.S. racial discourse, there and not-there at once. Wilderson's notion of Indigeneity as "liminal" is a prime example of this sort of disavowal produced to give coherence to a narrow framing of race discourse, politics, and antagonisms.

Although the notion of the trace is not my central analytic, given that it is a key term in Patrick Wolfe's argument it is worthwhile to set out what I am doing that is distinctive. Wolfe's "trace of history" refers to race itself, which he argues is a product of the foundation and maintenance of colonialism. For Wolfe, colonialism comes first and then "racialising practices seek to maintain population-specific modes of colonial domination through time."[20] Race is thus the trace of the history of colonialism, or as he puts it, "Race is colonial-ism speaking, in idioms whose diversity reflects the variety of unequal rela-tionships into which Europeans have co-opted conquered populations."[21] My study of the work of settler memory answers the question of what colonial-ism is saying through race in the U.S. political context, and what it is saying is "Nothing to see here, move along everyone!" It is fitting that these words sounds like something the police would say. The white settler roots of state surveillance and violence, policing, and incarceration are lodged in the back-ground of U.S. race politics in a way that undermines the ability to imagine and mobilize a coordinated vision of the abolition of white supremacy and racial capitalism and the decolonization of settler states and the territories claimed under settler rule. Specifically, the "nothing" in the "Nothing to see here" is settler colonialism and Indigeneity. As a result, settler colonialism's role in anti-Blackness and white supremacy is also disavowed because the subject position and political existence of the white settler garners minimal critical and political attention, if any at all.

Goenpul scholar Aileen Moreton-Robinson's innovative notion of the *white possessive* is formative for how I think about and deploy the concept of white settlerness.[22] Moreton-Robinson begins her 2015 book, *The White Possessive*, with this assertion: "The existence of white supremacy as hegemony, ideol-ogy, epistemology, and ontology requires the possession of Indigenous lands as its proprietary anchor within capitalist economies such as the United States." However, this fact is "rarely addressed in African American whiteness studies literature," and there is a noticeable "invisibility of Indigeneity within the early whiteness studies literature produced by white scholars."[23] This is a dynamic I will address directly in chapter 1 concerning, in particular, the po-litical memory of Bacon's Rebellion. In the course of calling out the produc-tive absences in U.S. race studies, Moreton-Robinson's wider aim is to show how "whiteness operates possessively to define and construct itself as the pinnacle of its own racial hierarchy."[24] This notion of white possessiveness is about relations to and domination over land and life, including the possession of human beings in enslavement and claims to and violence against gendered bodies. In this regard, the category of white settlerness that I most often deploy in this study builds upon Moreton-Robinson's argument by stipulating whiteness *as* property/possessive. As Moreton-Robinson notes and credits, critical legal and race theorist Cheryl Harris devised the concept and framework of whiteness as property as that which originated through the "appropriation of Indigenous peoples' lands and the subsequent enslavement of African Americans. However, the center of Harris's theory is how 'blackness' enabled whiteness as a form of property."[25] In a trend I see with other authors and narratives, Harris's groundbreaking piece acknowledges the role of Indigenous dispossession in an originary stage of the creation of whiteness, and then the trajectory of the argument conceptually and historically centers Blackness, as Moreton-Robinson notes, with less accounting for how whiteness and its propertied features continue to be shaped in relationship to Indigeneity and settler colonialism.

These deeply intertwined sets of racial and colonial formations and subject positions are complicated, fluid, and fraught. In my effort to define the relationship of settler memory to settler colonialism, I benefit greatly from Rita Dhamoon's insightful formulation: "Settler colonialism is not only a structure but also a process, an activity for assigning political meanings, and organizing material structures driven by forces of power. This process-oriented approach emphasizes that the dispossession of lands is temporal and ongoing, dynamic and continuous, and that the productive capacities of settler colonialism function to make and consolidate hierarchies of Otherness (e.g. among gendered people of colour, among Indigenous people, and between people of colour and Indigenous peoples across the borders of the nation-state)."[26] Dhamoon guides us to see settler colonialism not as a contained, unchanging, transhistorical phenomenon but more as an assemblage maintained in a "dynamic and continuous" process implicating socioeconomic, cultural, ideological, and political practices, discourses, institutions, and actors. Her extended definition implicates settler colonialism in the othering, oppression, and multilayered forms of conflict and hierarchy among peoples along lines of Indigeneity, race, class, gender, and sexuality. The key here is that race, gender, class, and sexuality are not add-ons to the place of Indigeneity and land dispossession in the structure of settler colonialism but are fundamental components to it. Dhamoon provides multiple avenues of intervention for grasping the function and inner workings of settler colonialism, and thus she helps us better explain and deconstruct its complicated workings and the extent of its reach by opening up rather than collapsing the concept. In this spirit, I posit settler memory as an unattended *productive capacity* of settler colonialism that as well as disavowing Indigeneity and settler colonialism also shields attention away from the standing, interests, and expressions of white settlerness. My study understands white settlerness as a subject position and structural formation secured through violent impunity over and exploitation of land and human and nonhuman life. However, the terms of the white settler position are never fully settled because the "dispossession of lands is temporal and ongoing" and thereby so is the effort of "assigning political meanings, and organizing material structures driven by forces of power," as Dhamoon reminds us. This is why the politics of memory, specifically concerning settler memory, plays a key role in the reproduction and securing of white settler status, land dispossession, and "hierarchies of Otherness."

In this book, I ask: How does settler memory shape race politics and discourse—what does it authorize, and how might it constrain this politics— and what would it look like if Indigeneity and settler colonialism were no longer faint traces but rather active constituents of contemporary politics and discourse in and of the United States? The basis for this question comes from my assessment that there is something fundamentally amiss with race analysis, discourse, and politics in the United States. As political theorist Jack Turner states, "Contemporary American race talk is stagnant." He sees this stagnation as rooted in debates that spin in circles because they lack due attention to the "interrelationship between history, social context, and personal freedom."[27] An underappreciated source of this problem is that most citizens and scholars of the United States are unable or unwilling to engage with settler colonialism and the politics of Indigenous peoples, or to the degree that they do this history and politics are often absent or marginalized from or barely attached to narratives of the story of race in the United States. This point recalls Moreton-Robinson's insights about the lack of attention to Indigeneity, settler colonialism, and land dispossession in U.S. race studies. She asks the question directly: "Why are the appropriation of Indigenous peoples' land and ensuing wars not perceived as having anything to do with the ongoing praxis of the United States as a white nation-state?"[28] Moreton-Robinson points to a tendency in antiracist Left critiques of white supremacy, especially those seeking to connect race and class in analyzing U.S. race politics, of eliding the role of settler colonialism, land, and Indigeneity in their analyses. This elision also occurs with liberal approaches to U.S. race politics that tend to center a race analysis without a serious consideration of class. Be it with antiracist Left or liberal analyses of race politics in the United States—and I will speak about both at different points in the book—there is a consistent tendency to leave Indigeneity, at best, in the background.

Since settler colonialism and Indigeneity stand as faint traces in popular memories of the history and present of race in America and in antiracist Left and liberal analyses and critiques, white settlerness is also a faint trace in the wider memory, conversation, and politics around race. Even more pointedly, I mean here to distinguish whiteness as a claim to racial superiority narrowly conceived from that of *white settler masculinity*. The latter phrase signifies a subject position that defines and binds racial status to a heteropatriarchal claim to land dispossessed from Indigenous peoples and to the enactment of violence against and the exploitation of human and nonhuman life. Critical attention to and political refusal of settler memory and its relationship to white settler masculinity helps open alternative modes of intervention regarding the complex relationship of Indigeneity, race, class, gender, and sexuality in U.S. political life.

Regarding the vital intersection of race and class that shapes the framework of a significant part of the antiracist Left, of which I include myself, Stuart Hall's definitive phrase continues to resonate for so many of us: "Race is . . . the modality in which class is lived, the medium through which class relations are experienced."[29] Hall's work is critical in this regard for taking heed of how class relations and experiences speak through and are shaped by race, as race is shaped by class. His vital lesson is that one cannot analyze or organize on class lines without addressing the differential racial experience of class in its socioeconomic, cultural, political, and ideological forms. I adapt Hall's formulation to the settler colonial context, and with a twist on Wolfe's idea that "race is colonialism" speaking, I argue that *whiteness is the major modality through which settler masculinity is lived*. To expand on what I mean by this, as noted, in the United States the concept of whiteness is an increasingly public feature of the scholarly and public discourse regarding race. However, the degree to which whiteness is a settler form of racial superiority is virtually invisible, rarely referenced or discussed in the public realm. This relative invisibility of the settler component of whiteness not only subsumes attention to and analysis of the role of land, dispossession, and settler violence in the ongoing racial formations of a settler colonial society; it also emboldens white masculinity by shielding its violent and possessive claims to land and human and nonhuman life, often in the name of defending the heteronormative white settler domestic realm. The normative status and practices of white settler masculinity reside at the heart of the wider racial and colonial system, in which sexual violence and heteropatriarchy are critical for "consolidating hierarchies of Otherness," as Dhamoon put it, and constituting and defending settler domesticity.

Kahnawà:ke Mohawk scholar Audra Simpson explains the role of sexual violence within a settler colonial system, linking the settler drives to prey upon land and upon women: "Feminist scholars have argued that Native women's bodies were to the settler eye, like land, and as such in the settler mind, the Native woman is rendered 'unrapeable' (or, 'highly rapeable') because she was like land, matter to be extracted from, used, sullied, taken from, over and over again, something that is already violated and violatable in a great march to accumulate surplus, to so called 'production.'"[30] Simpson does not collapse land and Native women as the same forms of bodies, of course, but rather argues that a defining feature of the settler perspective is seeing and acting upon them as both present as objects and absent as subjects. Land and Native women to the settler are, at once, objects of use, extraction, violation, and exchange while also not being subjects worthy of respect and reciprocity and of having a status as life capable of being harmed, of experiencing harm. To speak then of settler subjectivity is to speak necessarily of settler masculinity in which heteropatriarchy, enforced with violent impunity, is a central cohering element of settler colonialism as a "structure but also a process."

Even more precisely, settler masculinity in the U.S. context is fundamentally *white* settler masculinity, constituted through the violence of dispossession and the history of enslavement. In this light, I pair Simpson's insight with Saidiya Hartman's argument about the "sexual exploitation of slave women cloaked as the legitimate use of property and castration and assault of slave men. . . . In the case of slave women, the law's circumscribed recognition of consent and will occurred only in order to intensify and secure the subordination of the enslaved, repress the crime, and deny injury, for it is asserted that the captive female was both will-less and always willing."[31] Hartman thus sets out a presence-absence dynamic in terms of what the slaveholder and white supremacist legal system recognizes and does not recognize about the captive female. Enslaved Black woman are present as objects in the form of property and as *willing* subjects to satisfy white masculine desires while at the same time absent as those who can claim injury and a violation of their *will*.[32]

While the literal individuals carrying out settler violence against Indigenous peoples and the violence of the slave master may not be one and the same—although in figures like Andrew Jackson, to be discussed in chapter 5, we can see that they often were—the system of white settler rule in the United States is built on the intertwining of these two violent, possessive drives. In pairing Simpson's and Hartman's articulations, I posit the functioning of white settler masculinity as an encompassing subjectivity, not just as settler in one regard and white in another. To pinpoint white settler masculinity is not to deny the role of white settler femininity in emboldening settler masculinity and domesticity as norms against which other subject positions and relations are othered, constructed as threats, or deemed wanting, in need of correction or salvation. As Margaret Jacobs makes clear in *White Mother to a Dark Race,* white settler women in the United States and Australia actively served in the reproduction of and gained security through heteropatriarchal rule that positioned white settler femininity and the white settler domestic realm as ideals to be passed on to the lesser "darker races."[33] The disavowal of white settler masculinity through the work of settler memory thus also leaves white femininity and domesticity in the background of any effort to grapple with and challenge the ongoing reproduction and defense of white settler rule in contexts such as the United States. This brings me back to the politics of memory as a vital site of intervention and reimagination since it is, as Lee Maracle teaches us, a tricky, slippery, and powerful shaping force on individual and collective political life.

Everywhere we look, hear, smell, and touch, we can discover memory at work. As political philosopher Charles Mills sets out, we cannot neatly separate individual and collective memories because "when the individual cognizing agent is perceiving, he is doing so with eyes and ears that have been socialized. Perception is also in part conception, the viewing of the world through a particular conceptual grid. Inference from perception involves the overt or tacit appeal to memory, which will be not merely individual but also social. As such, it will be founded on testimony and ultimately on the perceptions and conceptions of others."[34] This testimony comes in narratives in which we encounter the entangled rather than distinct relationship between history and memory. Political narratives that make historical claims are necessarily making claims about memory—about what should matter to a people in their time, what is worth recalling and not. For this reason, analyses of these political claims need to take collective memory as seriously as they do history and, I would argue, even more seriously due to their inescapable role in politics. As Edward Said observed, "Collective memory is not an inert and passive thing, but a field of activity in which past events are selected, reconstructed, modified, and endowed with political meaning."[35] In this regard, Saidiya Hartman helpfully sets out how the collective memory of slavery and its afterlife is fundamentally shaped and intertwined with race politics in the present day:

So the point isn't the impossibility of escaping the stranglehold of the past, or that history is a succession of uninterrupted defeats, or that the virulence and tenacity of racism is inexorable. But rather that the perilous conditions of the present establish the link between our age and a previous one in which freedom too was yet to be realized. The past is neither inert nor given. The stories we tell about *what happened then,* the correspondences we discern between today and times past, and the ethical and political stakes of these stories redound in the present. If slavery feels proximate rather than remote and freedom seems increasingly elusive, this has everything to do with our own dark times. If the ghost of slavery still haunts our present, it is because we are still looking for an exit from the prison.[36]

While focusing on the "ghost of slavery" specifically, Hartman conveys that the deeper mnemonic issue with white majority settler nations such as the United States is not what we forget but how we remember, not just an "unknowing" but particular forms of knowing—"the stories we tell about *what happened then*." From the all-too-familiar white American claim "My ancestors never owned slaves" to mythologizing the memory of Martin Luther King Jr. by erasing his radical views, there are many examples of how the "stories we tell about *what happened then*" reproduce a form of American collective memory that shields white Americans from coming to terms with the nation's racist history and present. Hartman points us to the function of memory in the white settler imaginary in asserting that "the ghost of slavery still haunts our present," whereby the persistence of white supremacy and anti-Blackness are evidence of slavery's *haunting,* or "unresolved unfolding" in Christina Sharpe's words.[37] Hartman compels us to grapple with the fact that it is, in truth, present-day politics with which we are grappling, not past. Collective memory is a vital terrain of this political struggle, engaged not to settle the accounts of the past but to intervene in the social, economic, and political relations and crises of the present. And yet, for all its import, the politics of memory is both underexplored and ubiquitous and possibly underexplored because of its ubiquity. Like fish who do not know they are in water, we breathe collective memory every day, habitually, without giving it much thought.

It is in the function and practices of memory that I locate the means by which memory serves in the creation, mobilization, and reconstitution of a people, be it as citizens and subjects of state authority or of collectivities such as that of a nation, of a race, or as settlers. Just as memories make a house a home, collective memory can make a space into a place and speak to a collectivity's relationship to land and legacy that threads together a sense of identity and meaning over time. In discussing the memory that one of her Lakota ancestors, Mrs. Mosseau, had of her experience the day after the Wounded Knee Massacre of 1890, Layli Long Soldier understands Mosseau's memory as also her own in the collective sense:

> I refer to this as a collective memory because, as a people, we remember who we are from our families, from this land, from stories within the community, and from our senses. Yes, from our senses, we remember what's stored within us already. Maybe, sometimes, I/we cannot put words to it, but we feel something. I might call it *instinct*. It's an old sensation that cannot be named, for which there is no textual record or language to help us understand. Yet, it is there just below the skin and just like that. I feel it here, today.[38]

Here Long Soldier conveys the way in which memory, to recall Mills, is "not merely individual but also social." For Long Soldier and the Lakota, memory is central to one's sense of self, to one's connection to family and community, and to the land remembered and experienced not as a separate object but as a constitutive, relational element of individual and collective being. Long Soldier's articulation of what collective memory means to her and her people sets up an interesting contrast with the dominant forms of memory production in and of white settler colonial contexts such as the United States.

In a settler society, the work of collective memory serves to reaffirm the settler claim of belonging to, appropriation of, and authority over lands, on the one hand, and the disavowal of the genocide, dispossession, and alienation of Indigenous peoples, on the other hand. Collective memory is ubiquitous as a productive capacity of U.S. settler colonialism in this regard because in its many forms it serves to naturalize settlement through the habituated disavowal of Indigenous presence. Another way to put it is that settler memory is important to the reproduction of what Mark Rifkin calls "settler common sense," which comprises "an unstated set of nonnative inclinations, orientations, modes of perception, forms of networking, and durable lived assemblages shaped by processes of settlement and experienced as the stability of the given."[39] In referring to this as a habituated process, I draw from Henri Bergson's notion that "the past survives under two distinct forms: first, in motor mechanisms; secondly, in independent recollections."[40] This is the distinction between "*mémoirehabitude* (memory as habit) and *mémoiresouvenir* (memory as distinct recollection)."[41] Memory as habit refers to the motor mechanisms of collective life, the rituals by which a community replicates and passes on its myths, lessons, meanings, and identifications. Paul Ricoeur elaborates on Bergson's concept: "Habit-memory is the one we employ when we recite the lesson without evoking one by one each of the successive readings of the period of learning . . . like my habit of walking or of writing; it is lived and acted, rather than represented."[42] In many ways, chapters 1 and 2 of *Settler Memory* examine that which is habitually recited and enacted, rather than actively reimagined, in the lessons and meanings conveyed in political memories of Bacon's Rebellion and the Reconstruction era. Considering alternative ways to recast the memory and meaning of these eras may provide a way to clash and collide against the powerful and ever-slippery collective memories that predominate in white settler societies.

As concerns the colliding of memories in a settler colonial context, Edward Said speaks to the stakes of the politics of collective memory from his experience and knowledge of the Palestinian struggle and similar struggles of colonized peoples: "Perhaps the greatest battle Palestinians have waged as a people has been over the right to a remembered presence and, with that presence, the right to possess and reclaim a collective historical reality, at least since the Zionist movement began its encroachments on the land. A similar battle has been fought by all colonized peoples whose past and present were dominated by outside powers who had first conquered the land and then rewrote the history so as to appear in that history as the true owners of the land."[43] Said's words here could apply to Indigenous peoples and the U.S. settler colonial society. Historian Jean O'Brien of the White Earth Band of Ojibwe speaks to the role of memory in the U.S. settler context, in which she locates a form of remembering and disavowal in the manner in which "local narrators in New England simultaneously embraced and replaced Indian peoples in shaping their story about New England history. . . . Their arguments of the past, present, and future entailed a process of physically and imaginatively replacing Indians on the landscape of New England."[44] I deploy O'Brien's analytic of replacement to better understand the politics of settler memory at work in the sports names and mascots issue in chapter 4. I see settler memory as reproduced not only through the active recollection of storytellers and local narrators but also as a habituated process constitutive of peoplehood—of who a people is, who belongs and who does not, and why—for a white settler society. It is also a persistently contested process, as demonstrated by the ongoing and finally successful political struggle to change the Washington, D.C., National Football League (NFL) team's name, as one example.

Thus, my approach seeks to center the political struggle over memory. A key function of the work of settler memory is to shape collective and individual settler subjectivity, to legitimate settler governance in relationship to people, territory, and temporality, and to do so in a repetitive, persistent process in which Indigenous peoples are constantly woven into the American past and outside the political present. In settler societies, too often these memories are habitually reproduced as a contained and *settled* matter. It is important to be clear that this settler mnemonic process is not a simple forgetting of Indigenous peoples, of settler colonialism, and of white settler identity. The examples of Rachel Dolezal and Elizabeth Warren are not evidence of a forgetting of the history and present of Indigenous peoples but rather disavowals of their relevance to the contemporary political context. Dolezal and Warren do not make their individual claims outside of social and political contexts, for they would not even have deemed such claims to have meaning without that context and their implicit or explicit knowledge of it. Thus, the problem here is not a lack of memory or, as it is often diagnosed, amnesia. The diagnosis of amnesia and the cure of remembering are liberal rationalist ways to conceive the problem of, and solution to, forms of domination that emanate from the constitutive relationship of the past upon the present. The liberal rationalist approach imagines that if only we all knew better, had all the facts, read the right books, had the right conversations, and so on, then we would be on our way to addressing these historic injustices.[45] If disavowal is the problem, as I posit that it is, then the radical political cure is not historical knowledge on its own but rather a direct and antagonistic encounter with the commitments, interests, and forms of domination that maintain white settler societies. This requires, yes, getting the facts straight, but in the terrain of struggle over memory, facts do not speak for themselves as to their political meaning; rather, alternative memories need to be posed to reimagine the meaning of the past so they can be a source for radical and liberating interventions, lessons, and possibilities.

Here, I return to Dhamoon's view that settler colonialism is "not only a structure but also a process, an activity for assigning political meanings, and organizing material structures driven by forces of power."[46] Defining settler colonialism as a process and fluid collection of practices does not diminish the violence, domination, and dispossession that state and nonstate actors can and do enact. To the contrary, it can allow us to attend to the various levels of domination, surveillance, and terror enacted from multiple sources, many of whom are not official state actors. In this regard, consider Stefano Harney and Fred Moten's description of the intricacies and agencies of what they call state command. As they see it, white settlers from the Ku Klux Klan and pioneers of yore to their descendants in our time are the "citizen-deputies" of settler state rule whose violence is emboldened by such policies as Stand Your Ground laws: "Stand your ground—because man was not born to run away, because his color won't run, because again and again the settler must incant the disavowal and target the epidermalised trace of his desire for refuge—is only the most notorious iteration of this renewed dispersal and deputisation of state violence."[47] White settler subjects are the citizen-deputies of settler governance, called to arms not necessarily by official state actors but by the habituation of white settler memory itself as a shaping force on the imperative to defend the ground upon which they stand, that of white settler domestic space. Harney and Moten point to the fundamental role of the settler here when referencing the "incanting of the disavowal" through which these subjects enact their racialized, anti-Black—"epidermalised"—targeting. The specific thing disavowed here is that the ground these "citizen-deputies" so vigorously defend—the ground of the nation, of white standing, and of heteropatriarchal domesticity—is stolen from Indigenous peoples and cultivated over centuries by enslaved and exploited Black and Indigenous peoples and indentured migrant labor. This colonial conquest and settler theft of land is both a faint trace in U.S. history and disavowed as a matter of persistent contemporary political struggle. The work of settler memory serves to protect the idea that there are no truer claimants to this *ground* than white masculine and feminine settlers who maintain and preserve the sanctity of heteropatriarchal settler domesticity.

Here, it is important to make a key distinction on the matter of who and what count as the people, practices, and ideology that fall under the category of "settler." While anyone can habitually invoke in discourse, desires, and practice settler ideology and memory, as anyone can regarding those of white supremacy and heteropatriarchy—these discourses, ideologies and institutions are constitutive of the world in which we live, not attached essentially to any people—this is not the same as claiming that the analytic of the "settler" applies cohesively in the same way to all non-Indigenous peoples. In particular, for my study, as Harney and Moten's language suggests, there is no "settling" for Black people in a white settler society built on enslavement, dispossession, and the violent creation and defense of a white settler heteropatriarchal realm. As Zoé Samudzi and William C. Anderson put it in their 2018 book, *As Black as Resistance: Finding the Conditions for Liberation*, "Black Americans are residents of a settler colony, not truly citizens of the United States."[48] As they state later, "We are not settlers."[49] While Indigenous peoples were and are dispossessed of territories to generate this settler colony, Black people's permanent *settlement* is not a feature of the white settler social contract. Rather, Indigenous and Black people, in their own ways, have historically and to our time dealt with dispossession and displacement from their homes, be it through forced removals, state and nonstate terror, sexual violence, state policies, and racial capitalist economic practices that compel displacement and containment under the neoliberal guise of gentrification, privatization, and market forces.[50] Thus, while I engage in a critical rereading of what I deem to be the habituated lessons and settler memories reproduced in some of the key narratives, authors, and works in U.S. race studies, the effort here is not to dismiss them but rather to open up and dislodge presumptions so as to allow for a more expansive engagement and explain why this white settler dynamic is not more evident in the U.S. context.

In terms of my approach to the interpretations, arguments, and narratives I construct over the course of the book, I deem discourses such as those under examination to be practices that are as cohering and constitutive of political life as are those that may be constructed as more material in nature. In this regard, once again, I find Stuart Hall's words instructive: "Far from signaling just talk, the term 'discourse' suggests exactly the breaking down of the distinction between the two levels of 'pure ideas' and 'brute practice' in favor of the insistence that all human, social, and cultural practices are always both, that is they are always *discursive practices*. And this means we need to be cautious before too hastily trying to distinguish the discursive from the extradiscursive."[51] In this methodological, critical, and political spirit, chapters 1–3 of *Settler Memory* focus on the politics of memory and the role of settler memory in formative narratives and works in the study of race in the U.S. context. Chapter 1, "The Settler Memory of Bacon's Rebellion," examines a foundational narrative of race in U.S. political history. The chapter focuses on what I call the antiracist Left memory of Bacon's Rebellion in Virginia from 1675 to 1677. Bacon's Rebellion is the seemingly never-ending well of collective memory to which race scholars and commentators turn when thirsty for an origin story to ground and explain race as a fundamentally political concept—to mark the foundational moment of the political life of race in what would become the U.S. context. This narrative is shaped by settler memory in that it posits and then disavows, among other things, the constitutive role of white settler violence against Indigenous peoples, the presence of Indigenous peoples, and the intertwined functions of property and patriarchy. Chapter 2, "Reconstructing Political Memory," examines another origin narrative in the political life of race in the U.S. context, the story of the Reconstruction era in the late nineteenth century. It centers on a reading of W. E. B. Du Bois's classic work, *Black Reconstruction in America*. This chapter puts this analysis into the context of how and why contemporary writers and activists continue to turn to the Reconstruction era and *Black Reconstruction* to draw political lessons, what it means that important elements of these lessons remain constrained by settler memory, and how the Reconstruction era might be reimagined as a source for radical abolitionist and decolonization politics by refusing the work of settler memory. Following this, chapter 3, "James Baldwin and Cowboys and Indians," analyzes the work of possibly the most influential author in modern race discourse and thinking. I analyze Baldwin's nonfiction work and interviews with the critical and recuperative aim of showing how we can read Baldwin for the gestures he makes toward a settler colonial analysis of the political life of race in the United States. In so doing, I argue that Baldwin's work exemplifies the constraints settler memory places on race theorization while also showing what is possible by refusing settler memory.

Chapters 4 and 5 then turn to analyze two different contemporary political concerns through a perspective that refuses settler memory and seeks to show how doing so may open up alternative critiques and political possibilities. Chapter 4, "The Free Pass," analyzes Indian mascotry to reveal the constraints of racial liberalism for addressing what is, I argue, a white settler colonial practice. I also draw out how these names and mascots are premised upon deeply rooted anti-Blackness that exists compatibly with the erasure of Indigenous peoples as contemporary agents. Then, in chapter 5, "Mocking Disavowal and Cruel Celebration," I make the case for reading the rise of Trump and Trumpism through a perspective that attends to the settler colonial imperatives and desires of Trump and his supporters. I analyze what I call Trump's settler stanzas that reproduce the myth of Pocahontas in his attacks on Elizabeth Warren, which when woven together help link and underscore Trump's settler masculinity and white nationalism that manifest in his support for anti-Indian policies, anti-Blackness, oil pipeline development, border walls, sexual violence, and Israel's occupation of Palestine, among other things. In all, I discern in Trump and his supporters a consistent drive to celebrate U.S. settler colonial conquest and mockingly disavow Indigenous political agency and presence. This violent settler masculine drive for conquest and domination may well have taken its most literal form on January 6, 2021, when thousands of Trump supporters invaded the U.S. Capitol building to overthrow the 2020 presidential election results in order to take back *their* country and *stand their ground*. In this regard, attention to the settler masculine imperatives of Trumpism may also help explain why focusing on the function of whiteness alone may not be enough to make sense of the intensity and the reach of the support for Trump during and beyond his one term in office.

I conclude the book by first looking at liberal responses to the political candidacy and presidency of Donald Trump. A number of liberal critiques and assessments of Trump and racism in the country seek ways to redeem a liberal imaginary of an idealized and exceptional United States, one dependent upon the disavowal of Indigeneity and settler colonialism. After this discussion, I then transition to looking at the struggles and solidarities among, in particular but not exclusively, Indigenous and Black radical political movements. I do not idealize these relations as seamless or without tensions and discontinuities historically and in the present, but I do read Black and Indigenous radical movements as offering the disruptive interventions and active refusals of settler memory necessary for abolitionist and decolonizing politics and for conceiving and working toward a better world.

CHAPTER ONE

The Settler Memory of Bacon's Rebellion

"So I Dropped Indians"

In 1968, historian Winthrop Jordan published his award-winning and influential book *White over Black: American Attitudes toward the Negro, 1550–1812.*[1] A few years later, he admitted there was a problem with it. In 1974, Jordan published an abridged version of *White over Black*, titled *The White Man's Burden: Historical Origins of Racism in the United States*. In the preface, Jordan wrote about what happened to his original plan to include in the 1968 book the treatment of Indigenous people in the long history of American racism:

> First of all, when I began work on what became *White over Black* I started by analyzing white American attitudes towards blacks *and* Indians. It soon became obvious, as I then thought, that I could not attempt both, so I dropped Indians. But in continuing with attitudes towards Negroes, Indians kept creeping (to use the prevailing stereotype) back in. So in fact there is considerable discussion about attitudes towards Indians in this book. Secondly, I remain convinced that white American attitudes toward blacks have done a great deal to shape and condition American responses to other racial minorities.[2]

Jordan's telling language of "dropping" Indians from his analysis only to find them "creeping back in" resonates beyond his own experience to how the story of race and racism in the United States is generally constructed, remembered, and narrated. Jordan speaks to this point as it concerns U.S. historiography specifically when he notes in the book's appendix, "Suggestions for Further Reading," that "unfortunately, the tendency among historians is to separate ideas about Indians from ideas about Afro-Americans."[3] Note that his language is of the separation of ideas, not a lack of awareness of them.

Jordan implicitly acknowledges here that the problem with *dropping* Indigenous people is that the story of slavery and anti-Black racism is also one of settler colonialism, as anti-Blackness is a position not simply of the white subject but of the white *settler* subject. Since plantation slavery in the Americas required land from Indigenous nations, one cannot tell the story of white over Black without Indigenous dispossession and the construction of the "savage" other "creeping back" in, just as the narrative of whiteness and anti-Blackness informs and shapes the racialization and treatment of Indigenous people. These are a complicated, intertwined set of stories, to be sure, but not telling them together, or not putting them directly into conversation, constrains the potential reach and depth of the meanings one can draw from either story. The faint trace of Indigeneity that Jordan seeks to redress here speaks to his realization of the inherent limitations of his origin story of "American attitudes toward the Negro." The story of anti-Blackness can only get so far if settler memory does its work. As such, I argue that the corollary to anti-Blackness in the U.S. racial context is not anti-Indigeneity, simply put, but what I call necro-Indigeneity. I derive this from the concept of necropolitics, first defined by Achille Mbembe to refer to "the contemporary forms of subjugation of life to the power of death (necropolitics). . . . Necropolitics and necro-power [account for] . . . the new and unique forms of social existence in which vast populations are subjected to conditions of life conferring upon them the status of *living dead*."[4] I posit that necro-Indigeneity takes up a central role as the rarely seen structural support beam of the white-Black racial binary, of the U.S. racial hierarchy, and of U.S. political life in general.

Necro-Indigeneity is a key component of white settlerness because it is central to the settler practice of honoring or memorializing the "dead" as part of establishing the status and belonging of whiteness on territories dispossessed from Indigenous peoples. It thereby constructs Indigeneity today as eliminated or to be eliminated—marked for death by settler life. Furthermore, necro-Indigeneity also shapes the contours of racialized Blackness as split off from any claim to Indigeneity as a subject position, for as Shona Jackson argues, "Settler states that employed enslaved labor rely on two kinds of native death in perpetuity: the death of the Black as native and the death of the native occupant of the land."[5] Jackson is pointing to how the detachment of Blackness from Native identity confines Black subjectivity as a relationship to labor alone, not land, and the "death of the native" focuses on those people, Indigenous peoples of the Americas, who are obstacles to colonial claims upon territory. In this light, to consider the meaning of racism in relationship to necro-Indigeneity, racism takes the form and threat defined by Ruth Wilson Gilmore as "the state-sanctioned or extralegal production and exploitation of group-differentiated vulnerability to premature death."[6] Gilmore is referring to racism in general, but anti-Black racism epitomizes the historical and persistent "vulnerability to premature death" in the U.S. context, while necro-Indigeneity is the presumption of death already enacted, or to be marked for death that is not premature but overdo—the *living dead*, in Mbembe's words. Anti-Blackness and necro-Indigeneity are mutually entwined although not collapsed and seamless concepts. Addressing this complicated relationship has proven difficult for writers and analysts of race in the United States, thus the inclination to "drop the Indians."

This chapter examines the role of settler memory in the oft-repeated narrative of a historical event that many scholars take to be foundational for the political life of race in the U.S. context. This event is Bacon's Rebellion from 1675 to 1677, which has taken on a powerful mnemonic role for scholars, especially of the antiracist Left, as the moment when the *white race was invented*. It is also a story that in its most popular form consistently "drops Indians." To transition to this specific topic, I turn to critical legal and race studies scholar Michelle Alexander, finding in her work the effort to attend to the intertwined relationship of enslavement and dispossession while also replicating the tendency to "drop Indians." Alexander's most notable work, *The New Jim Crow: Mass Incarceration in the Age of Colorblindness*, published in 2010, has achieved the rare feat for an academic book of shaping the wider public discourse about the role of mass incarceration in reproducing the contemporary racial order, especially as it concerns disenfranchising and subordinating Black Americans. The deserved popularity of the book matters here to underscore that the work of settler memory is not marginal to the collective memory of the political life of race in the United States. Settler memory is a shaping force on the analyses and narratives of influential writers on race in the United States, from Jordan to Alexander and many others I discuss in this chapter and beyond.

In Alexander's book, Indigenous peoples and the history of colonial violence and dispossession make two notable, connected appearances. These both occur in the first chapter when Alexander sets out the origin story for her narrative that connects chattel slavery, the creation of the political meaning of race, the formal Jim Crow era, and the modern era of the prison industrial complex (the *new* Jim Crow era). The first appearance is an example of the increasing effort of scholars of race in the United States to *not* separate Indigenous and Black histories. In this sense, it is an important step in acknowledging the place of Indigeneity and settler colonialism as intertwined with the story of race and the institutions of structural oppression in the United States, such as mass incarceration.

In her discussion of the "birth of slavery," Alexander attends to the relationship of the violence toward racialized human beings and the colonial seizure of land required for plantation slavery: "The demand for land was met by invading and conquering large swaths of territory. American Indians became a growing impediment to white European 'progress,' and during this period, the images of American Indians promoted in books, newspapers, and magazines became increasingly negative. As sociologists Keith Kilty and Eric Swank have observed, eliminating 'savages' is less of a moral problem than eliminating human beings, and therefore American Indians came to be understood as a lesser race—uncivilized savages—thus providing justification for the extermination of the native peoples." Here, Alexander builds on the insights from the historical scholarship on slavery to make clear that the enslavement of kidnapped African people and their descendants in the so-called New World required the violent seizure of land from Indigenous nations. Alexander acknowledges and incorporates into her narrative the historical and socioeconomic relationship between the practices of settler colonial conquest and enslavement. At the same time, this specific narrative does end with her reproducing the familiar settler memory of the "extermination of the native peoples"—this being the logic of necro-Indigeneity. Thus, Alexander recalls the place and experience of Indigenous peoples and settler colonialism in serving one of two critical functions in the political life of race in the United States, which is to be the people sacrificed in the violence of dispossession necessary for eventually fostering the system of chattel slavery. After this sacrifice, Indigenous peoples and settler colonialism start to fade into the background in the political memory of enslavement, racism, racial injustice, anti-Blackness, and mass incarceration. This dynamic is particularly discernible in much of the antiracist Left scholarly memory about Bacon's Rebellion, which is the formative seventeenth-century political struggle that shaped the meaning of race, the racial hierarchy, and the white-Black racial binary, or so the story goes. This is the second critical function that Indigeneity and settler colonialism play in the story of the political life of race in the United States, before it drops out, and I begin with Alexander's discussion of it.

Bacon's Rebellion and the "Invention" of the White (Settler) Subject

In *The New Jim Crow*, Alexander immediately follows up her account of the dispossession and "extermination" of Indigenous peoples during the birth of slavery with a discussion of the historical impact of Bacon's Rebellion. This is the story, as Alexander puts it, of "Nathanial [*sic*] Bacon," a "white property owner in Jamestown, Virginia, who managed to unite slaves, indentured servants, and poor whites in a revolutionary effort to overthrow the planter elite."[7] Alexander does not claim to be a scholar of this particular rebellion or of seventeenth-century Virginia, but just as with her initial discussion of the "extermination of the native peoples" as foundational to the origins of chattel slavery, Bacon's Rebellion is de rigueur in many antiracist Left narratives of racialization in the United States. Alexander sets out the story of the rebellion:

> Varying accounts of Bacon's Rebellion abound, but the basic facts are these: Bacon developed plans in 1675 to seize Native American lands in order to acquire more property for himself and others and nullify the threat of Indian raids. When the planter elite in Virginia refused to provide militia support for his scheme, Bacon retaliated, leading an attack on the elite, their homes, and their property. He openly condemned the rich for their oppression of the poor and inspired an alliance of white and black bond laborers, as well as slaves, who demanded an end to their servitude. A number of the people who participated in the revolt were hanged [Bacon himself died of dysentery]. The events in Jamestown were alarming to the planter elite, who were deeply fearful of the multiracial alliance of bond worker and slaves. Word of Bacon's Rebellion spread far and wide, and several more uprisings of a similar type followed.

The next and crucial step in the narrative is the aftermath of the rebellion, in which resides the origin story of the political purpose and life of race in what would become the United States. As Alexander explains, the planter class responded to the rebellion and fear of future rebellions of this sort by taking a "step that would later come to be known as a 'racial bribe'":

> Deliberately and strategically, the planter class extended special privileges to poor whites in an effort to drive a wedge between them and black slaves. White settlers were allowed greater access to Native American lands, white servants were allowed to police slaves through slave patrols and militias, and barriers were created so that free labor would not be placed in competition with slave labor. The measures effectively eliminated the risk of future alliances between black slaves and poor whites. Poor whites suddenly had a direct, personal stake in the existence of a race-based system of slavery. Their own plight had not improved by much, but at least they were not slaves. Once the planter elite split the labor force, poor whites responded to the logic of their situation and sought ways to expand their racially privileged position.[8]

Alexander's outline of Bacon's Rebellion is a condensed version of the events as drawn from her main source, Edmund Morgan's *American Slavery, American Freedom: The Ordeal of Colonial Virginia*.[9] Positioned early in the first chapter of *The New Jim Crow*, it is also the final time in the book in which any Indigenous people or anti-Indigenous actions make an appearance in any way that is significant to the narrative and overall argument. In this regard, Alexander's narrative is not unique, as it follows a well-worn, habituated path in U.S. critical race histories of addressing and then moving on from Indigenous people's concerns. It is the work of settler memory that keeps writers and readers from steering off the course set by this path, as we can see through the habitual replication of the story and the meaning of the rebellion in the work of many other writers on race in the United States.

To start, Edmund Morgan's account of Bacon's Rebellion is one of the most cited by those who discuss it. In his chapter on the rebellion in *American Slavery, American Freedom*, Morgan provides detailed attention to the important role and presence of Indigenous nations, including the Susquehannock, Piscataway, Occaneechi, and Doeg. In so doing, Morgan is clear about Bacon's overt anti-Indian sentiments and the fact that what ignited the rebellion as much as anything was Virginia colonial governor William Berkeley's refusal to commission Bacon to lead his men in an attack against local Indigenous people—"to make war 'against All Indians in general.'"[10] After narrating the rebellion's demise, Morgan concludes the chapter by noting "an obvious lesson in the rebellion. Resentment of an alien race might be more powerful than resentment of an upper class. For men bent on maximum exploitation of labor the implication should have been clear."[11] While here he is referring to Indigenous people as the "alien race" driving Bacon's violent anti-Indian crusade, the larger lesson that English elites took from this was the political value of "racism, to separate dangerous free whites from dangerous slave blacks by a screen of racial contempt."[12] This contempt would be fueled through law, public policy, economic benefits, and social practices that racialized Blackness as signifying an enslavable people whom white people could denigrate, exploit, treat with violent impunity, and buy, own, and sell. The legal and informal capacity to treat Black people in this way came to be a defining feature of whiteness itself. To this end, "Virginia's ruling class," in a model that would be eventually followed in the emergent United States, "proclaimed that all white men were superior to black, [and] went on to offer their social (but white) inferiors a number of benefits previously denied them."[13] On this point, but even more directly, Theodore Allen in *The Invention of the White Race, Volume 2: The Origins of Racial Oppression in Anglo-America* argued that the rebellion was critical for *inventing* whiteness itself as a category and political identity with status and standing in relation to Black people, most notably. As Jeffrey B.

Perry states in the introduction to a new edition of this second volume, Allen's "major thesis" was that "the ruling class invented the 'white race' as a social control mechanism in response to labor solidarity as manifested in the later, civil war stages of Bacon's Rebellion (1676–77). To this he adds two important corollaries: (1) the ruling elite deliberately instituted a system of racial privileges in order to define and establish the 'white race'; and (2) the consequences were not only ruinous to the interests of African-Americans, they were also 'disastrous' for European-American workers, whose class interests differed fundamentally from those of the ruling elite."[14] In the work of other influential authors on the history and politics of race in the United States, one can find a similar pattern in how they tell the story of Bacon's Rebellion and, in so doing, reproduce its long-term meaning for political memory.

In her canonical 1990 article, "Slavery, Race, and Ideology in the United States of America," Barbara Fields's brief capsule of the rebellion begins with "reprisals by Indians, who understandably resented this encroachment by the aliens" and ends with the "suspicion and fear of the growing white lower class in the mind of the rich and powerful."[15] In his 2004 book *The Abolition of White Democracy*, Joel Olson begins with "hatred of Indians" as "an implacable enemy" and concludes his extended discussion of the rebellion, with its ultimate consequence being that "poor whites traded class solidarity for whiteness and its accompanying privileges. . . . The civil rights of the colonist not only served as the basis for American citizenship; they were simultaneously privileges reserved for the white race."[16] In more recent work, Ibram X. Kendi's *Stamped from the Beginning: The Definitive History of Racist Ideas in America* (2016) begins with Berkeley seeking to avoid a "war with neighboring Native Americans" and Bacon writing Berkeley that "the discourse and earnestness of the people is against the Indians" and ends with "poor Whites had risen into their lowly place in slave society—the armed defenders of planters—a place that would sow bitter animosity between them and enslaved Africans."[17] We find another example in a 2018 book, Asad Haider's *Mistaken Identity: Race and Class in the Age of Trump*, which as the title indicates is concerned with the politics of race and class in the contemporary moment. Haider sets out the historical context one needs in order to make sense of the twenty-first century political context, and this includes knowing that "what really changed everything was Bacon's Rebellion in 1676." His brief discussion of the rebellion that "changed everything" begins with a "brutal attack on Indigenous populations" and ends with "The insurrectionary alliance of European and African laborers was a fundamental existential threat to the colonial ruling class, and the possibility of such an alliance among exploited peoples had to be prevented forever."[18]

Each of these writers—as with Jordan, Alexander, Morgan, and Allen before them—is aware of Indigenous people's presence and to a different degree addresses and concurs with the claim that the history of genocidal violence and territorial dispossession against Indigenous nations was fundamental to the creation of the United States. However, due to the constraints of the politics, discourse, and study of race in the United States, Indigeneity and settler colonialism rarely make the final cut as it concerns the wider meaning embedded in the political memory of Bacon's Rebellion. The point of the Bacon's Rebellion story usually concerns the implications for white and Black people as racialized subjects. It almost never takes wider account of Indigenous people as those subject to racism and racist attacks or of Indigenous nations facing threats to their lives and land from the settler colonial society that will become the United States. There is a consistent settler memory pattern here, which shapes the meaning of Bacon's Rebellion as a racial origin story.

The pattern starts with a direct acknowledgment and account of the anti-Indian roots of Bacon's Rebellion, including the settler desire for Indigenous people's land, violent conflict with some Indigenous nations, and the anti-Indian sentiment of, in particular, white settlers led by Bacon. The popular memory of the Rebellion then shifts focus to what in antiracist Left discourse we would call a cross-race, class-based coalition among white (or English) poor and indentured workers and Black (or African) slaves uniting under Bacon's leadership to refuse Berkeley's and the Virginia elite's constraints on their actions and desires, in particular for violence against and land from Indigenous peoples. The next step is that this cross-race, working-class coalition initially directed toward Indigenous nations eventually turns against the elites, and violently so, leading Berkeley to escape and the rebels to burn Jamestown to the ground. The narrative then transitions to the next stage as the rebellion nears its symbolic end, with its leader Bacon dead and the Virginia elite mobilizing to quell the uprising; "one of the last groups to surrender was a mixed band of eighty Negroes and twenty English servants."[19] The "eighty slaves and twenty English servants" figure from Morgan's book is an oft cited historical fact deployed as an important mnemonic device in this origin story, calling forth the lost possibility of a cross-race form of class unity against elite economic and political power. For example, in "The Case for Reparations," Ta-Nehisi Coates discusses a 1704 Virginia law that further codified Black people as enslaved property subject to the most horrific forms of state-sanctioned violence. He follows this up by noting that "there would have still been people alive who could remember blacks and whites joining to burn down Jamestown only twenty-nine years before."[20] His insight about this historical transition from rebellion to institutionalized chattel slavery points to the final element in this pattern: white status over and against Black people is codified along the lines of who can be enslaved and who cannot, who is deputized to police whom, who can engage in racial and sexual violence with impunity, and who is subject to this violence. As this origin story goes, these formalized relations and sanctioned practices slowly institutionalize the white-Black binary in law, governance, economics, and sociocultural relations.

There is one more element in the pattern. It does not happen after the fifth step but rather threads itself slowly through the course of the entire narrative. This is the slow disappearance of Indigenous peoples and the violence against them that is first posited as critical to the *origin* of this origin story and by the end of the tale is but a trace embedded within it. This settler memory pattern allows for the habitual retelling of Bacon's Rebellion as starting with Indigenous peoples' presence and anti-Indian sentiment and ending with the creation of the white subject and the Black other. The path of this story is so well-worn that it is now more of a paved road with guardrails to contain the lessons to three: (1) the creation of the white-Black binary via the racialization of Blackness as enslavability, (2) the demise of a potential cross-race working-class coalition, and (3) the invention of whiteness as a privileged status. These are fundamental insights for race studies that draw from and find their historical and political grounding in the story of Bacon's Rebellion, but they are insights many thinkers on race in the United States arrived at after they "dropped Indians" from their narratives. But what if this story didn't drop Indians? What sorts of insights and alternatives might we garner, not to replace these three important lessons nor as a gesture of unhelpful multicultural inclusiveness but, to adapt Lee Maracle's words, to reimagine how we might "pull the moments of *this* story together, search for its possibilities," and re-pose it for our time?

Property and Patriarchy: Refusing the Settler Memory of Bacon's Rebellion

I turn first to American and Indigenous studies scholar J. Kēhaulani Kauanui (Kanaka Maoli), who is among the few writers to address directly how and at what expense Bacon's Rebellion so often plays a key role in the story of race in the United States. In a piece for a symposium on the life and work of Patrick Wolfe, Kauanui summarizes much of the left historiography of Bacon's Rebellion:

> Scholars and activists alike have perpetuated some romanticized accounts of the rebellion as a historical moment when poor Africans and Europeans united to fight their common exploiters (the English elite). Other accounts narrate it as a missed opportunity, given that poor Europeans eventually went the "white way," joining elites against those increasingly racialized as "black." Thus the Rebellion is also told as a genealogy of "whiteness" as a racial category and the "hidden origins" of race-based chattel slavery.... Today, Bacon's Rebellion is often evoked among the white Left as a reminder that elites will divide and conquer, keeping whites and Blacks from unifying. But what drops out in this lamenting account is that they were allied in challenging the English elites through their united efforts to commit genocide against indigenous peoples. This settler colonial context—imbricated with the North American institution of slavery— is often erased.[21]

Kauanui aptly describes the underlying tone of many left scholarly accounts of Bacon's Rebellion as "romanticized." The idea of romanticizing history speaks to the political role of memory. What we are witnessing here is the work of habit memory, not that of active recollection, given the consistency with which the pattern of the narrative of Bacon's Rebellion is reproduced by numerous scholars. The emphasis on habitual rather than active recollection speaks to the power of collective memory for reproducing the dominant presumptions, terms, constraints, and possibilities of the politics of race in the United States. This is the case such that some of the most insightful, groundbreaking, and radical scholars in the field reproduce it even while taking some account in their narratives of Indigenous presence and anti-Indigenous actions and sentiments. It is the seeing and disavowing of Indigeneity that we must take note of in discerning the implications of the settler memory pattern here, and in this important regard, my assessment of what is at work here differs a bit from that offered by Kauanui.

While I concur with much of Kauanui's reading and her call to reconsider how the rebellion is deployed for contemporary purposes, I argue that this is not about erasure but rather the simultaneous presence and absence of Indigeneity and settler colonialism and the disavowal of their relevance for politics. This is how necro-Indigeneity is a shaping force in U.S. race politics, discourse, and memory. An account that focuses on erasure conveys the idea that the anti-Indian violence of Bacon and his comrades is dropped from these "lamenting accounts," as Kauanui put it. But the previously noted excerpts from multiple authors on the rebellion show that they all, to some degree, incorporate Indigenous presence, settler violence, and territorial invasions against Indigenous nations as important starting points in their narratives. If the problem is erasure, then it can begin to be resolved by demanding presence in the narrative. However, Indigeneity and settler violence are both present and absent in the almost ritualistic retelling of the tale of Bacon's Rebellion. Refusing the work of settler memory in the lessons drawn from Bacon's Rebellion is not about refusing erasure, or at least it is not simply or sufficiently about that. Instead, we need to directly address what the absence *and* presence of Indigeneity, settler violence, and territorial dispossession mean for, among other things, the "genealogy of whiteness" and white settler masculinity, the roots of anti-Blackness, and the "missed opportunity" for a different form of coalitional politics that, as Kauanui rightly notes, are among the lessons many race scholars garner from the memory of the rebellion. Collective memory is tricky, fraught, and never seamless, so this is not about coming up with the correct or all-encompassing narrative; that is not possible and more of an epistemological matter than a political one. The aim is not to tell a completely different story but to tell the same story differently, to shift this seemingly two-dimensional memory slightly to draw out the three-dimensional (or more) features already embedded in it.

In his essay on "Bacon's Rebellion in Indian Country," James Rice argues that the story most often told about the key events and meaning of the rebellion "is not the story Indians would have told."[22] Historian Kathleen Brown would add that it is not the story women and men as gendered subjects would tell, as "out of armed conflict, petitions and postrebellion trials, a new lexicon for colonial masculinity emerged, one in which differences of birth meant less than the privileges of whiteness."[23] The insights provided by these two historians help me to tell the familiar story differently—to provide another set of threads for reweaving the political memory of this period. I will turn to them as I reconsider the familiar story of the rebellion, addressing also the productive function that the disavowal of Indigeneity serves to constrain the meaning usually drawn from this political memory.

For this reconsideration, I focus on Theodore Allen's aforementioned work, *The Invention of the White Race*, volume 2. This volume, published in 1997, builds on the insights of Jordan, Morgan, and the wider historiography and archives concerning slavery and race in the United States. Allen's central argument is that the white race was "invented" intentionally for the political and economic purpose of maintaining social control over, in particular, white labor, and Bacon's Rebellion was critical to this invention. This book has shaped the thinking of many critical race theorists and political theorists studying race and class. I count myself among this group. Joel Olson and Asad Haider made Allen's insight a fundamental premise and plank of their own work as well. I do not refute Allen's general argument, as the case he makes is persuasive and grounded. However, along with being an influential book in the field it is also the presence *and* explicit disavowal of Indigeneity and settler colonialism in the text—explicitly asserted by Allen himself—that draw my critical attention for constricting the book's political insights and reproducing the constraints in U.S. race politics and discourse more generally. I examine the implications of this disavowal because Allen's book is both influential for passing forward the habituated lessons of the rebellion and reflective of wider dynamics beyond the political memory of the Rebellion alone.

In *The Invention of the White Race*, Allen does not engage in Indigenous erasure, as it has a robust chapter on "Euro-Indian Relations and the Problem of Social Control." Instead, his chapter on the "Rebellion—and Its Aftermath" epitomizes the simultaneous absence and presence of Indigeneity and settler colonialism in political memory. Allen begins the chapter by directly discussing the presence of Indigenous peoples and anti-Indian violence in Bacon's Rebellion. He is clear and direct about his decision to disavow the idea that there is any significant long-term meaning one can draw from these facts concerning the origin story of the white race in the United States.

In Allen's words, "I have centered my attention on the second, civil war phase of Bacon's Rebellion—April 1676 to January 1677—rather than the first anti-Indian phase—September 1675 to April 1676."[24] He does so for four reasons, the first of which is a lack of sources from the Indigenous perspective, followed by these three:

> The basic Indian policy of the English ruling elite was motivated not primarily by consideration of social control over exploitable Indian bond-labor in Virginia, but rather a desire to exclude the Indians from English-occupied territory. . . . "White-race" identity was not the principle for which freemen were rallied for the anti-Indian phase of Bacon's Rebellion. The "not-white" and "redskin" classification of the Indian in Anglo-America would be the outcome of the invention of the white race, a transmogrification of the European-American that had not been accomplished in 1676. . . . And final consideration is that Bacon's Rebellion

was not primarily an anti-Indian war, although that was the tenor of the first call to arms by frontier plantation owners such as Nathanial Bacon and William Byrd, capitalists recently arrived in Virginia.[25]

To be clear on the matter, Allen then states why the Indigenous/anti-Indian part of this origin story has nothing, on its own, to teach us today: "The lesson of history to be drawn from the anti-Indian phase of Bacon's Rebellion is clear and retains its relevance today. The European occupation of Indian lands shows that, from Columbus to Custer, the bourgeois eye looks upon progress and genocide indifferently, as incidental aspects of the process of the accumulation of capital; the anti-Indian phase of Bacon's Rebellion was merely another example of that lesson."[26] The phrase "merely another example" does the dual work of making present anti-Indigenous violence by settlers and making absent any wider meaning for the rebellion itself.

To be clear, Allen's specific disavowal concerns the "relevance today" of Indigenous presence, anti-Indian violence, and settler aims in regard to the origin story of whiteness in Bacon's Rebellion itself. He does acknowledge that after this "invention" of whiteness, on in to the eighteenth century, there was the powerful lure of the frontier for "would-be planters," where "they went as 'whites'; resenting Negroes, not their slavery, indeed hating the free Negro most of all; ready now to take the land from the Indians in the name of 'a white man's country.'"[27] What is at stake here is the meaning of freedom for white people, which Allen understandably constructs in relationship to Black people who are enslaved and free, but at the same time, he places the white relationship to Indigenous peoples as a by-product rather than a mutually constitutive product of the meaning of white freedom in and beyond his origin story of the rebellion. The irony here is that the absence/presence of Indigeneity in Allen's argument is a critical component of the invention of the white race as he sets it out; the settler seeds of whiteness are sewn into the story he tells. This is so not despite but rather *because* of the sort of disavowal Allen articulates, which embeds settler masculinity into the constitutive background of the political meaning of whiteness *invented* during this time. Refusing settler memory in order to dislodge settler masculinity from the background of whiteness opens up alternative meanings and memories of the political struggle of Bacon's Rebellion in a way that can help us tell the story differently through the interwoven threads of anti-Blackness, enslavement, anti-Indigenous violence, land dispossession, and heteropatriarchy. Regathering the stories of the oppressive sides of the struggle also opens up political memory for theorizing anew the lost opportunities and lessons for collaborative resistance, or a convergence of interests, that one can draw from this story in considering "its relevance today."

To this end, in setting out how Indigenous nations were "central actors in the conduct of Bacon's Rebellion," James Rice makes the point that the rebellion was "neither two-sided (the governor vs. the rebel), nor three-sided (the governor vs. rebel vs. the Indians), but rather a multisided conflict in which most of the 'sides' lay within Indian country."[28] Rice helps us shift perspective slightly on Bacon's Rebellion in at least two interrelated respects as it concerns (1) how one identifies the peoples and interests involved in this political and military struggle and their relations with one another, and (2) the relationship of all these peoples to territory. First, the rebellion was a "multisided conflict" instead of "three-sided" because the many Indigenous nations in the area were not on the same side—there was intra-Indian conflict. Second, a good portion of the territory upon which the rebellion occurred was understood by the parties of the time as being "Indian country," while the rest was, as Allen himself put it, "English-occupied territory." In other words, the relationships that different peoples had with land took multiple and contested forms and shaped the identities, interests, and meaning of this conflict. Regarding the various "sides" involved, the Susquehannock Nation stood as "the most desperate and formidable enemy that Virginia had faced in over thirty years," while the "Piscataways and the Five Nations Iroquois" represented a strong "military threat" to the Susquehannock should the latter be drawn into a war with their old ally, Virginia.[29] This matters for Bacon's Rebellion—and the conflict between Bacon's and Berkeley's forces and their competing interests—because as Rice notes, "Berkeley wanted to fight only Susquehannocks, while the Baconites wished to rid Virginia of all Indians."[30] Thus, while Berkeley looked at the matter as a Virginia-Susquehannock battle in the midst of a multinational context, Bacon and his forces constructed and enacted it as a settler-Indian conflict in which settler freedom and security depended upon the elimination of Indigenous peoples and the opportunity to claim their territories. Rice offers us a way to read this story differently to show how Bacon's Rebellion involved the forging of a distinct settler identity through a racialized imaginary of and violent opposition to a singular group called "Indians," eliding the distinction between multiple Indigenous nations in the area. This forging of a dualistic settler-Indian fight also constructs a clear dividing line on relationships to territories: settler-occupied land, on the one hand, and a generalized notion of Indigenous territory that settlers desired, on the other. To be clear, this is not a description of the self-conceptions and practices of all the parties at this time—Rice sets out the complicated dynamics on the ground in this regard. It is to say that in reimagining the popular political memory of Bacon's Rebellion in a way that pays attention to the relationship of and among different peoples to land, one cannot drop the role of Indigenous peoples from the story without dropping important factors that shaped the identities and interests that the rebellion has come to represent. By disavowing the constitutive role of settler views and actions toward Indigenous peoples, the role of Indigenous nations themselves, and the identity and interests shaped through views of and relationships with land, the dominant left memory of Bacon's Rebellion narrows and limits the possible meanings and lessons that can be garnered from it. Notably, settler identity through the Baconite perspective is in no small part formed racially through the construction of a racialized Indian identity expressed and manifested through anti-Indian violence and in the desire for land to secure economic benefit and settler freedom.

By contrast, Theodore Allen directly disavows that the genocidal effort to remove or keep Indigenous people out of occupied land—"exclude the Indians from English-occupied territory," as he says—matters for the rebellion's relationship to race and to the political lessons of this moment. His disavowal of the relevance of settler views of Indigenous people and their desire for Indigenous territory narrows the lesson regarding the interests and identity of the emergent white working class to matters of labor—the "social control of labor"—but not also land. Allen splits off the relationships that implicate labor from those concerning land as regards how Bacon's Rebellion shaped racialized subjects and meaning. Allen's analysis constrains the meaning of the invented white race in this moment to labor interests, the legacy of which he and many others, as noted, say we live with to this day. We see this when he asserts that "white-race" identity was not the principle for which "freemen were rallied for the anti-Indian phase" of Bacon's Rebellion. To Allen, the roots of the conflict that would lead to the invention of the white race were fears of Indigenous peoples, settler colonial desires for territory, and the conflicts with Indigenous nations fueled by and that further fueled violent anti-Indian racism. While I would not refute Allen's claim that this transformation to whiteness had not been accomplished by 1676, it is not clear as to why settler anti-Indianism is not then deemed a constitutive root of this emergent invention of the white race, of what he calls "a transmogrification." The logical, historical, and political core of Allen's claim is that the invention of whiteness is a product of the effort to resolve conflicts, reconcile competing claims, and dissolve threats to elite interests. This process of racial creation through and as a means to address conflicts fits well with Michael Omi and Howard Winant's definition of race as "a concept which signifies and symbolizes social conflicts and interests by referring to different types of human bodies."[31] In other words, the racialization of bodies is a product of politics and political, economic, and symbolic interests, not a product of biology or essence. Allen sees and acknowledges the motivating principle of settler identity at this stage, but this is a settler identity he splits off from that of white race identity. This process goes hand-in-hand with his splitting off the political meaning and conflicts regarding land from those concerning labor. Settlerness and whiteness are distinct for Allen, as are land and labor interests, and this is the case for many others who follow this lead in understanding the political life of race in the United States. But how can one grasp the meaning of whiteness in this moment without a relationship to settlerness or the meaning of land politically and socially without accounting for human relations to and claims over land? This question is about not only settler claims to land for the sake of property ownership and economic benefit but also the process of shaping white settler masculinity through seeing and desiring land as foundational to securing the rights of patriarchy and the defense of the domestic realm, of women and children, from threats posed by racialized others. In this regard, gender, patriarchy, and masculinity are underattended suturing forces in shaping the meaning of white settlerness, which need to be dislodged from the background of whiteness to help us tell the story differently.

This brings me back to Kathleen Brown's work, which tells the story of the rebellion differently by focusing on the constitutive role of gender in shaping the terms of the cross-class coalition that drove a wedge between white servants and Black bonded labor and slaves. Here we weave together the story of how the Baconites' anti-Indian violence and territorial desires and actions were, in no small part, a reaction to a racialized threat they perceived to their patriarchal privileges and their capacity to defend the settler domestic realm; to defend the women and children of their settler households. Brown draws out this insight from the archives, where she finds that "most suspected rebels described themselves as the innocent victims of Indians or insisted that the pleas of wives and children compelled them to take action. . . . Provoked by the suffering of family members, men claimed to enter the fray actively because of the exigencies of being providers and protectors."[32] Here the fear of Indians—which was a racialized imaginary and real in terms of the on-the-ground conflicts and violence between settler communities and Indigenous nations—is premised upon both the existence of and the need to defend the settler domestic realm. To be clear, these patriarchal assertions are also reflective of a concern among white elite and working-class men about women who were defiant, or at least not subordinate enough, to male authority. Brown refers often to women as religious dissenters, gossipers, and those inclined toward defiant speech, including "the threat presented by the small number of women in each county who had crafted powerful community identities through property ownership, legal learning, or reputations for defiance."[33] Thus, as Brown puts it, in many ways the rebellion is the story of the consolidation of a "new constellation of honor and manhood—rooted in property and patriarchy—that ordinary men were demanding for themselves."[34] This drive and concern for property and patriarchy shaped the terms and components of a distinctly white settler masculinity for servants and laborers, one that pivoted around many things, including the need and right to have guns to defend the white settler realm. As Roxanne Dunbar-Ortiz points out, decades before Bacon's Rebellion the "Virginia militia was founded for one purpose: to kill Indians, take their land, drive them out, wipe them out. European settlers were required by law to own and carry firearms. . . . Militias were also used to prevent indentured European servants from fleeing."[35] The guns that were first used against Indigenous people, enslaved Africans, and European indentured servants were eventually turned on English elites in Virginia during the rebellion. For elites, dissolving this threat was an important element of the postrebellion aftermath to forestall further resistance from white non-elite men, as Brown states: "The colonial government conceded its need for these men to fulfill responsibilities as householders. Berkeley's attempts to ban arms and ammunition in the aftermath of the rebellion were soon overturned by complaints that the absence of weapons left individuals vulnerable, unable to defend their households against Indians, or feed their families."[36] Thus, "in the aftermath of Bacon's Rebellion, the inherent honor of white manhood became increasingly based on the right to carry a gun."[37] Here the story ties together settler fears of Indigenous people as threats to settler domesticity with the efforts of Virginia elites to stoke settler fears about the loss of patriarchal standing to help foster a white male bond between elites and workers.

The colonial government's effort to secure for white working men the rights and privileges of settler masculinity in the aftermath of Bacon's Rebellion was another way that white and Black people were driven apart, made enemies rather than allies, in which gender, race, class, and colonialism thread together a story told differently than that usually offered. When Theodore Allen seeks to split off the anti-Indian and civil war phases of the rebellion, he bifurcates the relationship of settler identity and whiteness in a way that collapses rather than opens up the sites and subjects of oppression under white supremacy and the meaning of freedom for white men. Opening up this story compels us to attend to how masculinity and patriarchy shape the contours of white settlerness in a tripartite relationship to Indigenous peoples whom are deemed threats to the domestic realm, to Black people who symbolize the enslavement that white men feared could become their condition, and to women who represent, at once, dependency and a defiance of male authority. The role of gender in relation to racial formation is critical here, for it served to divide, in particular, white men from Black men. Brown sets this out: "During the last quarter of the seventeenth century, white legislators systematically stripped enslaved men of the trappings of masculinity enjoyed by white men: property ownership, gun possession, and access to white women. In doing so, they transformed the rebellious potential of autonomous white men into a form of domestic patriarchy that reinforced rather than undermined the social order."[38] It is important to be clear about three elements at work here: (1) "Property ownership" implicates dispossession of Indigenous territories; (2) "gun possession" references the seeming threat to settler domesticity that gives meaning to land as not only about accumulating capital and economic security but also securing a notion of freedom built upon a gendered and racialized relationship of standing and domination over one's domestic realm, defended at all costs; and (3) "*access* to white women" denotes the gendered and sexualized privileges of white men in a patriarchal relationship to white women, just as it also makes Black women invisible, as nonsubjects. To this latter point, it is worth recalling Saidiya Hartman's words from chapter 1 that "the captive female was both will-less and always willing." Thus, a story told differently about the colonial government's "racial bribe" to English servants that attends to settler masculinity in demarcating whiteness from Blackness thereby draws out the racialized meaning of gender to divide white men from Black men through a norm of settler masculinity that positioned white women as subordinated subjects, Black men and women as subordinated will-less objects, and Indigenous men and women as subject to genocidal elimination. The function of white settler masculinity in this story reveals a notion of freedom based in property ownership (actualized or desired) and the right to defend the settler domestic realm and the rights and privileges of patriarchy through the barrel of a gun directed at racialized others and as a means of access to gendered others. Inspired by Maracle's words, if we "pull the moments of *this* story together" in this way, how then do we remember Bacon's Rebellion differently in order to reimagine and open it up, "search for its possibilities," instead of trying to tell a completely different story that would itself disavow important features?

I suggest considering the narrative possibilities for political memory of Brown's words about the demands of "ordinary men" for a "new constellation of honor and manhood—rooted in property and patriarchy." In short, let us say that the racial bribe to white working-class men in the aftermath of Bacon's Rebellion was based in the promise of *property and patriarchy.* Property and patriarchy in this context coimplicate the role of land, labor, race, gender, and colonialism in a differently posed memory of Bacon's Rebellion. Brown connects these elements of the emergent racial, colonial, and patriarchal orders as an intersecting oppressive formation during this time: "In the aftermath of the rebellion, white men received political recognition as providers, masters, and potential patriarchs, but the law defined enslaved men as incapable of these attributes. Caught in the racist undertow of the crusade against Indians, the political reaction to civil war, and the economic need for a new source of labor, male slaves were systematically stripped of the privileges of white manhood."[39] Here we see a particular example of the development about which Aileen Moreton-Robinson writes regarding the history of the *white possessive*: "From the seventeenth century onward, race and gender were markers that divided humans into three categories: being property, owning property, and being made propertyless."[40] Black people's bodies and their progeny become property in which, as Saidiya Hartman put it starkly, "slavery conscripted the womb."[41] White people gain the right to own property in the form of human and territorial bodies. Indigenous peoples are violently dispossessed of their territory that white settlers transform into property. The legal, political, and socioeconomic developments in the decades after Bacon's Rebellion secured access to and the rights of *property and patriarchy* that codified the invention of white settler masculinity, backed by the gun with which white settler men could *stand their ground* against Indigenous invaders and rebellious Black slaves. This is not a completely different story from the popular memory and lessons of the rebellion. I agree with Allen that the "white race" in the pre-U.S. context was invented as a political identity around this time, but he has a narrowed imaginary of the *invention* itself and thereby what one is seeking to dismantle in abolishing it. However, by refusing settler memory and compiling the story a little differently, the property and patriarchy dimension emerges from the background to reimagine the narrative and the implications of this popular political memory, offering a chance to reconsider its relevance for today.

Recall that, in Allen's terms, we get the invention of whiteness through the process by which Virginia elites broke the English-African labor coalition of Bacon's Rebellion, but not in advance of it. Whiteness and Blackness, and thus anti-Blackness as a designation tied to enslavability, are thereby coproduced in this political moment, out of which we get the white-Black binary. By reading the "'not-white' and 'redskin' classification of the Indian in Anglo-America" as a by-product rather than one of the key elements in turning the European-Americans into the white race, Allen disavows how settler desires for land and thus property are imagined to secure patriarchal domain over the settler domestic realm, an important component of this newly invented whiteness, of white settler masculinity. When settlerness is left to lurk in the shadows of whiteness, thus does lurk the relationship to land and heteropatriarchy too. In so doing, Allen is then unintentionally disavowing how settler masculine desires, fears, and actions around property and patriarchy also shape and fuel anti-Blackness, as part of the racial bribe. Settler desires for control over land, women, and racial others are at the propertied and patriarchal root of the production of white standing that formalizes the anticitizenship and enslavability of Black people—of anti-Blackness—and the genocidal elimination and dispossession of Indigenous peoples—of necro-Indigeneity. I pose this as an intervention into this powerful political memory in U.S. race studies, as a refusal of Allen's disavowals that shape for his contemporary audience what do and do not count as the politically pertinent factors that comprise and maintain the white race. To Allen, the key pillars of whiteness are the social control of labor and enhanced rights and privileges in relation to Black people, which then need to be critiqued, opposed, and dismantled in an antiracist, especially abolitionist, politics. I agree with him as far as he goes, but his story does not go far enough. The politics of land, colonialism, Indigenous peoples, and the interconnected formations of heteropatriarchy and settler domesticity are, by this logic and narrative, not deemed to be among the pertinent political lessons one can garner from the antiracist Left memory of Bacon's Rebellion as it concerns defining the aims of abolishing whiteness and white democracy. But let's connect stand-your-ground laws in our time to the political memory of Bacon's Rebellion so as to deploy this memory to imagine a convergence of interests to oppose this contemporary policy that is utilized primarily by white people, especially men, to defend with violent impunity their domestic realms and bodies from perceived threats by racial others. A narrative of the rebellion as the invention of white settler masculinity through the violent right to defend property and patriarchy offers a much more coherent mnemonic connection than does the constrained political memory Allen offers. After all, from whence comes the ground upon which the white man stands and that he defends, and what in all its heteropatriarchal glory is he defending?

I bring up the example of stand-your-ground laws to think differently about Bacon's Rebellion, keeping in mind Allen's concerns with, in his words, that which "retains its relevance today." The work of settler memory in Allen's narrative is his disavowal of the historical and contemporary political relevance of anti-Indian actions during Bacon's Rebellion, which limit its political relevance today to whiteness and race politics narrowly conceived, including what fuels anti-Blackness, the race/class divide, and the lessons one can take about missed opportunities for radical political coalitions. As to the latter point, as noted, Kēhaulani Kauanui suggests that one consequence is that "instead of seeing Bacon's rebellion as a missed opportunity for poor European and poor Africans, the historical event reveals a lost chance for alliance politics between African and Indigenous peoples."[42] Kauanui points us toward the deeper problem, which is that far too often the idea that Bacon's Rebellion could offer us any lessons for Black and Indigenous collaboration or Black and Indigenous political struggles on their own or in relation to one another is foreclosed in advance if settler memory is not refused. By contrast, a political memory of the rebellion that frames it around a racial bribe with property and patriarchy as its core enticements opens up the possibilities for centering collaboration less around possible coalitions than around central sites of struggle and contention. These central sites are the forms of oppression required to maintain the rule of property and patriarchy in a white settler state that coimplicates white supremacy, capitalism, settler colonialism, and heteropatriarchy. But when settler memory remains lodged in the background of the white-Black binary in U.S. race discourse, it is much more difficult to make such a connection between the past and the present, to draw out the features of the "past that is not past," in such laws as stand your ground or the similarly directed castle doctrine.[43] These types of laws are created out of and reproduce the notion of innocent white victims facing racialized threats to their settler domestic realms, and thus these laws immunize homeowners in their use of violence to defend property and patriarchy. These laws are subject to critique in our time, and in that light one might consider how telling the story of Bacon's Rebellion differently offers ways for students, scholars, and activists to imagine and theorize how to enact coalitions and collaborations in opposing such legalized defenses of white supremacy, capitalism, colonialism, and patriarchy. A differently told memory of Bacon's Rebellion may be able to help with theorizing convergent sites of resistance rather than divergent sites that, say, construct political interests and subjectivities around primarily labor for Black and white people and around land for Indigenous peoples, with a disengagement from the role of heteropatriarchy.

The lesson of a reimagined Bacon's Rebellion that does not "drop Indians" is that one cannot split off land from labor when the human bodies that are laboring as enslaved people, as gendered subjects, and as exploited wage workers or indentured laborers are produced through their relationships to lands dispossessed from Indigenous peoples, just as the meaning of the land is defined in relationship with and through the meaning making by human beings in law, politics, economics, and culture. Remembering the rebellion differently provides a vehicle for reshaping contemporary imaginaries, possibilities, and critiques in a world in which scholars and activists are constantly searching for ways to assess and refigure the terms and practices of solidarity, collaboration, and coalition and the accompanying lines of antagonism.

Reconsidering America's Original Sin(s)

I close with a ready example of reimagining U.S. collective memory, with the words of Michelle Alexander from 2016. Like Winthrop Jordan, she, too, had an epiphany about "dropping Indians." On her Facebook page in February 2016, Alexander recommended an article about the history of the incarceration of Indigenous people that featured a photograph of the late nineteenth-century handcuffs used on Indigenous children who were dragged away from their families and sent to boarding schools to be, in the language of the time, "civilized." In her recommendation, Alexander said the following:

> This is a lengthy yet powerful account of the history that gave rise to the mass incarceration of Native Americans, a subject that has received almost no public attention or acknowledgement. On occasion, I've made the mistake of referring to slavery as America's "original sin," which ignores the fact that our current democracy would not have been possible without the genocide of indigenous people. I think we should speak of "original sins"—in the plural—if we want to give an accurate account of our nation's formation. I do not believe there is any way to repair the harm that has been done, but I do believe this history ought to guide us as we strive to tell the whole truth about the past and consider what must be done to build not only a new justice system, but a new America. This picture of tiny handcuffs made for Native American children says it all. (Facebook, February 25, 2016)

Alexander checks herself on her and the nation's inattention to not only the genocidal killing and incarceration of Indigenous people but also the various ways in which this history gets subsumed, even disappears, relative to slavery's place in the story of the nation's formation. Importantly, she addresses the degree to which this absence then limits our grasp of the history and present of mass incarceration and the violence of policing.

Alexander refuses this erasure by recasting the political memory of U.S. practices and institutions of white supremacy as also being settler colonial in nature, as original *sins*, plural. She is not alone in this reconsideration of the nation's founding as conveyed in the collective memory of the United States. Dr. Cornel West poses the matter similarly: "To tell the truth about the history of this grand experiment in democracy is prophetic fightback. We're grounded on the dispossession of land of our precious indigenous brothers and sisters and the violation of their bodies. People talk about slavery being America's original sin. That's not true. The treatment of our indigenous brothers and sisters was our original sin. Slavery was second."[44] Alexander and West offer a compelling way to reimagine and reshape the collective memory of the foundational oppressions of the United States as a means for mobilizing radical collaborations and imaginaries in the present. In this regard, a reframing of what counts as the nation's original sins calls forth a powerful and deep rhetorical legacy in the United States, one that has understandably centered on Black enslavement.

The first recorded use of the phrase to refer to the American "sin" of slavery and involvement in the slave trade was by James Madison in 1820: "All these perplexities develope [*sic*] more & more the dreadful fruitfulness of the original sin of the African trade."[45] A Google search for "original sin of slavery" turns up over twenty-seven thousand hits, mostly concerning the United States. A search of "America's original sin" comes up with over forty-five thousand hits, with slavery and racism as the constant referent. By contrast, a search for "the original sin of genocide" turns up eight results, only half of which have a reference to Indigenous peoples in the U.S. context, and a search for the "original sin of Native American genocide" turns up exactly one result—and various word permutations using "Indigenous," "American Indian," or "Native" lead to no better results. While a comparative tally of Google search results is a snapshot of this question, it does suggest another way in which slavery and racism are central, and uniquely so, in the American national narrative, with dispossession, genocide, and colonialism in the background. This does not mean the reframing to original *sins* cannot take hold, but it raises questions about what sort of political struggles, antagonisms, and visions it suggests.

The language and meaning of sin implies redemption, or at least the possibility of it, and efforts to achieve it. However, in a settler colonial context built on the dispossession of Indigenous peoples from their lands, a fundamental element of any path toward redemption would have to involve the decolonizing return of territory to Indigenous nations and a radically rethought and practiced human relationship to land, to one another, and to nonhuman life. Would redeeming the original sins of the United States mean a collaborative decolonization and abolitionist politics, which dismantles the rule of property and patriarchy? I don't know, but I would be interested in hearing the answer from those who suggest we remember the story of the United States differently in this way, and it is the sort of question that a critical engagement with the politics of memory should ask in response to such invocations. As with the origin story of Bacon's Rebellion to which so many race theorists turn to fuel liberating imaginaries via the lessons of the past, be they tales of caution or of lost potential, Alexander's and West's framing of "original sins" both holds out hope for an expansive and radical vision while also having to grapple with its potential limitations. I find a similar dynamic with the way in which writers turn to the period after the American Civil War of 1861–1865, when it seemed like another violent conflict and rebellion might open up a path to liberation. Next, in chapter 2, I examine the role of settler memory in the political lessons and memory drawn from the story of the Reconstruction era, which formally lasted from 1865 to 1877. The Reconstruction era is another origin story to which writers and activists turn for radical mnemonic fuel.

CHAPTER TWO

Reconstructing Political Memory

The Reconstruction Era and the
Faint Trace of Settler Colonialism

The Mirror of Reconstruction

While Bacon's Rebellion has powerful mnemonic appeal for many who study race and class politics in the U.S. context, the Reconstruction era that formally lasted from 1865 to 1877 has a more wide-ranging, persistent role in the politics of American collective memory. In his 1980 address as president of the American Historical Association, John Hope Franklin spoke to the importance of the Reconstruction era to the nation's collective memory: "If every generation rewrites its history, as various observers have often claimed, then it may be said that every generation since 1870 has written the history of the Reconstruction. And what historians have written tells as much about their own generation as about the Reconstruction period itself."[1] The title of his address and eventual publication was "Mirror for Americans: A Century of Reconstruction History."[2] Franklin's words capture how in the political life and memory of race in the United States, the Reconstruction era has foundational resonance. The metaphor of the mirror speaks to how in the Reconstruction era each subsequent generation sees what it wants to see, what it needs to see, in order to intervene in and define the imperatives of its time. This remains true.

In 2015, Eric Foner, an eminent historian of Reconstruction, wrote an editorial for the *New York Times* titled "Why Reconstruction Matters," in which he concludes: "Citizenship, rights, democracy—as long as these remain contested, so will the necessity of an accurate understanding of Reconstruction. More than most historical subjects, how we think about this era truly matters, for it forces us to think about what kind of society we wish America to be."[3] To Foner, an engagement with the memory of the Reconstruction era can help us grasp the conditions, challenges, and possibilities of the present day. He is not alone. In 2017, Ta-Nehisi Coates published a collection of essays titled *We Were Eight Years in Power: An American Tragedy*. The book traces Coates's emergence as a writer and his assessment of, in particular, U.S. race relations during the eight years of Barack Obama's presidency from 2009 to 2017. However, the title is not a direct reference to Obama's eight years as president; it is a quote from the Reconstruction and post-Reconstruction eras. The title comes from the words of Black American Thomas Miller, a South Carolina congressman who in 1895 appealed to delegates at the state's constitutional convention to support voting rights—a failed effort in the end—in a statement that began with "we were eight years in power." Miller was referencing eight years in the midst of the Reconstruction era when Black American citizens and elected officials ran the state government that built and rebuilt the infrastructure of South Carolina and "placed it on a road to prosperity."[4] There is no significant mention of Reconstruction in the rest of *We Were Eight Years in Power*. Rather, with the title Coates deploys Miller's words as a political memory that gestures to the symmetries between the past and present of race politics in the United States.

We can see this mnemonic connection to the Reconstruction era in political organizing, such as in the Moral Mondays and New Poor People's Campaign movements led by Reverend Dr. William J. Barber. The title of Barber's 2016 book asserts that we need *The Third Reconstruction*. The "Second Reconstruction" refers to the mid-twentieth-century civil rights movement and the Civil Rights Acts of the 1960s that the movement produced. To grasp the urgency of the present political condition, Barber directs his readers to the past: "You couldn't understand America's deep need for a Third Reconstruction without studying our history of partial progress, which has been met, time and again, by immoral destruction."[5] On this point, he notes: "In both the First and Second Reconstructions, it took the extremists more than a decade to mount an effective reaction. . . . We are participating in the embryonic stages of a Third Reconstruction."[6] As it concerns this political project, Robert Greene in *Dissent* magazine in 2018 argued that "if the left wishes to make the most of the Third Reconstruction—not just defeating a revanchist right wing at the polls but fundamentally changing the nation for the better—we can draw important insights from these two previous eras of civic revolution." A key lesson to be drawn is that "in each of the previous two Reconstructions, an inability to unite across various identity fault lines contributed to the collapse of the progressive insurgency." Thus, "what we should take from the idea of a Third Reconstruction is an awareness of how issues of race, class, and gender continually intersect to shape people's lives."[7] Greene hopes those shaping a Third Reconstruction will learn this lesson.

For contemporary writers and activists, especially those concerned with the persistence of racial inequality, the mirror of Reconstruction reflects what might have been in terms of bringing into fruition a radical vision of freedom and liberation and what could still be if we heed the hard-earned lessons of the past. The political focus of these memories attends primarily to race and class inequality. The turn to the first Reconstruction to help us think through the political challenges of our time also provides a chance to open up this tricky, slippery, and powerful memory to consider how it might be told differently if one were to attend to the conditions, struggles, and claims of Indigenous peoples and the functions of settler colonialism.

For the most part, the histories of Indigenous nations and of U.S. settler colonialism during the late nineteenth century are disconnected or split off from the political story and habituated memory of the Reconstruction era. This splitting constrains the possibilities for reimagining and theorizing the political meaning and lessons of this era. Echoing Winthrop Jordan's comment that the "tendency among historians is to separate ideas about Indians from ideas about Afro-Americans" from chapter 1, historian W. Fitzhugh Brundage writes: "In recent years historians have exposed the interrelated processes of pacifying the postwar South and wresting the American west from its previous inhabitants. . . . Americans both then and since seem to have quarantined the memories of Reconstruction and the conquest of the West from each other. Somehow the Reconstruction of the South stands outside of the national narrative while the conquest of the West is enfolded within it."[8] I concur with Brundage's claim that there is an almost "quarantine-like" separation of the Reconstruction and Western conquest stories in U.S. collective memory. However, in the case of the antiracist Left memory of this period I find there to be a reversal of the dynamic he denotes in which Reconstruction is placed outside the nation's story and Western conquest is enfolded into it. For those seeking to call forth memories and devise transformative visions for abolishing white supremacy and capitalism, the Reconstruction era and its aftermath are central to the narrative of a post–Civil War white supremacist nation shaped by the political and economic imperatives of what we now call racial capitalism.[9] On the other hand, the story of U.S. expansion and conquest that occurs at the expense of Indigenous peoples is often positioned if not fully outside, then as juxtaposed with the defining events, structures, and critical forms of contention of this period. It is not that this history is unknown but rather that it is not acknowledged as constitutive enough of the nation's past on these matters when this era is invoked to inform our contemporary political condition. A major consequence of the quarantining of Reconstruction from the conquest of the West is the reproduction of a conceptual mapping in political memory that quarantines a focus on labor from one that attends to the role of land. What also falls through the gaps of this divide is attention to gender and sexuality in relation to settler domesticity and the coimplicated imperatives of securing the regimes of property and patriarchy.

The solution here is not, as Joseph Genetin-Pilawa astutely cautions, "simply wedging Indian affairs into the story of Reconstruction," as that "obscures more than it reveals."[10] Rather, my approach is to draw out the way in which land is present and absent from the story of Reconstruction—present in a distinct and vital way but also absent as to its source, meaning, and relevance for not only Indigenous peoples but Black Americans too. There is a settler memory of land at work in Reconstruction memory, which is a cause and consequence of positioning Indigenous peoples, settler colonial practices, and white settler masculinity in the background of left political memories of this era. To dislodge them from their background positioning, I take a closer look at the canonical text of antiracist Left understanding and memory of the Reconstruction era, that which historian Moon-Ho Jung called "the greatest book that the US historical professional has ever produced."[11] That is, W. E. B. Du Bois's *Black Reconstruction in America: 1860–1880*, published in 1935. The mirror of Reconstruction for many left scholars, writers, and activists reflects back an image shaped through Du Bois's powerful study.[12]

Du Bois's *Reconstruction* of Political Memory

With *Black Reconstruction*, Du Bois rejected the narrative of the likes of the Dunning School that placed the blame for Reconstruction's failure at the feet of Black Americans and white Northerners for being some combination of incompetent, corrupt, slothful, and licentious. Du Bois retold the story of the Reconstruction era from the perspective of many interests and parties to it, but in particular that of Black Americans as "ordinary human beings" critical to engineering the defeat of the Confederacy and bringing about political achievements despite the fact that the effort to reconstruct the South and "make black men American citizens was in a certain sense all a failure, but a splendid failure."[13] The "splendid" element came in the manner in which Black freedmen across the South, with "all the wealth and all the opportunity, and all the world against" them, took on the rigorous and committed task of a "great and just cause; fighting the battle of the oppressed and despised humanity of every race and color."[14] The many accomplishments produced by Black legislators in the South during this time included the creation of public schools and historically Black colleges and universities that exist to this day.[15] In reweaving the story of Reconstruction—clear-eyed about its failures and the reasons for it; diligent in foregrounding the "splendid" accomplishments and radical potential it offered—Du Bois challenged and effectively shifted the politics of memory of the period. It is thus no coincidence that the book's last chapter is "The Propaganda of History," in which he provided the summary lesson of his study.

In this final chapter, Du Bois blasts historians of his time: "One is astonished in the study of history at the recurrence of the idea that evil must be forgotten, distorted, skimmed over. . . . We must forget that George Washington was a slave owner, or that Thomas Jefferson had mulatto children, or that Alexander Hamilton had Negro blood, and simply remember things we regard as creditable and inspiring. The difficulty, of course, with this philosophy is that history loses its value as an incentive and example; it paints perfect men and noble nations, but it does not tell the truth."[16] He surmises that an American child "would in all probability complete his education without any idea of the part which the black race has played in America; of the tremendous moral problem of abolition, of the cause and meaning of the Civil War and the relation which Reconstruction had to democratic government and the labor movement today." Du Bois then turns his attention to his main targets: "The treatment of the period of Reconstruction reflects small credit upon American historians as scientists. We have too often a deliberate attempt so to change the facts of history that the story will make pleasant reading for Americans."[17]

His critique resonates today in the tendency to avoid ugly truths about the past. In many ways, the lesson Du Bois provides here inspires my own reexamination of Black Reconstruction, drawing out presumptions lodged in the background. In this case, I mean to attend to the subtle forms of settler memory at work in the book. In posing my intervention in this way, I am not pointing out a major flaw in the book as if it should or could have been otherwise or implying that Du Bois approved of Indigenous people's violent treatment or dispossession. His substantial oeuvre and his own political history show that is not the case. For example, Du Bois was an associate member of the Society of American Indians and accompanied Santee Dakota Charles Eastman to the Universal Races Congress in London in 1911.[18] Du Bois wrote about the Reconstruction era while living through the Jim Crow era, which shaped his political imperatives regarding the intervention he sought to make with the book. To recall John Hope Franklin, Du Bois was addressing the urgent matters of his generation by reexamining the history and reposing the political memory and meaning of the Reconstruction era. In this spirit, attending to the story of land in Black Reconstruction offers a way to tilt the angle on this mirror a bit so as to examine and recast some of its embedded presumptions that forestall alternative, potentially anticolonial, imaginaries and lessons to be taken from this era.

The Story of Land

At the end of the first chapter of *Black Reconstruction*, on "The Black Worker," Du Bois writes that the "emancipation of man is the emancipation of labor and the emancipation of labor is the freeing of that basic majority of workers who are yellow, brown, and black."[19] This vision of emancipation is a story of labor solidarity and liberation from class oppression grounded, literally and figuratively, in the role of land. Eric Foner argues that "Du Bois was the first historian to stress [land's] centrality to the era's history," and the "land issue was crucial to the fate of Reconstruction as was the struggle over control of the labor of emancipated slaves."[20] Land is central to Du Bois's narrative and analysis. Control over, claims to, and efforts to redistribute land are pivotal in the racial and class power struggle of this era, to the hopes for and the demise of Reconstruction. Du Bois maintained a clear focus on land as central for securing the economic and political freedom of Black people over the long term and to building a cross-race, class-based coalition with working-class white people in particular. Political struggles over land and the aims for land redistribution are explicit features of this vision of cross-racial class solidarity even more directly than is the case in the antiracist Left memory of Bacon's Rebellion.

However, while land is crucial and ever present in the story of Reconstruction as Du Bois tells it, what I call *the story of land* remains in the background of the wider narrative. I am referring here to the story of how land comes to have its political, economic, and cultural meaning and value in the political struggles of this period. This is necessarily a story of dispossession of land from Indigenous nations and its transformation and mobilization for other purposes, be it as the basis for the liberation of working classes or for consolidating the hegemony of racial capitalism. Thus, the story of land is also a story—many stories—of people, of many different peoples, and in particular of Indigenous peoples.

In the general period in U.S. history from the American Civil War through Reconstruction and its aftermath, Indigenous nations were dispossessed of their lands at a considerable rate, Indigenous nations resisted and fought back against white settler state invasion, and brutal anti-Indian violence involved historic massacres and devastating removal and eliminatory practices. Two

U.S. federal policies that led to significant dispossession of Indigenous territory bookend this historical period. These were the Homestead Act of 1862, through which around three hundred million acres of collectively held Indigenous territory was made available at a low cost to railroad companies and to settlers, and the General (or Dawes) Allotment Act of 1887, which broke up Indigenous tribal reservations, allotted individual parcels of land provisionally to Indigenous male heads of households primarily, and sold the rest of the lands off to non-Indigenous purchasers, white settlers for the most part. By 1934, the Dawes Act had turned ninety million acres of Indigenous collective territory into settler-owned private property.[21] In the midst of these two policies, the U.S. federal government also instituted President Ulysses S. Grant's "Peace Policy," starting in 1868, which aimed to confine Indigenous peoples to reservations and tasked missionaries—backed by U.S. soldiers— with imposing Euro-American norms of dress and farming as well as Christian beliefs, including heteropatriarchal family structures and gender roles. In 1871, through a rider to an Indian Appropriations Act, the U.S. Congress legislated an end to formal treaty making with Indigenous nations, signaling a turning point in U.S.-Indigenous relations. Thus, this era in U.S. Indian policy witnessed the aggressive and accelerated breaking up and dispossession of Indigenous territorial landholdings and the imposition of Euro-American heteropatriarchal forms of family and gender roles. In other words, property and patriarchy continued to be twin pillars of settler colonial rule in the post– Civil War period.

Indigenous people and nations were by no means passive actors in the face of all this. For example, in 1870 Sarah Winnemucca of the Paiute Nation wrote to Tonawanda Seneca Ely S. Parker, the commissioner of Indian Affairs from 1869–1871 (the first Indigenous person in this federal role), to protest the treatment of her people under Grant's Peace Plan. She did so in order to decry the prospects of life on a reservation for the Paiutes. The letter, subsequently published in such newspapers as the *Chicago Tribune*, protested that "if this is the kind of civilization awaiting us on the reserve, God grant that we may never be compelled to go on one, it is more preferable to live in the mountains and drag out an existence in our native manner." Winnemucca's critical analysis of the U.S. government's plans for her people leads her to close the letter with a compromise proposal to Parker, stating: "On the other hand, if the Indians have any guarantee that they can secure a permanent home on their own native soil, and that our white brethren can be kept from encroaching on our rights after having a reasonable share of ground allotted to us on our own, and giving us the required advantage of learning, etc., I warrant that the savage, as he is called to-day, will be a law abiding member of the community fifteen or twenty years hence."[22] As she did throughout her fascinating and underexplored career, Winnemucca balances her assertion of Indigenous political and material demands for life, land, and freedom from white settler invasion with the strategic need to appeal to white settler norms, even while underscoring that the notion of the "savage" is a colonialist and racist view with the qualifier "as he is called to-day." Winnemucca is one of many Indigenous people whose voices and actions were consistent features of the politics of the post–Civil War U.S. context. For example, at the collective level, notable Indigenous military resistance to settler invasion during this period included the Oceti Sakowins' (the Great Sioux Nation) 1866 victory over the U.S. Army garrisoned along the Bozeman Trail, which led to the 1868 Treaty of Fort Laramie. More famously, as well, the Sioux and allied nations were victorious at the Battle of Greasy Grass (Little Big Horn) in 1876 against a military invasion led by General George Armstrong Custer.

These forms of resistance are some of the examples of Indigenous efforts to defend their lives and land in the face of genocidal violence perpetrated by state and nonstate actors during this formative period from the American Civil War on through to the end of the nineteenth century. In the midst of and beyond the war, settler state violence against Indigenous peoples occurred in such notorious forms as the 1862 U.S. state execution by hanging of thirty-eight Dakota men in Mankato, Minnesota. This remains the largest formal mass state execution in United States history, authorized by President Abraham Lincoln only days before he signed the Emancipation Proclamation. These executions occurred after the Dakota Uprising and the U.S.-Dakota War of 1862 that was sparked by the failure of the United States to live up to its treaty promises, which left the Dakota without payment for land they ceded and literally starving. Layli Long Soldier gets to the heart of the matter in her poem "38": "One should read 'The Dakota people starved' as a straightforward and plainly stated fact. As a result—and without other options but to continue to starve—Dakota people retaliated. Dakota warriors organized, struck out, and killed settlers and traders. This revolt is called the Sioux Uprising."[23] The Dakota people were punished, with thirty-eight executed, for rebelling against a settler state that took their land and left them to die. This execution was followed not long after by the Sand Creek Massacre of 1864 in which upward of five hundred Southern Cheyenne and Arapaho Indians were murdered by U.S. troops. This pattern of eliminatory settler colonial violence against Indigenous peoples that continued during the post–Civil War period of U.S. settler state advancement is notably bookended by the Wounded Knee Massacre of 1890, in which the U.S. Seventh Calvary killed up to three hundred disarmed Lakota Sioux on the Pine Ridge Reservation.[24] In 1990, the U.S. House of Representatives and the U.S. Senate passed a resolution of "deep regret" to apologize for the Wounded Knee Massacre.[25]

Furthermore, in a settler eliminatory practice that in some ways persists into the early twenty-first century, during this period thousands of Indigenous children were stolen from families and communities by settler nonstate and state organizations to assimilate them into white settler heteropatriarchal norms of dress, language, gender, and liberal, free market individualism. As historian Margaret Jacobs explains, this policy was driven in great part by white settler women in a "maternalist politics" in which they had the often sincere self-image of being the *Indian's Friend*. And "by depicting indigenous women as the degraded chattel of their men who failed to measure up to white, middle-class Christian ideals, many white women missionaries and reformers created a pathological view of indigenous women and gender relations that became yet another justification for the removal of indigenous children."[26] This policy of removing Indigenous children to boarding schools was driven by the effort to impose ideals of white settler domesticity and European gender and sexuality roles and norms while breaking up Indigenous collectivities. In this effort, the boarding school's role was to "kill the Indian and save the man," in the words of Colonel Richard H. Pratt of the Indian School in Carlisle, Pennsylvania, in 1879.[27]

These stories of land and their implications for so many peoples reside in the background as a trace within Du Bois's narrative of the Reconstruction era. Across the entirety of *Black Reconstruction*, repeated references to land reveal its centrality in the book, undergirding his scholarly study as it does for the era as a whole. When writing about "The White Worker" in chapter 2, Du Bois sets out "How America Became Labor's Promised Land," when "land was free and both land and property were possible to every thrifty worker."[28] This is a tale of the unacknowledged dispossession of territory from Indigenous peoples that takes political form in the ideological imaginary of the United States as the "Promised Land." Here is a sampling of more references to land in the book. Threaded from the beginning to end, Du Bois refers to the "continual supply of fertile land, cheaper slaves," "endless land of richest fertility,"[29] "free rich land and cheap labor,"[30] "access to the soil, South and West, to the free laborer,"[31] "land hunger—this absolutely fundamental and essential thing to any real emancipation of the slaves,"[32] "one clear economic ideal and that was his demand for the land,"[33] and "demands for land and education."[34] Then, near the end of the book, at the conclusion of chapter 14,

"The Counter-Revolution of Property," he proclaims that "the rebuilding, whether it comes now or a century later, will and must go back to the basic principles of Reconstruction in the United States during 1867–1876—Land, Light, and Leading for slaves, black, brown, yellow, and white, under a dictatorship of the proletariat."[35] At the beginning of *Black Reconstruction*, Du Bois writes of liberating the "majority of workers who are yellow, brown and black," and by the end of the book, Du Bois has added white workers to a future cross-racial class alliance, with land as central to the hope of one day bringing this dictatorship of the proletariat into being. Notably, however, the absence in this alliance of "red"—a popular racial signifier for Indigenous people in the U.S. schema—is a cause and consequence of how land is positioned and pivotal in the book's narrative. Specifically, the marginalization of the story of land itself goes hand in hand with the disavowal of Indigeneity and colonialism in the political memory of Reconstruction. We see this settler memory dynamic at work in the book in the slippage that occurs in the deployment of the concepts of *land* and *property*.

Keeping in mind the consistent references to land, take note of how Du Bois defines the terms, interests, and aims of class conflict during the Reconstruction era in chapter 14. This is a critical chapter not only for diagnosing the core reason for the "splendid failure" of Reconstruction but also for offering one of the political lessons Du Bois seeks to pass on to subsequent generations. In setting out the conditions and priorities for generating political and economic freedom during Reconstruction, he states: "In the South universal suffrage could not function without personal freedom, land and education, and until these institutions were real and effective, only a benevolent dictatorship in the ultimate interests of labor, black and white, could establish democracy."[36] This effort failed, as we know, and he explains why:

> There is no doubt that the object of the black and white labor vote was gradually conceived of as one which involved confiscating the property of the rich. This was a program that could not be openly avowed by intelligent men in 1870, but it became one of the acknowledged functions of the state in 1933; and it is quite possible that long before the end of the twentieth century, the deliberative distribution of property and income by the state on an equitable and logical basis will be looked upon as the state's prime function.
>
> Put all these facts together and one gets a clear idea, not of the failure of Negro suffrage in the South, but of the basic difficulty which it encountered; and the results are quite consistent with a clear judgment

that Negro and white labor ought to have had the right to vote; that
they ought to have tried to change the basis of property and redistribute
income; and that their failure to do this was a disaster to democratic
government in the United States.[37]

As Du Bois explains, elite political and economic interests brought Reconstruction to an end out of fear of a political movement based on property redistribution and cross-racial labor solidarity.[38] This was the threat posed by a
radical vision of abolition-democracy based on economic and political freedom, rather than that of a liberal form of abolition-democracy based on the
latter alone without attending to economic needs and redistribution. Du Bois
does not give up on his vision but rather poses this radical political memory
as seeds of possibility for his time, or for later on in the century. What he also
reproduces for political memory is a slippage in the transition from land to
property. This issue matters because as Tonawanda Seneca scholar Mishuana
Goeman argues, "A consequence of colonialism has meant a translation or
too easy collapsing of *land* to *property*, a move that perpetuates the logic of
containment" by which Indigenous people's relationships and practices with
land are contained within and by settler colonial parameters.[39] As Goeman
explains, "By thinking through *land* as a meaning-making process rather than
a claimed object, the aspirations of Native people are apparent and clear,"
which is a perspective and lived set of practices at odds with and threatened
by land as "property . . . a distinctly European notion that locks together (pun
intended) labor, land, and conquest. . . . As such, property is not just material, but it is also constructed through social relationships."[40] Building on Goeman's insight, when the concept of *property* becomes a ready stand-in for the
meaning of *land* then Indigenous people's social relationships in and with
land are rendered illegible to the settler eye, other than as a threat and obsta-
cle to settler colonial, capitalist imperatives and social relationships.

As I read the text, Du Bois tends to refer generally to *land* in structural or
aspirational terms—requirements of land for plantation slavery, desires/de-
mands of free laborers and freedmen for land or soil—and to *property* to reference the power of elites as the "propertied" class and as a specific commodity
to be seized and redistributed. Still, this is not always so seamless, and there is
a slippage and collapsing of these concepts in a way that raises questions about
the most memorable demand of the Reconstruction era—the memory of
which lives on in contemporary debates about reparations for slavery—that
of "forty acres and a mule." Du Bois sets out and analyzes the response to the
potential impact of this order:

Surprise and ridicule has often been voiced concerning this demand of Negroes for this land. It has been regarded primarily as a method of punishing rebellion . . . but so far as the Negroes were concerned, their demand for a reasonable part of the land on which they had worked for a quarter of a millennium was absolutely justified, and to give them anything less was an economic farce. On the other hand, to have given each one of the million Negro free families a forty-acre freehold would have made a basis of real democracy in the United States that might easily have transformed the modern world.[41]

Du Bois's reference to creating a "real democracy in the United States" that might be globally transformative speaks to the abolitionist aim of destroying the white supremacist democracy through the redistribution of its undergirding economic foundation and accompanying redistribution of political power. In the final section of the chapter, I will discuss the meaning we might take from the fact that Black Americans for the most part were denied this promise of land as a potential basis of economic and political security, which I consider in relation to Indigenous peoples' dispossession from their territories. I consider what alternative stories of the forty acres of land might be on offer through a framework that is not only one supporting a radical abolitionist-democracy but also one committed to decolonization. For now, I want to consider further the slippage or collapse of land to property, and how this relates to patriarchy and settler domesticity.

To start, the *forty acres* promise stemmed from William T. Sherman's Special Field Order No. 15, which sought to turn over to Black Americans up to four hundred thousand acres of land seized from Southern white property owners. Here is the pertinent directive from Sherman's order:

III. Whenever three respectable negroes, heads of families, shall desire to settle on land, and shall have selected for that purpose an island or a locality clearly defined, within the limits above designated, the Inspector of Settlements and Plantations will himself, or by such subordinate officer as he may appoint, give them a license to settle such island or district, and afford them such assistance as he can to enable them to establish a peaceable agricultural settlement. The three parties named will subdivide the land, under the supervision of the Inspector, among themselves and such others as may choose to settle near them, so that each family shall have a plot of not more than (40) forty acres of tillable ground, and when it borders on some water channel, with not more than 800 feet water front, in the possession of which land the military authorities will afford them protection, until such time as they can protect themselves, or until Congress shall regulate their title. The Quartermaster may, on the requisition of the Inspector of Settlements and Plantations, place at the disposal of the Inspector, one or more of the captured steamers, to ply between the settlements and one or more of the commercial points heretofore named in orders, to afford the settlers the opportunity to supply their necessary wants, and to sell the products of their land and labor.[42]

The distribution and management of these acres fell under the purview of the Bureau of Refugees, Freedmen, and Abandoned Lands, better known as the Freedmen's Bureau, which lasted from 1865 to 1872. This policy and state institution were to provide a foundation for political and economic freedom for Black Americans after emancipation. This ideal of economic and political freedom also linked the role of property and patriarchy in the effort to secure a settler domestic realm for Black Americans that would be safe and productive, for them and for the settler capitalist and heteropatriarchal system.

The directive pairs heteropatriarchal domesticity with the expectations of productivity in relationship to land and labor in a market system—in short, property and patriarchy in a settler colonial system. To parse it, the directive sets out that the U.S. government seeks "three respectable negroes, heads of families" who "shall desire to settle on land" to be supported to engage in "peaceable agricultural settlement" with state protection "until Congress shall regulate their title" and with assistance to be able "to sell the products of their land and labor." Land is central and explicit in this pivotal story of forty acres, but the implicit *story of land* here is one in which there is a collapsing of land into property by means of the effort to recruit and produce productive and peaceable settler households as the basis for Black freedom secured in the marketplace for land and labor. The forty acres plan never came to be, a major failure in the splendid failure. Still, the story told here about what was lost is worth denoting with regard to the heteropatriarchal and settler domestic norms constituted in relationship with and through the potentiality of property holding. This was to be Black-male-owned property, with male labor having the status to earn in the marketplace, ideally, although not in reality of course, whereas Black women's labor would be not just subsumed but owned by her husband. This settler heteropatriarchal model of the household was not an implied expectation for Black Americans but rather was designed, instituted, and required by the Freedmen's Bureau. In her work on marriage as a political institution in the United States, Priscilla Yamin explains, "When the Freedmen's Bureau designated the husband as head of household, it insisted that men sign contracts for the labor of the entire family and established wage scales that paid women less for identical work. In other words, labor contracts were structured to promote and enforce the patriarchal principles of marriage so that the wife's wages were not her own but belonged to her husband."[43] To repurpose Aileen Moreton-Robinson's triad regarding property, postemancipation Black Americans went from *being property*, to the prospect of *owning property*, to being made, for the most part, *propertyless*. This occurred in no small part due to, as Du Bois puts it, the "deep resentment and irritation" of Southern whites, including those "white poor [who] were determined to keep the blacks from access to richer and better land from which slavery had driven the white peasants."[44] Du Bois points here to how land shapes the meaning of whiteness via a resentful and often violent relationship to Black people, whereby the racial prerogative of access to land demarcated a position of standing and status of white over and against Black; a position white settlers fought to maintain. At the same time, Black women were not only dispossessed of the prospects of owning land in the form of property in this story of land; their labor became the property of their husbands at the behest, even the dictate, of the Freedmen's Bureau. In short, while undermined by the white supremacist, capitalist overthrow of Reconstruction, the Freedmen's Bureau set out and imposed an ideal of settler domesticity for Black people through the prospect of property holding secured through agricultural settlements that were to adhere to and reproduce heteropatriarchal familial and gendered forms and practices.

As it concerns heteropatriarchy, Du Bois did not ignore the role of gender and sexuality in *Black Reconstruction*, especially early in the text when the focus is on the antebellum period. As he notes, "Sexual chaos was always the possibility of slavery, not always realized but always possible: polygamy through the concubinage of black women to white men; polyandry between black women and select men on plantations in order to improve the human stock of strong and able workers."[45] Here Du Bois calls forth the perpetual threat and enactment of rape in a climate of "sexual chaos," the structural role of rape in the form of white slaveholders' concubines, and the role of Black women compelled to breed the next generation of slaves. In discussing the "moral sense of the planters," Du Bois argues that "they could not face the fact of Negro women as brood mares and black children as puppies."[46] That said, Saidiya Hartman finds that Black women's role as laborers lacks the status of that of Black men in Du Bois's narrative: "In *Black Reconstruction*, women's sexual and reproductive labor is critical in accounting for the violence and degradation of slavery, yet this labor falls outside of the heroic account of the black worker and the general strike."[47] Alys Eve Weinbaum also points out that while Du Bois discussed the function of racialized sexual violence and patriarchy in the antebellum period, he did not continue to draw out its constitutive role in assessing white supremacy in the Reconstruction era. She states, "In the recursive historical rhythm of Du Bois's book as a whole (he moves from antagonism, to revolt, to crisis, to re-entrenchment, and then again to antagonism), the gendered and sexualized reproductive contradictions that are constitutive to the narrative at the outset go missing from the story of war and Reconstruction that eventually unfolds."[48] To bring this back to the slippage between land and property, Hartman and Weinbaum signal how the story of gendered bodies and the story of land are similarly there and not there in the left memory of Reconstruction implicit in this text—each is a constitutive presence/absence of the wider narrative. This matters for how we think about the meaning of dispossession regarding who or what is subject to it and how, as Alyosha Goldstein puts it, "dispossession as a social relation of deprivation, impoverishment, and displacement suggests a constitutive relationship between land and bodies that is often overlooked."[49] In other words, the collapsing of land and property that Goeman flags as a colonialist logic is also necessarily "a social relation of deprivation, impoverishment, and displacement" that shapes the meaning and treatment of bodies in gendered, racialized, classed, and colonialist ways. To draw out the story of land then is to draw out the story of people and life in relationship to the land, in stories that invoke oppressive experiences while potentially offering liberating alternatives about how to live in relation to one another and to land.

With this in mind, I return to the colonial logics of dispossession implicit in the *collapsing* of land and property to excavate further its logic and implications for land and the peoples who exist in relation with it and one another. To be sure, Du Bois was assessing the political and economic situation during Reconstruction as he found it, with the status of property as hegemonic. Still, as contemporary readers of this text we should not reproduce the slippages and elisions in this collapsing of meanings around *land/soil* and that of *property*. To this end, consider Robert Nichols's argument that the concept of dispossession has a "recursive logic" to it as "a mode of *property generating theft*."[50] That is, dispossession produces its own referent, this being the *possession* that is rendered subject to theft in the act of turning land into property in a system of exchange. This insight is particularly pertinent to settler colonialism, for as Nichols states, "Colonization entails the large-scale transfer of land that simultaneously recodes the object of exchange in question such that it appears retrospectively to be a form of theft in the ordinary sense. It is thus not (only) about the transfer of property, but the transformation into property."[51] Thus, the invocation of property itself implicates dispossession as always already at work. In white settler colonial contexts as well, this process exists in a mutually constitutive relationship with the racialized and gendered production of the people deemed the rightful and deserving owners of property and those who are not worthy of it. Brenna Bhandar argues that racialization and the construction and application of the logic of property in colonial sociopolitical systems go hand in hand. To Bhandar, property logics work in tandem with the production of the white liberal possessive subject, and thus "the undoing or dismantling of racial regimes of ownership requires nothing less than a radically different political imaginary of property."[52] Her insights compel us to consider how the story of land that becomes property is a vital component of the story of how people come to see themselves as white in a settler colonial system. With this racialized story of land dislodged a little more from the background, take note of Du Bois's claim later in chapter 14 of his book that "the overthrow of Reconstruction was in essence a revolution inspired by property, and not a race war."[53] To Du Bois, the race war served as an instrument in preserving the power of the propertied class but was not the fundamental antagonism at issue; not the essence of the matter. This argument has a great deal of merit, of course. However, by elevating the role of land as property over the imperatives of racial prerogatives in this instance, Du Bois risked eliding the identity and interests of white settlers as a subject position formed in great part through a colonialist relationship to land transformed into property or potential property and thus premised in dispossession. This elision of settlerness and the story of land shape the background of one of the most well-known and habitually repeated concepts from *Black Reconstruction*. This concept is the so-called wages of whiteness,[54] which refers to the *racial bribe* to white laborers during this era. This is a bribe that could no longer include the promise to white people to not be enslaved, as was the case in the aftermath of Bacon's Rebellion. It had to take a postslavery, late nineteenth- and early twentieth-century form to divide white workers from, most notably, Black workers.

Du Bois argues that in the aftermath of Reconstruction white workers formed a cross-class racial alliance with the white capitalist class, instead of a cross-racial alliance with Black workers, in exchange for a "sort of public and psychological wage" for being white, even while receiving a "low wage" in the sense of monetary compensation for their labor.[55] Du Bois details what the "white group of laborers," as he calls them, receives with this "wage":

They were given public deference and titles of courtesy because they were white. They were admitted freely with all classes of white people to public functions, public parks, and the best schools. The police were drawn from their ranks, and the courts, dependent upon their votes, treated them with such leniency as to encourage lawlessness. Their votes selected public officials, and while this had small effect upon the economic situation, it had great effect on their personal treatment and the deference shown to them. White schoolhouses were the best in the community, and conspicuously placed, and they cost anywhere from twice to ten times as much per capita as colored schools. The newspapers specialized on news that flattered the poor whites and almost utterly ignored the Negro except in crime and ridicule.[56]

Du Bois's brilliance is evident by the fact that with minor adaptation this paragraph could apply to the public and psychological wages many white people still earn in the twenty-first century. While he deemed there to be minimal economic benefit or compensation from this package of "wages," one can discern and extrapolate the socioeconomic benefits white working-class people would gain from better schools, public employment such as policing, freedom to act in extralegal ways, and a greater influence on the courts and legislatures. However, even if one accepts the claim that there was not much of an economic benefit to this racial bribe, the notable absence in this discussion of these *wages* is that of the formal and informal racial prerogative of access to land dispossessed from Indigenous peoples and thus the possibility of being property owners. The work of settler memory here is in the detachment of whiteness from settlerness, lodging settler interests and identity into the background of whiteness. This matters because the status, desires, and alliances formed by the white worker are vital to Du Bois's assessment of the politics of the period in terms of his radical vision for an abolition-democracy and the reasons for its failure, especially the failure of the cross-racial class coalition between white and Black laborers. It is not only public deference, the best schools, and access to courts and voting but also the background factor of the story of land that is key to this failure. Bringing the story of land out of the background does not replace Du Bois's story but rather animates what is implicit in it to tilt the angle of the mirror to help us take a different look at our time through the political memory he handed down to us.

As to the availability of land for white settlement, Du Bois notes that the Homestead Act of 1862 "threw open western lands to settlers on easy terms" but that a great deal of these "gifts of public lands were showered upon the railway builders, amounting to half of the area opened by the Homestead Act."[57] While railroad companies did exploit the desire of settlers for land by extracting high prices, this still left a significant amount of land from the so-called public domain out West to be claimed and transformed by settlement and settlers, be they farmers, new immigrants, or those moving from the East Coast during and after the American Civil War. In her study of poor white people in the antebellum South, Keri Leigh Merritt points out that "during early Reconstruction, while many former slaves questioned the actual socio-economic benefits of their emancipation, poor whites experienced a time of mostly positive change." These changes included the public and psychological wages to which Du Bois referred, but Merritt also includes the fact that the "Homestead Act of 1862, along with the Southern Homestead Act of 1866, allowed tens of thousands of poor whites to join the ranks of landholders. Many poor whites migrated westward, to seek new opportunities and economic independence."[58] Roxanne Dunbar-Ortiz also informs us that "Under the Homestead Act, 1.5 million homesteads were granted to settlers west of the Mississippi, comprising nearly three hundred million acres (a half-million square miles) taken from the Indigenous collective estates and privatized for the market."[59] While the Homestead Act did not formally exclude Black people, one could only be eligible as a full citizen, and that would not occur until a few years after the American Civil War with the passage of the Fourteenth Amendment in 1868. Thus, prior to that year the noncorporate beneficiaries of the act were predominantly white settlers. Due to the levels of legal and violent intimidation directed against Black people after abolition, white settlers claimed significant benefit from this and other Homestead Acts. This meant that access, or the prospect of access, to land *as* property was a "wage" conferred to whiteness as a socioeconomic benefit with vital political and social meaning during the late nineteenth-century consolidation of the racial and colonial capitalist system of the United States.

Keri Leigh Merritt provides specific figures on the extent to which white settlers and their ancestors benefited, and still benefit, from the Homestead Act, in contrast to Black Americans:

> Combined with the claimants of the original Homestead Act, then, more than 1.6 million white families—both native-born and immigrant— succeeded in becoming landowners during the next several decades. Conversely, only 4,000 to 5,500 African-American claimants ever received final land patents from the [Southern Homestead Act of 1866.] The

Homestead Acts were unquestionably the most extensive, radical, redistributive governmental policy in US history. The number of adult descendants of the original Homestead Act recipients living in the year 2000 was estimated to be around 46 million people, about a quarter of the US adult population. If that many white Americans can trace their legacy of wealth and property ownership to a single entitlement pro-gramme, then the perpetuation of black poverty must also be linked to national policy. Indeed, the Homestead Acts excluded African Americans not in letter, but in practice—a template that the government would propagate for the next century and a half.[60]

What Merritt's insights and data underscore here is how Black and Indige-nous relationships to land in their distinct form, be they historical, actualized, collective, relational, individual, or aspirational, were obstacles to white set-tler and corporate ambitions for land and territorial expansion. In his time, Du Bois would not have had the full benefit of this historical and empirical detail on the impact of the Homestead Act. Still, the white racial prerogatives and anti-Blackness baked in to the presumptions of the purpose and appli-cation of the Homestead Acts and the importance of the role of land made available by these acts were quite discernible to him. This is evident in his discussion of Andrew Johnson in the chapter on "Transubstantiation of a Poor White." Du Bois positions Johnson's story as the exemplar of the "un-conscious paradox and contradiction" of the "dreary destiny of the Poor White South that, deserting its economic class and itself, became the instrument by which democracy in the nation was done to death, race provincialism deified, and the world delivered to plutocracy."[61]

Prior to becoming vice president in 1865 under Lincoln and then president upon the latter's assassination in April 1865, Andrew Johnson had been in Congress for over two decades, first in the House and then as a senator from Tennessee from 1857 to 1862. While he owned eight slaves, Johnson also loathed the slave-holding aristocracy and was a fervent advocate of white democracy, as he could not imagine including "Negroes in any conceivable democracy."[62] Johnson's advocacy of the Homestead Acts was a critical ele-ment in his pursuit of a white democracy and an anti-aristocracy political agenda, eventually leading to the act signed into law by Lincoln in 1862. As Du Bois notes, in Congress Johnson "championed free Western lands for white labor, and favored the annexation of Cuba for black slave labor," and in the Senate when Johnson "asked that plantations be divided in the South and lands in the West, he had in mind white men, who thus become rich, or at least richer. But for Negroes, he had nothing of the sort in mind, except the bare possibility that, if given freedom, they might continue to exist and not die out."[63] Johnson's political life provides a telling arc for Du Bois, as "he had begun as a champion of the poor laborer, demanding that the land monopoly of the Southern oligarchy be broken up, so as to give access to the soil, South and West, to the free laborer," but once "thrust into the Presidency . . . he dropped his demand for dividing up plantations when he realized that Negroes would largely be beneficiaries . . . and [he] made strong alliance with those who would restore slavery under another name."[64] To Du Bois, Johnson's life and career symbolize and enact the "tragedy of American prejudice made flesh; so that the man born to narrow circumstances, a rebel against economic privilege, died with the conventional ambition of a poor white to be the associate and benefactor of monopolists, planters, and slave drivers."[65] In Du Bois's narrative, Johnson is a key figure for embodying the tensions between race and class interests that led to or symbolized the roots of the demise of a potential cross-race, working-class coalition of white and Black laborers. Johnson's working-class antagonism toward the aristocracy could not supersede or compel him to reassess his racial hatred of and inability to imagine equality, never mind alliance, with Black people.

At the same time, the unstated settler colonial dynamic at work here is that these so-called free Western lands are Indigenous peoples' territories that Johnson sought and eventually succeeded in making available to, for the most part, white but not Black free laborers as part of his effort to disempower the aristocratic class—a failed effort, as it turned out. Thus, Johnson helped preserve planter aristocracy in the South at the expense of the capacity of Black people to become landowners while maintaining the availability of Western lands dispossessed from Indigenous peoples. The colonial logics of territorial dispossession and the necro-Indigenous logic of elimination do a lot of work in the background of this narrative, while they remain but a mnemonic trace in this story of Reconstruction due to the work of settler memory. The territorial dispossession of Indigenous peoples is remembered briefly by Du Bois, such as when he notes that a Black Congressman "championed relief of the Cherokee Indians . . . opposed the restriction on Chinese immigration, and arraigned our selfish policy toward Indians."[66] However, dispossession is otherwise positioned in the background of his narrative regarding the consistent and important function of land in the economic, political, and racial relations of this period. The role of land in Du Bois's narrative is, at once, ever present as the site for contesting the power of the aristocracy and as the basis for enabling the freedom of laborers, while the *story of land* is relatively absent in terms of its formative role in the meaning of white racial identity and freedom. In short, land is present as it concerns what groups of people want, but it is absent in terms of informing us about who groups of people are in racial, gendered, classed, and colonialist terms and what this land means to them. To tell this tale a little differently, the story of land for Johnson is one in which land means white settler freedom, power, and democracy defined through racially exclusive access not simply as a payoff or bribe from or as a tool of elite monopolists but as a meaningful identity and set of material interests defined directly against the interests and freedom of Black people and structurally and implicitly at the expense of the lives and territories of Indigenous peoples. This is what the story of land—a settler colonial story—helps to tell us regarding how settler identity and interests shape the meaning of whiteness and anti-Blackness in the postemancipation period, amid the splendid failure of Reconstruction.

The familiar left memory of white alignment with the capitalist class via the public and psychological wages of whiteness often presumes, following Du Bois's lead, that white laborers did not get much out of it materially, as low wages persisted, but in exchange they benefited in other ways. The lure of the material and sociopsychological benefits and the political value of access to land are not usually incorporated into the explanation of the interests and identities shaping the alliances, and nonalliances or antagonisms, of white people at this time. If they were so addressed, it is more likely that one would read white working-class subjects as citizen-deputies of settler state expansion as well as class traitors. By drawing out of the background the implicit meaning of Du Bois's consistent references to the role of land, we can tell the story differently to open up alternative political memories to apply to the challenges and aims of our era. For example, a recomposed memory of Reconstruction can tell the story of what I call the layers of dispossession experienced by Black and Indigenous peoples, with attendant lessons and models of resistance to go along with those provided by Du Bois.

Layers of Dispossession

The expansionary white settler democracy of the post–Civil War United States was built on accelerated territorial dispossession of Indigenous nations through federal policies and wars, the effort to dismantle and destroy Indigenous communities' lives through the imposition of settler domestic norms, and the deputization of white settler citizens to enact a great deal of this for their own sake and on the state's behalf. It also required that the vast majority of Black people be without wealth, property, and opportunity, leaving them precarious and thus more readily exploitable in the political and economic system. As Du Bois famously puts it, millions of Black people were the ex-slaves who "went free; stood a brief moment in the sun; then moved back again toward slavery."[67] This movement back toward slavery was caused in significant part by their dispossession from land and the prospect of owning land. To call upon the regrettable memory of Andrew Johnson one last time, in May 1865 he issued a proclamation of amnesty by which property, except slaves, was to be returned to those white Southerners who pled fealty to the United States. Du Bois sums up the consequences: "The pardoning power was pushed and the land all over the South rapidly restored. Negroes were dispossessed, the revenue of the Bureau reduced; many schools had to be discontinued."[68] Du Bois's words here lead me to consider Lenape scholar Joanne Barker's prescient question: "If dispossession is understood as formative of the US empire, might it be necessary to treat it as a component of the economic disparity not only of Indigenous people but also of others so indentured within/to the state?"[69] Barker compels us to consider the wider reach of dispossession, one not quarantined to a particular axis of oppression or subject position. In this spirit, a political memory that builds upon Du Bois's perspective while telling the story a little differently considers the layered work of dispossession that has an impact on Indigenous and Black peoples.

With layers of dispossession, I mean to reimagine the memory of Reconstruction as one shaped through the interrelationship of the dispossession of Indigenous peoples from a great deal of their lands during this time period and the dispossession of Black people from much of the forty acres per household promised or acquired postemancipation. These two dispossessions are not the same. For Indigenous peoples, territorial dispossession threatens an ontologically central relationality to the lands and the human and nonhuman life residing on and through it.[70] As noted through Nichols's theorization, this process of dispossession recursively creates the concept of theft by turning Indigenous land into a possession as property in the development and maintenance of settler colonialism. This is a different process and consequence from the popular conception regarding the failed promise of forty acres and a mule, according to which Black Americans lost or did not gain access to the property and resources needed for agricultural settlement deemed vital for their economic and political security in a system that remained, still, settler colonial. In this case, white settler dispossession revoked Black property claims and squashed the vision of an abolitionist-democracy through, in no small part, securing and expanding white settler prerogatives to property through state and nonstate means.[71] As Du Bois states, "The restoration of the lands [to Southern whites] not only deprived Negroes in various ways of a clear path toward livelihood, but greatly discouraged them and broke their faith in the United States Government."[72] In addition, historian Treva B. Lindsey writes of Black women's broken faith in the U.S. government after Reconstruction's demise: "The failure of Reconstruction as a long-term solution for the tremendous legacy of slavery and for the lack of citizenship rights for all blacks contributed to New Negro womanhood's emergence. In addition to struggles against white supremacy and societal sexism and patriarchy, many African American women remained cynical about the promise of either racial advancement or women's rights movements for African American women."[73] Thus, the layers of dispossession that haunted Black and Indigenous communities during this period, while distinct in meaningful ways, also reveal resonant coinhabitative experiences of dispossession by, domination from, and frustration with a white settler heteropatriarchal nation in the aftermath of the American Civil War. The layered but not collapsing connection of these social relations of dispossession are often absent from the political memories and lessons of Reconstruction because the politics around land and around labor are usually split off or quarantined from one another, as if the former concerns Indigenous peoples alone and the latter that of workers "black, brown, yellow, and white."

In the case of the political life of race in the United States, this splitting occurs due to what Alyosha Goldstein calls the "not given" of "the sociality of land and bodies—the restless and multiple stories of place, the agonistic possibilities of collective life otherwise."[74] Recall Goldstein's notion that "dispossession as a social relation of deprivation, impoverishment, and displacement suggests a constitutive relationship between land and bodies that is often overlooked." As it concerns the period discussed in the chapter, Goldstein sets out the history of land claims and dispossession for Black Americans and Indigenous peoples as an intertwined story of the post–Civil War white settler state and society: "From General William Tecumseh Sherman's Special Field Order 15 in 1865 promising land to freed slaves to Reconstruction and its collapse to the General Allotment Act of 1887 and its aftermath, U.S. land policy moved from ostensible redistribution and assimilation to reasserting unbridled white nationalism and accelerated white settlement. After antebellum era laws prohibiting enslaved blacks from acquiring land [were overturned], the brief and quickly recanted effort to provide arable land to the formerly enslaved shifted to Jim Crow segregation and racial terror."[75] Goldstein speaks to how the period from 1860 to 1890, to extend Du Bois's time line by a decade, can be recalled to memory as a time when Black and Indigenous experiences, claims, and resistances were built out of their relationships to land and their struggles to resist dispossession and maintain their social relationships. Dislodging resistance to dispossession and to imposed social relations from the background of the Reconstruction-era story means centering "the restless and multiple stories of place, the agonistic possibilities of collective life otherwise" experienced by Black and Indigenous peoples.

In terms of the connection between the stories of land and of a people, consider how Du Bois posits the response of Black people to the failed promise of Sherman's order: "What is the use of giving us freedom if we can't stay where we were raised and own our own house where we were born and our own piece of ground?"[76] While the likes of Eric Foner have noted that land is a central matter in Du Bois's analysis, this has not led to a great deal of analysis centering the practices of dispossession against Black Americans as one of the stories of land of this period—of what land means to a people's social relationships.[77] The usual narratives of Black dispossession focus on the loss of access to property, strictly understood, but there is less attention to the experiences and memories of Black people's relationship with lands that do not have to be centered in a property logic but that could speak to a deeper form of relationality rarely reflected in political memory.

To tell the story of land refuses settler memory by deeming Indigenous people's experience, claims, and resistance as neither quarantined from nor collapsed with Black people's experiences, claims, and resistance but rather as indicative of a coinhabitative relationship to white settler colonialism. By coinhabitative, I mean that in their experiences and practices Black and Indigenous communities engaged in distinct forms of resistance to white settler state and society domination, exploitation, and dispossession that when considered in their totality represent the active presence of abolitionist and decolonizing alternatives that could serve to reinfuse and reshape radical political memories of this era. This may be something the contemporary generation wants or needs to see in the mirror of Reconstruction, such as in relation to contemporary critiques of and resistance to racial capitalism. As Jodi Melamed argues, without critical attention to contemporary Indigenous people's resistance and practices such as the "thinking of land and relating to land that lies outside the permissible rationality of racial capitalist settler coloniality," then "resistance to racial capitalism can shore up settler colonialism despite the fact that both rely on the violences of primitive accumulation."[78] Her point is that to historicize, theorize, and politicize racial capitalism along labor, racial, and class lines in a way that quarantines concerns with land, Indigeneity, and colonialism presupposes and reproduces as a settled condition the dispossession of Indigenous peoples from their lands and the state and nonstate settler violence that maintains it.[79]

This is not to erase tensions and incompatible objectives. In the post–Civil War era, the Cherokee Nation was compelled against its wishes—and still did in certain respects in to the twenty-first century—to provide full recognition of and support to the ancestors of the nation's ex-slaves, Cherokee freedmen, as codified in their 1866 treaty with the U.S. government.[80] As well, a fair number of Black men served as so-called buffalo soldiers in the U.S. military's effort to invade, attack, and remove Indigenous peoples from their territories west of the Mississippi.[81] To be sure, then, "the restless and multiple stories of place" of Indigenous and Black peoples are fraught, disjointed, and impossible to bound within a singular encompassing political memory. These are restless and multiple memories—slippery and tricky—to be grappled with, composed, and recomposed with an eye to the lessons and alternatives for "possibilities of collective life otherwise." For example, two major U.S. federal government measures during this period that concerned land and the relationship among peoples were the U.S. federal government's treaties with Indigenous nations, on the one hand, and Sherman's Special Field Order No. 15, on the other hand. Both exist in political memory and have their distinct place but these are stories of land that are usually told in quarantined mnemonic bubbles. What if they weren't? What coinhabitative story of the lost possibilities—of splendid pursuits and historic failures—might we recompose for our time in an alternative political memory of Reconstruction?

As it concerns treaties, one in particular stands out: the aforementioned 1868 Treaty of Fort Laramie between the Great Sioux and Arapaho Nations and the United States. With this treaty, the U.S. government was "essentially suing for peace" in the wake of the victory of the Oceti Sakowin—the "seven nations of the Dakota-, Nakota-, and Lakota-speaking peoples"—over the U.S. Army garrisoned along the Bozeman Trail in 1866.[82] The 1868 treaty "pledged peace to both sides"; "reserved the area West of the Missouri River and east of the Rockies for the 'absolute and undisturbed use' of the Sioux" for as long as the buffalo should range there; pledged U.S. government support for the tribes in the form of education, "seed and clothing for Indian farmers, and set up agencies for the distribution of aid"; and "recognized the Bozeman Trail area as 'unceded Indian territory' where whites would not be allowed to settle and within which there would be no military posts."[83] As Lower Brule Sioux historian Nick Estes asserts, for Lakota leader Red Cloud the "1868 Treaty was not just an agreement between two human nations, but also an agreement among the nonhumans as well—including the buffalo nations."[84] Here we get a decidedly contrasting story of land that concerns the relation of land and life, human and nonhuman. Land is not collapsed as property in this relationship set out in a treaty with the United States, by which the Oceti Sakowin make clear the priority of their relational land practices and that white settlers are a threat to them. As has been the case with hundreds of other treaties signed with Indigenous nations, the U.S. federal government did not live up to its promises, and in this case this involved the U.S. military and settlers eradicating millions of buffalo as a means to undermine the spirit and rule of the treaty and the life of the Oceti Sakowin.[85] In 1980, the Great Sioux Nation won a court case against the U.S. government for the latter's seizure of unceded territory in the Black Hills, and the courts awarded a settlement of over $100 million dollars. The Sioux Nation refused and continues to refuse the cash settlement (with accrued interest it is now over $1 billion dollars in value), holding fast to the demand for the return of the land.[86] We see here a modern example, connecting the past of the Reconstruction era to the present, of the story of land and its meaning as not that of a fungible commodity, as is the case in the colonial, capitalist logic of white settler societies. One can refuse settler memory here by reflecting on how the radical politics and positioning of the Oceti Sakowin in the late nineteenth century can meaningfully shape the political legacy and lessons of that era for our time. This political memory is based in the Oceti Sakowin's relationship to territory defined and lived as well as possible on their own terms as a practiced vision of "the agonistic possibilities of collective life otherwise" compared to that of the white settler colonial society.

With the 1868 Treaty of Fort Laramie in mind and in political memory, I return to the forty acres promised in Sherman's Special Field Order No. 15. Along with the directive noted earlier regarding the Freedmen's Bureau's effort to create households led by men according to an ideal of settler domesticity, Sherman's other directives included those that spoke to the structure and possibility of Black collective self-governance on the land:

I. The islands from Charleston, south, the abandoned rice fields along the rivers for thirty miles back from the sea, and the country bordering the St. Johns River, Florida, are reserved and set apart for the settlement of the negroes now made free by the acts of war and the proclamation of the President of the United States.

II. At Beaufort, Hilton Head, Savannah, Fernandina, St. Augustine and Jacksonville, the blacks may remain in their chosen or accustomed vocations—but on the islands, and in the settlements hereafter to be established, no white person whatever, unless military officers and soldiers detailed for duty, will be permitted to reside; and the sole and exclusive management of affairs will be left to the freed people themselves, subject only to the United States military authority and the acts of Congress.[87]

The form of Black self-governance proposed here still involves the military to secure safety and invokes the plenary power of Congress, but it was also a vision of a region comprising seized ex-Confederate Southern territory "set apart" for "respectable Negroes" to form "settlements" on lands in which "no white person" who was a civilian was "permitted to reside." The "sole and exclusive management" of this territory was "left to the freed people themselves." One can discern tensions and symmetries with this model of land relations and self-governance compared to the path toward and meaning of sovereignty set out in the 1868 Treaty of Fort Laramie. On the one hand, as noted, the order sets out that freed Black people would be settlers whose relationship to land was to be as property owners in a patriarchal system, which exists in tension—if not directly at odds—with an Indigenous ethic and practice of the sociality of land and bodies based in traditional practices and relationality with territory and life and thus not one of ownership, patriarchy, extraction, and commodification. But even my framing it in that way is oversimplified.

For example, as Adrienne Monteith Petty notes, over the course of the late nineteenth century Black Americans struggled to figure out ways to gain land that could allow them to live in peace and some level of prosperity in the face of threats and challenges against Black life in the post-Reconstruction era. In these efforts, Black women in particular were "central to land acquisition" by taking "the lead in purchasing farms," in particular with the innovation of "dual tenure," whereby "freedpeople and their descendants worked as sharecroppers and slowly accumulated their own property at the same time." African Americans bought "land in groups" to overcome "their limited economic base," just as Black Union soldiers "organized to buy large tracts of land, especially in the upper South states of Virginia, Maryland and North Carolina."[88] The story comes to a familiar end, as Monteith Petty concludes: "Ultimately, African American farmers never achieved the freedpeople's vision and expectation of widespread control of southern land. Nevertheless, their aspirations endured through the generations in ways that scholars should continue to investigate. Their efforts to acquire land, whether the most modest snippets of land or thousands of acres—constituted a form of resistance to a capitalist system that relegated African Americans to the most precarious and exploitative roles."[89] These efforts should also be included as part of the "splendid failure" of Reconstruction, for they offered a model of Black collective landholding and self-governance in resistance to brutal exploitation and dispossession of their property, just as the Oceti Sakowin did and continue to do in their fight against domination and dispossession. At the same time, one lesson to be drawn is that Black ownership of property is not a radical form of resistance to a capitalist system that is, more precisely, a *racial colonial capitalist system*, for which the exploitation of Black labor and life compose a major pillar. In this regard, Nik Heynen reminds us that in the wake of Andrew Johnson's edict to restore land to Southerners, "racial capitalism won another victory when President Johnson suggested that despite losing their lands, freed people occupying those lands be offered contracts to work the lands for the original owners (many instances their former masters), which was tantamount to a new form of wage servitude that quickly evolved into sharecropping."[90] In short, dispossession from land was central to the production of the precarity of Black labor, which speaks to the need for bringing together, not quarantining, matters of land, labor, and life in political memory. Recomposing the lessons of these tensions in these stories of land offers up ways to reimagine the relationship of antiracist, anticolonialist, and anticapitalist visions in, say, a possible Third Reconstruction. This could involve recalling and suturing the visions of Indigenous and Black self-governance that the memory of Reconstruction does provide.

Sherman's directive affirming the creation of a Black self-governing region that forbids the presence of white settlers is strikingly similar to the provisions in the 1868 Treaty of Fort Laramie that prohibit white settlement. There is also a coinhabitative parallel in the manner in which these self-governance projects and agreements were a consequence of Black and Indigenous resistance by enslaved Black Americans in the form of the "general strike" walk-off from slave plantations and fighting to defeat the Confederacy and by the Oceti Sakowin and allied Indigenous nations against U.S. military invasion. Thus, without disavowing potential tensions and conflicting visions and interests regarding the stories of land and their meaning for Black and Indigenous communities, there are symmetries and experiences in common that can be the basis for alternative political memories of Reconstruction. The radical Black governance in Southern states during the Reconstruction era that Du Bois offers as one of the *splendid* elements of the "splendid failure" and the Special Field Order No. 15 vision of Black self-governance free from white settlers coexisted in political time and space with the Oceti Sakowin's successful military effort to force the U.S. government into a peace agreement that legally recognized their claim to territory and self-governance free from white settlers. This coinhabitative set of political projects did not come to fruition as promised, but it remains available to our political memories as we seek to challenge, rethink, and fuel contemporary ideas about radical liberation and solidarity.

To offer alternative "restless and multiple stories of place" to those which predominate, I conclude this section by first turning to the memory offered by Kendra Field in her powerful historical study of Black families who moved West after the American Civil War, in particular to the Indian Territory that became the state of Oklahoma in 1907 and the relationship of Black, Indigenous, and Black Indian communities therein. To start, Field sets out a vital point: "One of the most profound aspects of African-American and Indian history lies in the unwitting abandonment of one's homeplace, one's spiritual markers, and the remains of one's ancestors."[91] Here Field references the layers of dispossession that provoke and disrupt relationships to place and that could be fodder for more radical political memories and imaginaries concerning the "sociality of land and labor" and of life in general. To this end, Field expands upon and illustrates the intimacy and ontological import of land relations for Black Americans during this period: "Throughout the postemancipation years, freedpeople took many measures to maintain links with particular lands. They did this by walking or riding home to see loved ones. They did this by visiting family gravesites. They did this by planting on the old homeplace after they take up residence elsewhere. By such measures, the rhetorical shorthand of 'forty acres and a mule' barely captures the breadth and depth of freedpeople's land claims, revealing the cost of leaving one's homeplace and the complicated social and emotional burden of 'making freedom real.'"[92] Field does not romanticize the relationship of Black and Indigenous people in such contexts as Indian Territory, for it featured, as a start, "Native Americans as slaveowners" prior to emancipation and "African Americans as settlers on Indian land" during and beyond Reconstruction.[93] This was a fraught relationship, made tenser by the layered dispossession of Indigenous peoples from their ancestral territories and of Black people from their postemancipation property claims. These layers of dispossession were not simply contiguous practices. They reinforced one another to constitute neither solely a white supremacist nation nor a settler nation but rather a white settler nation. In resistance, Field's discussion of Black land relations offers a vision of a mode of relationality that carries lived and mnemonic power for challenging a settler colonial capitalist view of a people's relationship to land often articulated in the popular memory of the failed promise of "forty acres and a mule." This is a model one can draw forth to refuse what a property-based vision might mean in our contemporary context and by connection provide mnemonic sustenance for how an abolitionist politics could be brought into productive collaboration with a decolonial one.

A start but not the finish to such a radical imaginary in practice could begin with "black, brown, yellow, and white" accomplices—those laborers Du Bois called forth as the prospective coalition of the dictatorship of the proletariat— declaring in their own practices that the United States live up to its agreements with Indigenous nations, not in cash payouts but in territory and respect for Indigenous self-governance. This demand also opens up the social and political meaning around land itself to refuse the limiting land/labor distinction, which too easily quarantines settler colonialism from white supremacy. One finds a coinhabitative spirit that refuses such a divide in the contemporary *Black/Land Project*, which "gathers and analyzes stories about the relationship between Black people, land and space."[94] Stories from the Reconstruction and post-Reconstruction eras such as that provided by Field that refuse settler memory and the hegemony of property logics fit into the Black/Land Project's mission. In the words of project member T. G, for "particularly people of color and certainly Africans and Native peoples, land is not just simply dirt. It's not just simply space and stuff. It is a part of who we are. I think it is part of how we define ourselves. It really is."[95] Political approaches that support treaty land commitments to Indigenous nations and non-property-based narratives of the relationship of Black life to land resist the layers of dispossession imposed on Indigenous and Black peoples. To this end, an approach that refuses the settler memory of the Reconstruction era reveals to us a period of time when radical Black and Indigenous governance did coinhabit on these lands, even for brief and staggered moments in time.

Conclusion

In Colored No More, Treva B. Lindsey calls attention to the fact that during the 1893 World's Columbian Exposition, the name of which celebrated the four-hundred-year anniversary of European contact with the Americas, a distinct politics of memory was in play. As she states, "Despite being only twenty-eight years past the Civil War and sixteen years past the formal end of Reconstruction, the exposition anchored this new moment in U.S. history in the discovery of the New World by Europe, and indirectly, though perhaps intentionally, in the subsequent annihilation and marginalization of the First Nation and

Indigenous peoples of the Americas and the enslavement of African people."[96] Lindsey speaks to the relationship between necro-Indigeneity and anti-Blackness in constituting the American national self-image presented to the world in the late nineteenth century; a political memory produced just decades after the demise of Reconstruction.

The political memory of the Reconstruction era still has a strong hold on the politics and discourse concerning race in the United States. This is especially so on the political left whereby, in the midst of the ever-more public rise of white settler nationalism in the twenty-first century, it makes sense to look to the past for models and lessons that can help guide our way forward. My invocation to refuse settler memory does not mean refusing the memory of Reconstruction; rather, in reconsidering this period as a source for radical imaginaries it is time to rethink the meaning and practices of solidarity and the scope of the radical political aims we seek to garner from it. As scholars and activists inspired by Du Bois continue to look to the Reconstruction era for the regenerative fuel of lost potentiality, a blended abolitionist and decolonizing approach could turn the meaning of this era into something new and germinal for contemporary theorizing of solidarity, coinhabitation, governance, and resistance. This approach requires rigorous attention to the ways in which the disavowal of Indigenous people and settler colonialism undermines not only the effort to attend to important structural components of the U.S. political context but also the attempt to excavate and analyze the deeper roots of white supremacy, anti-Blackness, heteropatriarchy, and capitalist domination. Dislodging the story of land, as opposed to just the *role* of land, can help to foster this recomposition and shake up the habitual political memories of Reconstruction. In the next chapter, I have the same aim of thinking through the limitations and possibilities for radical political imaginaries as I analyze the work of possibly the most insightful and influential twentieth-century writer on race in the United States.

CHAPTER THREE

James Baldwin and Cowboys and Indians

"What Do You Mean, We?"

In 1963, James Baldwin toured the United States to promote his new book, *The Fire Next Time*. The speeches he gave followed roughly the same template and arc. One such speech was at the Second Baptist Church in Los Angeles in April 1963, where he spent significant time discussing the "several things" that "we did" to "conquer the country," beginning with the foundational role of genocidal violence against Indigenous people. Baldwin stated bluntly, "We promptly eliminated them. We killed them."[1] Later in this chapter, I will analyze at greater length this section of his speech, but to start I turn to something Baldwin said in the midst of his discussion of the "several things" done to create the United States. Soon after referencing the foundational role of Indigenous genocide, James Baldwin told this joke:

> There used to be an old joke going around among Negroes, if you
> remember the Lone Ranger, I think he had a sidekick called Tonto,
> an Indian, there's always a good Indian, he rode around with the Lone
> Ranger and according to my version of the story, the version I heard,
> Tonto and the Lone Ranger ran into this ambush of nothing but Indians.
> The Lone Ranger said "What are we going to do Tonto?" And Tonto said,
> "What do you mean, we?" Well, I tell that joke in order to point out
> something else. It's a Negro joke. One of the other things we did in order
> to conquer the country, physically speaking, was to enslave the Africans.[2]

The punch line turns on the question of who constitutes the "we." In the context of the joke, the white masculine settler "Ranger," who always had an Indigenous man by his side despite the moniker of being "Lone"—another example of the production of Indigenous absence and presence in American mythology—is left dangerously alone, surrounded by Indigenous warriors, when Tonto refuses incorporation into the "we." The joke is on the white man. In telling the joke to this particular audience, Baldwin could seem to be offering a gesture of Black-Indigenous solidarity, whereby Tonto, the Indian ambushers, the "Negroes" who tell the joke, and the people in the predominantly Black audience listening and laughing (as the audiotape makes clear) compose the "we" positioned against and laughing at the white settler figure. While one could read this as an expression of solidarity, it also seems to serve other purposes and raises some questions.

Ultimately, the joke is for a Black audience as a form of vicarious identification with the political condition of Indigenous people in relationship to white oppressors, which could be but is not necessarily the same as an expression of political solidarity. This matter of who Baldwin means by the "we" is further confused by the fact that the joke is preceded by his assertion that "we" killed and eliminated Indigenous people and immediately followed by stating that enslaving "the Africans" was "one of the other things we did." The "we" in this regard is the American nation as a whole, into which Baldwin implicates himself, although fitfully. I start with this passage because the question "What do you mean, we?" exemplifies Baldwin's own grappling with the relationship of Black people to the past, present, and future of an American nation built upon and sustained through white supremacy. The joke's role in the context of this speech also shows that the treatment of Indigenous peoples has a constitutive place in this story for Baldwin, but more so to transition Baldwin from Indigenous genocide to the enslavement of Africans in his story of the nation. The narrative arc in the 1963 speech that begins with colonial "conquering" and Indigenous genocide and ends with slavery and Black subjugation is not an isolated example in Baldwin's career.

In 1985, just two years before his death, Baldwin published an essay in *Playboy* magazine titled "Here Be Dragons." The essay's title and in many ways its subject matter were inspired by Baldwin's public debate and discussion with poet Audre Lorde in 1984. Their conversation centered on the role of gender and sexuality in the Black community and in the wider system of U.S. white supremacy. It was during this 1984 debate that Lorde referred to the intersection of racism, patriarchy, and sexism that shapes U.S. political society as "the dragon we have been born into."[3] Lorde challenged a number of Baldwin's assumptions about gender and sexuality, and she seemed to make him rethink a number of things in that regard as evidenced in "Here Be Dragons." In that 1985 essay, Baldwin argues that oppressive norms of gender and sexuality idealized a particular expression of masculinity that is central to the ills of the American nation. Here is how he frames the problem: "The American ideal, then, of sexuality appears to be rooted in the American ideal of masculinity. This ideal has created cowboys and Indians, good guys and bad guys, punks and studs, tough guys and softies, butch and faggot, black and white. It is an ideal so paralytically infantile that it is virtually forbidden—as an unpatriotic act—that the American boy evolve into the complexity of manhood."[4] As in

1963, Baldwin's narrative begins with references to the settler colonial context in the relationship of "cowboys and Indians" and ends with the racial one of "black and white." However, instead of using a joke the path he follows from colonial binaries to racial ones traverses the realm of sexuality and gender. This is also not a random pattern.

The "paralytically infantile" form of sexuality and gender Baldwin is referring to is the white settler masculinity of the cowboy, of the Lone Ranger, and even more often for him that of Gary Cooper and John Wayne. To reference white settler masculinity as "paralytically infantile" is not to diminish or qualify its dangerous implications. Through these iconic white masculine figures, Baldwin implicitly signals the need to attend to settler masculinity, heteropatriarchy, and whiteness. To make this point is not to claim that Baldwin had a fully articulated and thought out argument about the interrelationship of settler colonialism, gender, sexuality, and white supremacy. Rather, I argue that there is a telling symmetry in Baldwin's fraught attention to settler colonialism and to gender and sexuality in the expanse of his work, especially his nonfiction work that often focused on the political life of race in the United States. By fraught, I mean the difficulties he faced in consistently addressing them and their connection to his wider themes.

In this chapter, I focus my attention on Baldwin's implicit and explicit references to Indigeneity, settler colonialism, and the politics of memory in his nonfiction work, speeches, and interviews. In so doing, the role of gender and sexuality will prove to be important for grasping how he seeks to understand, articulate, and connect settler colonialism to white supremacy via the function of white settler masculinity. He does not refer to settler colonialism by name, but by using this term in my analysis, I mean to indicate the implied or explicit substance of many of his references to the history and present of U.S. violence toward Indigenous peoples, the dispossession of their lands, and the practices of white settlement. The other important matters in this regard concern Baldwin's discussions of whiteness and the American relationship to history and memory. To Baldwin, whiteness in America was defined through a hostile relationship to history. While Baldwin was not a theorist of settler colonialism or Indigenous peoples' history in the United States, by paying close attention to settler masculinity, whiteness, and the politics of American memory we can see how he attends to the role of settler colonial practices that reside at the heart of U.S. white supremacy. This chapter is about how and what it means that Baldwin is constantly grappling with the settler colonial roots and resonance of U.S. white supremacy that he detects but cannot quite fully or thoroughly name and analyze as such. One can locate this as a consistent trope and touchstone throughout his career. Doing so, however, requires being honest and clear about the difficulties that one of the nation's most insightful writers faces when, in some way, he seeks to address the constitutive role of settler colonialism and Indigenous people's history in the political life of race in the United States. These difficulties may be just one of the reasons why Baldwin's discussion of Indigenous people and genocide is largely ignored in the significant literature analyzing his work, even as many turn to him to help make sense of our moment.

James Baldwin may be as popular and influential now as he was over fifty years ago when he wrote *The Fire Next Time*. Along with the 2017 documentary *I Am Not Your Negro*, which was nominated for an Academy Award for Best Documentary, recent years have witnessed the inauguration of a new journal, the *James Baldwin Review*, in 2015, and the publication of collections inspired by his work. In her introduction to the 2016 collection, *The Fire This Time: A New Generation Speaks about Race*, Jesmyn Ward writes about how in the wake of the killing of Trayvon Martin by George Zimmerman in 2012 and the latter's acquittal in 2013, she could not find the words to speak her outrage. She then came across Baldwin's *Notes of a Native Son*: "It was a revelation," as she had "never encountered that kind of work, work that seemed to me, to know I needed it." She subsequently "picked up *The Fire Next Time*," which inspired her to "call on some of the great thinkers and extraordinary voices of my generation to help me puzzle this out." In putting together the collection of essays inspired by Baldwin, Ward came to realize how "inextricably the past is in the present, how heavily that past bears on the future; we cannot talk about black lives mattering without reckoning with the very foundation of this country."[5] Eddie Glaude, in his 2020 book *Begin Again: James Baldwin's America and Its Urgent Lessons for Our Own*, finds Baldwin's contemporary relevance in how "activists throughout the Obama years ... sought out his works as a way of making sense of a country on the cusp of change, because they were protesting in the streets and walking the corridors of power demanding that change."[6] Similarly, Susan McWilliams, editor of the 2017 collection *A Political Companion to James Baldwin*, started her introduction by referring to students and organizers of the Black Lives Matter movement "reading Baldwin, quoting Baldwin, rediscovering Baldwin." McWilliams notes the longstanding influence of his work: "Before and since Baldwin's death almost thirty years ago, the American political experience, and particularly the racial politics that lie in the bloody and battered heart of that experience, keeps turning us back and back to the importance of turning back to Baldwin." In short, she writes, "This is still Baldwin's America."[7]

Yet therein resides the issue. While it may not seem necessary to focus on the role of Indigeneity and settler colonialism in Baldwin's work—for has he not provided us with enough already?!—the intervention does matter in order to consider what this "America" is in Baldwin's eyes that leads people to "turn back" to him to understand it. For Baldwin, this America includes both his searing critique of its constitutive failures and his consistent, if difficult, effort to imagine a path to redeeming or rebuilding the nation. Thus, it is not merely interesting but in fact urgent to take serious account of what may seem like marginal or peripheral references in Baldwin's work, those concerning Indigenous peoples and settlement, and place them at the center of an analysis. Baldwin could not escape seeing the relationship of white supremacy to settler colonialism; he was just not always sure what to do with it. In this regard, how he fumbles and also addresses these challenges reflects and, in some ways, shapes how so many today still struggle to understand and articulate the relationship of Indigeneity and settler colonialism to the political life of race in the country.

I turn next to the function of settler memory in Baldwin's work, which raises questions about what might be the limitations of his critique of the United States and his vision for a better world. I then make the case that in examining Baldwin's own challenges in addressing matters of gender and sexuality we find not only a similar, even constitutive, dynamic to that of settler memory but also an alternative, possibly expansive analysis of the problems of race in the United States. From that basis, I argue that Baldwin's view of the role of whiteness as the core ill of the United States is grounded in the story of *settlement*, which implicates the role of settler masculinity and the American hostility to history. To be clear, I am not making an intellectual history argument that over time Baldwin gains greater clarity regarding a position that accounts for Indigeneity and settler colonialism, as the tensions with the reproduction of settler memory persist. I am making the case that this critical intervention allows us to grasp Baldwin's thinking in a slightly different way so we can better interrogate the "America" he sought to understand, critique, and even reimagine.

"This Particular Indian": Baldwin's Settler Memory

James Baldwin liked to talk about cowboys and Indians. He did not do so often, but he did so persistently throughout his career. When he did, the form and content of his points were often striking in imagery and ripe with meaning. The most famous example, particularly because it featured in *I Am Not Your*

Negro, occurred in 1965, during a formal debate between Baldwin and William F. Buckley Jr. at Cambridge University on the question "Is the American Dream at the expense of the American Negro?" Early in his argument for the "yes" side, Baldwin made the following statement: "It comes as a great shock around the age of 5 or 6 or 7 to discover that the flag to which you have pledged allegiance, along with everybody else, has not pledged allegiance to you. It comes as a great shock to discover that Gary Cooper killing off the Indians, when you were rooting for Gary Cooper, that the Indians were you."[8] Gary Cooper is the iconic on-screen portrayer of noble, tragic white American settler masculinity, someone Baldwin mentions often. In this memory, the young Baldwin's fear is not that he will be killed on the American frontier by a white settler as if he were an Indigenous person but rather that the Gary Cooper cowboy character represents the threatening white cop patrolling the inner city. One can surmise this because in "Down at the Cross: Letter from a Region in My Mind" in *The Fire Next Time*, Baldwin recounts his experiences as a young boy who was beaten, tortured, harassed, and sexually humiliated, as well as on the receiving end of racist invective, at the hands of the New York City police.[9] Still, that does not resolve the issue of Baldwin positioning himself as an Indigenous person in this memory and imaginary about the Black experience in the United States.

Baldwin's reference to being one of the Indians received little critical attention in the generally praiseworthy commentary on *I Am Not Your Negro*. One observer did raise a serious critique on this matter. Historian Kyle Mays, who is Black and Saginaw Anishinaabe, argues that Baldwin's and the filmmaker's choice of images "used the history of settler colonialism as a prophetic tool, a prop to Black Americans to say this: if you don't resist white supremacy and racism, if you don't fight oppression, you will be treated just like the 'Indians.'" Mays continues:

> It perpetuates the settler state's major goal of cementing the fact of indigenous disappearance. We did not all disappear, and we remain, fighting, still. These scenes create a tension not only between blackness and indigeneity, both in how the settler state constructs the parallel but different treatment of Black and Indigenous Peoples historically and today, but also how Blacks construct an idea of liberation. This is not to say that all Black radicals uncritically use indigenous genocide as a tool for Black liberation; indeed, many seek solidarity and acknowledge that they are on indigenous land. However, at least historically, Black radicals and intellectuals have used the history of indigenous genocide as a

prophetic tool, and it is this discursive practice that needs to be challenged and critiqued.[10]

Mays speaks to the wider concern with how Indigenous peoples and claims serve as vehicles for conveying the condition and status of non-Indigenous peoples. Mays is pointing to the settler memory dynamic at work whereby Indigeneity and settler colonialism are present and absent in Baldwin's illustration of anti-Blackness in the United States.

This is not the only time Baldwin made this sort of settler memory claim. There are shades of it in the 1963 speech, in which Indigenous people are present as forms of active resistance in a joke that speaks to the Black political condition. Then, in a 1972 interview, after referring to the "will of the American people" that put "Nixon in the White House and Ronald Reagan in the governor's mansion," Baldwin stated, "And the effect on the American people of the presence of such men in high office is that they are justified in their bigotry, they are confirmed in their ignorance, they are all similar or greater John Waynes." Throughout Baldwin's career he often used the metaphor of the Hollywood film cowboy for U.S. political leaders to illustrate the "paralytically infantile" white settler masculine figure that white America keeps electing. Interviewer John Hall followed up Baldwin's point here, leading to this exchange:

> HALL: That reminds me that you once remarked upon the difficulty of growing up in a world of John Waynes, once you discover that you're the Indian.
> BALDWIN: That's right, exactly. But it's not going to work that way it did before. They're not going to be able to kill off this particular Indian. In fact they're not going to be able to kill off these particular Indians.[11]

His reference to Black people as "these particular Indians" is a direct political usage "of Indigenous genocide as a tool for Black liberation," as Mays puts it. Here, the "they" refers to the white settler masculine rule of the American nation in which Black Americans stand as the modern "particular Indians" threatened with genocide. Baldwin employs this trope to embolden or forewarn of Black resistance and survival in the face of white settler masculine violence carried out by the nation's John Waynes.

These are just a few of the examples of how settler memory is often present in some way in Baldwin's references to Indigenous peoples and *cowboys and Indians.* I do not deem Baldwin to be making casual references here. I argue he is seeking to grasp the persistence of U.S. white supremacy, and the politics of resistance to it, as shaped unavoidably by a history of colonial genocide, a history that Americans refuse to acknowledge. In short, while Baldwin does reproduce settler memory, we can also discern moments, some implicit and others more direct, where he also refuses it. The trick is to understand him to be variably reproducing and refusing settler memory, and sometimes he does so in the course of a single passage. It is through this fraught, at times contradictory, but also fertile dynamic of Baldwin's work that I argue he seeks to find a way to attend to the settler colonial roots of the political life of race. We can trace this complicated effort through two distinct pathways. One concerns the function of gender and sexuality in his work. The second concerns his insights on the meaning and role of whiteness in the United States. The link between both of these is the production, maintenance, and meaning of white settler masculinity.

Settler Sexuality and White Settler Masculinity

At times, Baldwin spoke about gender and sexuality in a way that has a familiar ring with the settler memory pattern he occasionally utilized when discussing Indigeneity and colonialism. One of the most notable examples in this regard came during a 1968 appearance on the *Dick Cavett Show*. The relevant quotation was in *I Am Not Your Negro* as well as the 1989 documentary *The Price of the Ticket*. An oft utilized video clip, it conveys Baldwin's argument about being Black in the midst of modern U.S. white supremacy. In this encounter, Baldwin was responding to Yale philosophy professor Paul Weiss, who claimed that there was too much attention to race and group-based thinking at the expense of universal and individual perspectives. This led Baldwin to state the following:

> I don't know what most white people in this country feel, but I can only conclude what they feel from the state of their institutions. I don't know if white Christians hate Negroes or not, but I know that we have a Christian church which is white and a Christian church which is black. I know as Malcolm X once put it, "the most segregated hour in America is high noon on Sunday." That says a great deal to me about a Christian nation. It means that I can't afford to trust most white Christians and certainly cannot trust the Christian church. I don't know whether the labor unions and their bosses really hate me. That doesn't matter. But I know that I'm not in their unions. I don't know if the real estate lobby has anything against black people, but I know the real estate lobby keeps me in the

ghetto. I don't know if the board of education hates black people, but I know the text books they give my children to read and the schools that we go to. Now this is the evidence! You want me to make an act of faith risking myself, my wife, my woman, my sister, my children on some idealism which you assure me exists in America which I have never seen.

Baldwin's response to Weiss undercuts the white liberal emphasis on individual motivations, beliefs, personal biases, or good intentions regarding racial equality by shifting attention to the institutional realities and experiences— "the evidence!"—of being Black in America. His focus on the institutionalized racial and class bifurcations and exclusions along the lines of religion, employment, housing, and education is an elegant illustration of life for Black people under racial capitalism. Then, with a passionate crescendo that can be properly experienced only by watching the clip, he concludes this statement by personalizing the matter. Baldwin positions himself as a Black heterosexual married man with children who is concerned with protecting "my wife, my woman, my sister, my children" from white supremacy and the false idealism of the American mythos.[12] Baldwin's homosexuality was never much of a secret, not that he discussed it much publicly, and he also never married or had children. So, then, what to make of the pose of heteronormativity here by Baldwin? What might be the connection between this pose and Baldwin's occasional pose of being one of the "Indians"? To address the first question I turn to Black queer theory assessments of Baldwin's approach and to Black feminist perspectives on the role of heteronormativity in political life and then transition to address the second question.

Dwight McBride, in his 1998 article "Can the Queen Speak? Racial Essentialism, Sexuality, and the Problem of Authority," argues that in this 1968 response Baldwin is affecting the position of the representative "race man," which is the "image of the black man as protector, progenitor and defender of the race," and "the truth of this rhetorical transformation—the hard, difficult worrisome truth—is that in order to be representative race man, one must be heterosexual." McBride continues, "And what of women? They would appear, in the confines of race discourse, to be ever the passive players. They are rhetorically useful in that they lend legitimacy to the black male's responsibility for their care and protection, but they cannot speak any more than the gay or lesbian brother or sister can."[13] He sees this as a moment when Baldwin donned the "racial representative mask" at the "expense of effacing (even if only temporarily)" his sexual identity.[14] To McBride, what gets lost is the principle that "if I am thinking about race, I should already be thinking about gender, class and sexuality," and the "point is not just one of intersection—as we have thought of it for so long—it is one of reconstitution."[15] More generally, Black feminist scholar Brittney Cooper's germinal notion of the "black radical spectacular" speaks to the performative function of the representative race man in positioning Black women as secondary or supportive players in radical Black politics. Cooper deploys this concept to analyze the marginalization of Black women from the 1963 March on Washington for Jobs and Freedom: "Wherein Blackness and black radical politics are placed on spectacular display and deployed for radically disruptive and productive ends. . . . The charisma of those who speak for the crowd is important for political efficacy. On the other hand, this moment reinscribed the subordination of Black women's political issues to the more pressing concerns of a Black male-centered liberation narrative."[16] Thus, Cooper in general and McBride with specific concern for Baldwin's words in this exchange call forth the function of heteronormativity in political life and the urgency of an intersectional approach to reconstitute the meaning of racial oppression itself as always already infused by oppressive dynamics along the lines of gender, class, and sexuality. To McBride, in these moments Baldwin fails his audience by masking the degree to which heteropatriarchy is constitutive of rather than additive to white supremacy.

Marlon Ross, in his 2013 article "Baldwin's Sissy Heroics," takes up the challenge brought forth by critics such as McBride to take seriously "what it means for Baldwin to speak from, and be read through, the habitus of black queer subjectivity."[17] Ross reads Baldwin as engaged in a refusal rather than a reproduction of heteronormativity not through a direct articulation of his sexuality and sexual politics but rather in the performance of what Ross calls Baldwin's *sissiness*, by which he does not mean weakness or passivity—to the contrary. To Ross, one can discern Baldwin's "sissy heroics" through his body language, ideas, deeds, and tone of voice and in those words that defy heteronormative masculine expectations and demands in his nonfiction work. This is to be distinguished from Baldwin speaking and writing about homosexuality as such. As Ross explains it, "I suggest that the sissy formation, when distinguished from incipient or teleological homosexuality, can perform productive theoretical work for us, as it did for Baldwin. Implicit in this inquiry, then, is the idea that the sissy must be thickly contextualized in relation to not only nonconforming gender roles but also to recognizable racial formations."[18] Ross is arguing that we read Baldwin the "sissy" as a position that refuses the binaries and dictates of heteronormativity as a key feature of Baldwin's critique of racial formation in the United States. Ross sees a connection, not a tension, between the two. To support this claim, he points to Baldwin's posture—quite literally his physical posture in the way he sits and gestures in photographs and in interviews—as evidence of a bodily refusal of heteronormativity, which to Ross is necessarily a racist heteronorm.

An anecdote from Baldwin's 1972 memoir, *No Name in the Street*, about a white Southern political leader sexually accosting him, "his wet hands groping for my cock," provides Ross another stark example of Baldwin's efforts to address how sexuality and gender are fundamentally linked with race.[19] Baldwin's reaction to this sexual assault is to think in terms of the power that this white man had—"With a phone call, [he] could prevent or provoke a lynching."[20] Baldwin does not react to this assault due to his concern for those who could be lynched if he upset this man.[21] Instead of reacting with open indignation or rage, Baldwin reads the situation as one in which this man's aggressive sexual act is by definition a racial act. To be clear, it is not *also* a racial act but rather, at once, a sexual and racial assault that is not about the man being a "faggot," in Baldwin's words. It is about the white Southern man utilizing the gendered racial power that white men have deployed since the time of slavery on up to the modern era to do whatever they want to do. Race, gender, and sexuality are not disaggregated in Baldwin's reflection of this incident. Rather, in the spirit of McBride's notion of "reconstitution," they compose one formation. In this way, Baldwin draws our attention to the fundamental role of white masculinity in the political life of race, such that whiteness defines masculinity as masculinity defines whiteness. Looking forward to chapter 5, one can foresee the connection between the Southern man grabbing Baldwin's penis in the Jim Crow South and Donald Trump running a race-baiting, xenophobic campaign in 2016 that led to him winning the U.S. presidency even after he was caught on tape gloating that he can grab women "by the pussy" and get away with it. The lesson here is that there is no understanding of the history, structure, and practice of whiteness without understanding the role of gender and of sexuality and, specifically, of masculinity. What is still missing, however, is the function of settlerness.

In this regard, I see a similarity with how one can read Baldwin's complicated relationship to gender and sexuality and how one can read his references to Indigeneity and the history of U.S. settler colonialism. Consider Ross's conclusion as it concerns Baldwin and heteronormativity: "If Baldwin sometimes voiced a heterosexual script—raging against the emasculation of black men by the Jim Crow regime—he as frequently, and as trenchantly as anyone I've ever encountered, also proffered the most devastating critique of the racist heteronorm in a wide range of genres."[22] As Ross summarizes, in Baldwin's nonfiction writings, speeches, and interviews one can find ways in which he reproduces racist heteronormativity and also trace his effort to criticize and refuse it. Baldwin engages in a similarly fraught struggle regarding the acknowledgment of Indigeneity and settler colonialism. This is not a coincidental dynamic. Baldwin's efforts to grapple with settler colonialism and heteronormativity are intertwined matters. To understand the dynamics of each requires accounting for the other.

Baldwin positing that he is a straight man with a wife and children in one setting and as one of the Indians threatened with death in another are connected by the idea that both positionalities are responses to the oppressive functioning of settler sexuality and settler domesticity in a white supremacist society. To elaborate, I build upon the notion of *settler sexuality* as defined by Scott Lauria Morgensen: "In the United States, the sexual colonization of Native peoples produced modern sexuality as 'settler sexuality': a white and national heteronormativity formed by regulating Native sexuality and gender while appearing to supplant them with the sexual modernity of settlers."[23] In their work on decolonizing feminism, Maile Arvin (Kanaka Maoli), Eve Tuck (Unangax̂), and Angie Morrill (Klamath) set out the process and purpose of the imposition of settler sexuality: "The heteropaternal organization of citizens into nuclear families, each expressing a 'proper' modern sexuality, has been a cornerstone in the production of a citizenry that will support and bolster the nation-state. Thus, as settler nations sought to disappear Indigenous peoples' complex structures of government and kinship, the management of Indigenous peoples' gender roles and sexuality was also key in remaking Indigenous peoples into settler citizens."[24] For her part, Lee Maracle speaks to the political imperatives at work here for settler colonial rule: "The aims of the colonizer are to break up communities and families, and to destroy the sense of nationhood and the spirit of co-operation among the colonized. A sense of powerlessness is the legacy handed down to the colonized people."[25] This process also produces a heteronormative settler memory of Indigeneity, as Joanne Barker puts it, "Imperialism and colonialism require Indigenous people to fit within the heteronormative archetypes of an Indigeneity that was authentic in the past but is culturally and legally vacated in the present."[26] These Indigenous studies scholars all point to the need to understand the imposition of heteropatriarchy and settler domesticity as a central component in the creation and maintenance of settler nation-states premised in the logic of the elimination of Indigenous peoples. As Morgenson notes, this settler sexuality is racialized as white, and thus while it is built through colonial violence and forced assimilation in the effort to eliminate Indigenous nations, it also shapes the racialized terrain of gender and sexuality for the settler nation as a whole, across the racial spectrum. Thus, in his 1968 encounter with Weiss, Baldwin's pose of being a representative race man with a wife and children can be read as reproducing for tactical purposes settler sexuality and heteropaternalism in his performance of the "Black radical spectacular." To be sure, Baldwin was trying to negotiate the terrain of white settler masculinity by finding a mode of discourse to get his point across to the audience of *The Dick Cavett Show*. This is not to excuse this move, but it puts it in the context of the hegemonic parameters of white settler sexuality Baldwin confronted at this moment. One can better map this terrain by taking account of the mutually constitutive role of race, gender, sexuality, and coloniality in shaping the terms of political discourse and the socioeconomics of racism in the United States, which is what Baldwin was directly addressing in the exchange on *The Dick Cavett Show*.

Baldwin addressed the relationship of race, gender, sexuality, and colonialism in a more nuanced way when pushed by Audre Lorde during two exchanges in their 1984 debate, held in Amherst, Massachusetts. The first exchange begins with the topic of racism:

JB: You use the word "racism."

AL: The hatred of Black, or color.

JB: But beneath the word "racism" sleeps the word "safety." Why is it important to be white or Black?

AL: Why is it important to be a man rather than a woman?

JB: In both cases, it is assumed that it is safer to be white than to be Black. And it's assumed that it is safer to be a man than to be a woman. These are both masculine assumptions. But those are the assumptions that we're trying to overcome or to confront.

AL: To confront, yeah. The vulnerability that lies behind those masculine assumptions is different for me and you, and we must begin to look at that.

Baldwin speaks to a key element of white settler supremacy, which is the dream of safety and of the role of masculinity in embodying and securing this safety. Lorde is pushing him to take heed of how the norms of white patriarchal society shape the viewpoints and relations among Black men and women and how these norms need to be refused, not reproduced. Upon this basis, the two of them start to find some common ground, and the language they agree on is one of combat, not within the Black community but against that which threatens it as a whole. The call of the enemy is coming from inside the house, and that house is the American nation:

AL: Yeah, we're at war.

JB: We are behind the gates of a kingdom which is determined to destroy us.

AL: Yes, exactly so. And I'm interested in seeing that we do not accept terms that will help us destroy each other. And I think one of the ways in which we destroy each other is by being programmed to knee-jerk on our differences. Knee-jerk on sex. Knee-jerk on sexuality.

JB: I don't quite know what to do about it, but I agree with you. And I understand exactly what you mean. You're quite right. We get confused with genders—you know, what the western notion of woman is, which is not necessarily what a woman is at all. It's certainly not the African notion of what a woman is. Or even the European notion of what a woman is. And there's certainly not [a] standard of masculinity in this country which anybody can respect. Part of the horror of being a Black American is being trapped into being an imitation of an imitation.[27]

A notable distinction Baldwin makes here concerns the Western, African, and European notions of a woman. By "Western," rather than African or European, he seems to be suggesting a white settler colonial norm of "what a woman is" and of the "standard of masculinity in this country," the United States. He ends with how Black Americans are trapped by these standards, and his reference to this being a Western product is an implicit reference to "the heteropaternal organization of citizens into nuclear families" by settler nations seeking "to disappear" the collective life of Indigenous peoples, as Arvin, Tuck, and Morrill put it. These are the roots of settler colonial domesticity in relation to which Baldwin feels trapped into being "an imitation of an imitation" in that well-traveled 1968 clip in which he challenges white supremacy in the defense of "my wife, my woman, my sister, my children." In so doing, he is in a paradoxical position of contesting while struggling not to reproduce the standards and expectations imposed by what Morgenson calls "the sexual modernity of settlers." In drawing out the role of settler sexuality and domesticity at work here, we get not only a better sense of what Baldwin is grappling with but an illustration of what is required and implicated in a politics of resistance to settler colonialism and white supremacy against the constraints of U.S. political memory. With this aim in mind, I next examine how Baldwin accounts for and analyzes myths about the settlement of the land that would become the United States.

White Settler Masculinity and the Story of Settlement

With white settler masculinity and settler sexuality in mind, Baldwin's repeated references to the likes of Gary Cooper and John Wayne come to have a deeper logic to them. With these references, Baldwin is driving at something while also seeking to derive something. This is evident in his 1963 speech "A Talk to Teachers," in which he mocks and refutes one of the American nation's founding tales and political memories:

> What passes for identity in America is a series of myths about one's heroic ancestors. It's astounding to me, for example, that so many people really appear to believe that the country was founded by a band of heroes who wanted to be free. That happens not to be true. . . . They were hungry. They were poor. They were convicts. Those who were making it in England, for example, did not get on the Mayflower. That's not how the country was settled. Not by Gary Cooper. Yet we have a whole race of people, a whole republic, who believe the myths to the point where even today they select political representatives, as far as I can tell, by how closely they resemble Gary Cooper. Now this is dangerously infantile, and it shows in every level of national life.[28]

Baldwin is retelling the settler story here to refute its mythology and to link the mythos produced through national collective memory to white American desires and political decision-making in the late twentieth century. He is speaking to the power of political memory. Desire and decision-making are politically intertwined in the myths of "a whole race of people, a whole republic" that longs for paternalistic protection provided by white settler men. Baldwin is not saying that all myths are bad or that a people can live without myths. He is pointing to the damage done through the dominant myths shaping the political memory of the American nation as it stands and its direct impact on the nation's political life. This 1963 reference to Gary Cooper in "A Talk to Teachers" also complicates and provides background to the Cooper reference he made in the debate with Buckley in 1965. In 1963, in the context of a tour to support his searing diagnosis of race in the United States in *The Fire Next Time*, Baldwin was calling out the myths about "how the country was settled," specifically those concerning the political and erotic power of settler masculinity as the racialized heteronormative protector in chief. This characterization of white settler masculinity as dangerously "infantile" persisted throughout his career, from 1963 to his reference to it in "Here Be Dragons" in 1985. The noble protective figure of Gary Cooper, who as Baldwin made clear in the 1965 exchange with Buckley is the one killing the Indians, is the model of settler masculinity that white America continues to elect to this day. The example of Gary Cooper or other such cowboy figures he kept turning to also demonstrates that the history and memory of settler colonization and the mythos of white settler masculinity are not ancillary to the story Baldwin told about race in the United States; they are foundational. This is not to say that Baldwin consistently refused settler colonial mythologies of the United States. Rather, the fact that he veered between reproducing and refusing settler memory makes his arguments and formulations richer for understanding U.S. political memory because they demonstrate—through the lens of one of the most sophisticated writers on race—the constraints and challenges in resisting and refusing the hegemonic parameters around race discourse and race politics in the United States. These parameters produce Indigeneity and settler colonialism as the constitutive outside of the political life of race in the United States.

For example, in "Down at the Cross: Letter from a Region in my Mind," the longer letter of the two that comprise *The Fire Next Time*, Baldwin mentions Indigenous people twice and only once as it concerns a claim about their condition or status. He states: "And today, a hundred years after his technical emancipation, [the Black American] remains—with the possible exception of the American Indian—the most despised creature in this country. Now, there is simply no possibility of a real change in the Negro's situation without the most radical and far-reaching changes in the American social and political structure."[29] What such radical changes might look like for Baldwin is a more open question that I will return to a little later in the chapter. For now, I want to take note of Baldwin's tendency throughout his career to view Indigenous people as the one group in U.S. history who may have been treated and viewed worse than Black Americans.[30] In 1967, writing on the International Crimes Tribunal in the midst of the U.S. war on Vietnam, Baldwin states, "A racist society can't but fight a racist war—this is the bitter truth. The assumptions acted on at home are also acted on abroad, and every American Negro knows this, for he, after the American Indian, was the first 'Vietcong' victim. We were bombed first."[31] We see this again in his words from 1979: "A very brutal thing must be said: The intentions of this melancholic country as concerns black people—and anyone who doubts me can ask any Indian—have always been genocidal. They needed us for labor and for sport. Now they can't get rid of us. We cannot be exiled and we cannot be accommodated. Something's got to give."[32] Then in 1984, in his blistering essay "On Being White . . . and Other Lies," published in *Essence* magazine, Baldwin writes: "America became

white—the people who, as they claim, 'settled' the country became white—-
because of the necessity of denying the black presence, and justifying the
black subjugation. No community can be based on such a principle—or, in
other words, no community can be established on so genocidal a lie. White
men—from Norway, for example, where they were 'Norwegians'—became
white by slaughtering the cattle, poisoning the wells, torching the houses, massacring Native Americans, raping Black women."[33] Not long after this passage, in this short essay's conclusion, he makes a precise claim: "It is the black
condition, and only that, which informs us concerning white people."[34]

As with his *Mayflower* comments from 1963, in his work in 1984 Baldwin
talks about how the concept of whiteness must be understood in relation to
how people, "as they claim, 'settled' the country." This is another consistent
but underexamined thread throughout his career. As Lisa Beard argues, Baldwin in this passage is setting out the case that the "Western world and white
racial identity are irrevocably tied to oppression—in that they are *defined by*
and *generated through* violence. That civilization projects its own violence
onto black people, indigenous people, immigrants—and onto antifascist freedom struggles."[35] Baldwin's references to Indigeneity and settler colonialism
are not the same sort as those noted earlier in this chapter. Baldwin is not
positioning himself or Black people as Indigenous. Still, there is a clear settler
memory impulse here when he invokes genocidal violence toward Indigenous
people as a prophetic warning in the 1979 quote claiming that if "they cannot
get rid of us" through exile or accommodation, "something's got to give." The
overriding similarity in these references is that Baldwin positions Indigenous
people, in his own words, as the "exception," as those people one can "ask" for
confirmation about the genocidal lie at the heart of the nation because they
were first to experience it. This is an example of Indigeneity and settler colonialism being the constitutive outside of the story of race in the United States;
the story that begins "after the American Indian." It is a prophetic use of Indigeneity for Black political purposes, to recall Mays's formulation. Here Baldwin deploys his knowledge of genocidal violence toward Indigenous peoples
to illustrate the precarious condition of Black life in the United States. There
is a constitutive absence and presence of Indigeneity and settler violence at
work here because for Baldwin one cannot understand the United States and
the political life of race for white and Black people, in particular, without grasping the nation's colonial underpinnings and the violent anti-Indigenous practices that brought whiteness into being. He positions Indigenous people as
the foundational recipient of expansionary imperial-colonial violence but then
asserts that Black Americans "were bombed first." The violence toward Indig-

enous people is both there and not there—foundationally relevant but not politically relevant, it seems. Yet, at the same time, his discussion of the origins of whiteness—specifically white settler masculinity—takes it a little further, which shows how he toggles between reproducing and refusing settler memory.

One of Baldwin's major contributions to race studies is the theorization of whiteness as a political identity. He was clear that whiteness is not based upon genetics or culture but rather on power that is "not a human or a personal reality; it is a political reality."[36] In other words, it concerns who has the "judges, the juries, the shotguns, the law."[37] As much as any other modern writer, Baldwin turned the lens of the "race problem" around from that which focused on people of color, especially Black people, as the ostensible problem that needed to be solved to making the case that the problem is white people or, more accurately, the concept of whiteness itself. On this matter, Baldwin had an unwitting (on both their parts) contemporaneous Indigenous ally in Standing Rock Sioux scholar, writer, and activist Vine Deloria Jr., who is a central and founding figure in Indigenous studies. In his 1968 canonical work, *Custer Died for Your Sins: An Indian Manifesto*, Deloria calls out the myth and problem of whiteness: "The white as we know him in America is an amalgam of European immigrants, not a racial phenomenon. . . . And we are taught to speak of the *Negro problem*, the *Indian problem*, and so forth. White has been abstracted into a magical nebulous mythology that dominates all inhabitants of our country in their attitudes toward one another."[38] As I discussed in previous work, in *Custer Died for Your Sins* Deloria positioned the demands and condition of Indigenous politics in contrast and relationship to Black politics, especially in the post–World War II period in the United States.[39] It does not appear that Deloria and Baldwin ever met, but their critiques converge from distinct yet connected experiences of living under white settler colonial rule. They each engage in their deconstruction of the myths, lies, and violence at the center of the foundation and maintenance of the United States. That Deloria is much less known than Baldwin is itself a product of settler memory, and thus in the rest of the chapter, I will note a couple of other areas where one can imagine meeting points in their thought at the intersection of anticolonial and antiracist critique.

In Baldwin's discussion of whiteness, I see him pointing to the function of white settlerness, or white settler masculinity, specifically, and the racist heteronorm it reproduces and represents. His wording in "On Being White" is direct on the matter, as he states that "being white" is constituted through the paired combination of genocidal and racialized sexual violence—"massacring

Native Americans, raping Black women"—and by the violence done to non-human life and to the land and water in the colonization process—"slaughtering the cattle, poisoning the wells." To grasp Baldwin's powerful words about whiteness in "On Being White," we must attend to the intersection of settler colonialism, gender, sexuality, and white supremacy. Anything less is a limited reading and understanding of whiteness as he defines and characterizes it and of the practices of settlerness that make whiteness possible. In "On Being White," Baldwin defines the concept of white masculine settler identity as dependent upon the enactment and reenactment of violence to land and life. His wording also implicates the role of settler sexual violence in the transformation of "Norwegians" into white men. Thus, when Baldwin asserts that it is *only* the Black condition that "informs us" about white people, his own words earlier in the piece have already refuted this claim. Here again, we run into the tensions and difficulties he has in grappling with the settler colonial resonance and roots of U.S. white supremacy.

Baldwin provides us a case study of settler memory in "On Being White." In the short span of this piece, he recalls in striking detail the formative past of genocidal and settler sexual violence against Indigenous peoples and Black women to explain how a Norwegian becomes a white American man. He then disavows the experience and status of Indigenous peoples and violent colonialist practices as having political relevance for "informing" us about whiteness itself. We saw this in the chapter on Bacon's Rebellion, especially in the disavowal of Indigeneity and settler colonial violence for the meaning of whiteness that emerges from the rebellion. In Baldwin's case, the dilemma of what to make of these tensions in this passage, as we have seen with his words in other contexts, leads me to the question of the meaning and extent of his radical political views: How radical are they?

The question to ask is: Out of Baldwin's work, can one garner a radical vision, one that is anticolonial and antiracist in its political memory and decolonial and abolitionist in its vision of a better world? Moon-Kie Jung says no. He argues that beyond Baldwin's difficulty in seeing outside the white-Black binary, whereby in discussing "non-Black peoples of color, Baldwin tends to see only the commonalties they share with Blacks," the deeper problem with positing his work as radical is Baldwin's identification with and attachment to America.[40] In making this point, Jung references many of Baldwin's claims about genocide against Indigenous people (a number of which I have noted already) and then asks a prescient question: "What would radical decolonization look like for indigenous peoples, for example, would it be possible to achieve without abandoning 'America' or 'Americans'"?[41] To Jung, Baldwin's unwillingness or inability to abandon America—to detach himself from the "we" of the nation in order to focus on the "they" of white American settler supremacy—fundamentally delimits the radical potentiality of his ideas and critiques, including forestalling what would be required to seriously address Indigenous people's demands for the decolonization of the United States. Lawrie Balfour, on the other hand, argues that criticisms of Baldwin as either an assimilationist or a militant miss the mark because his "message is more radical than either critique suggests." Specifically, the radicalism of his "essays consists in their capacity to trace the workings of race consciousness at so many levels of American experience. It consists as well in Baldwin's acknowledgement of the inescapable tension between human beings' dependence on the circumstances that have made them and the aspiration to create something truly new."[42] The parameters of what it means to create something new in Baldwin's perspective are not limited by a commitment to redeeming a specifically *American* project, according to Balfour, for the "radicalism of Baldwin's social criticism consists in his recognition that a commitment to social change means a willingness to give up the pretense that outcomes can be controlled or identities fixed, an openness to a new order whose parameters cannot be specified in advance."[43] This can only occur if the circumstances that have created the present context, those that are constraining the ability of people to imagine and enact a better world, are challenged as neither simply true nor false but as products and subjects of contestation in order to open up space for alternative political memories, mobilizations, and visions of collective existence.

An important contextual and structural circumstance that constrains imagining and enacting a better world concerns the hegemonic status of property itself. On this matter, Jack Turner argues that for Baldwin one of the key elements of whiteness that lends to its stubborn and oppressive persistence as a political identity is how it purports to fulfill the previously noted "dream of safety" for those who can claim it. To Turner, Baldwin's demand that whiteness must be abandoned or abolished to achieve a real postracial community requires letting go of the dream of safety, and this demand carries with it radical implications. Turner states, "Most provocatively, the surrender of safety would require at least the partial surrender of the vested right to property—that is, of a right to goods beyond what one needs to lead a life of equal freedom."[44] Turner is referring to a radical rethinking of the relationship of humans to one another, to nonhumans, and to the world around them, including the land and the goods required for our survival. Turner is not speaking about decolonization here or claiming that Baldwin is, but he is claiming that the United States as we know it can only become a place that in some way fulfills Baldwin's vision if it becomes a radically different place, an almost unrecognizable one. We see this claim in Turner's argument that, for Baldwin, "sensible Black Americans do *not* seek inclusion. Such inclusion is tantamount to being 'integrated into a burning house.' Sensible Black Americans seek instead a democratic reconstitution of society—starting with the standards by which we judge our lives."[45] From the Biblical prophecy "no more water, the fire next time" that ends and marks the title of his 1963 book to the reference to the United States as a "burning house," Baldwin was not subtle in his metaphorical references to the American nation being destroyed, burnt to the ground, if it does not address its racial ills. For his part, writing not about Baldwin but rather the aims of the civil rights movement in *Custer*, Vine Deloria Jr. argued that "to survive, Blacks must have a homeland where they can withdraw, drop the façade of integration, and be themselves."[46] Deloria's vision is not even necessarily one of a "democratic reconstitution," although possibly on decolonial terms, but it is certainly one that advocates abandoning any political vision that involves inclusion into this burning edifice of America.

The question Jung's provocation poses about Baldwin's thinking, however, is whether burning the house to the ground is a necessary precondition for real change in the first place, rather than retribution for a lack of change. I think there is more to draw from Baldwin in this regard than Jung may allow, but his skepticism is warranted. Settler memory is a shaping force in many of the ways in which Baldwin posits the place and meaning of settler colonialism and Indigeneity in the United States. A radical critique of U.S. white supremacy needs to reflect and speak to the vision of an intertwined abolitionist and decolonizing politics. Baldwin is clear on the former as it concerns abolishing white standing and whiteness, but he is less direct or consistent on the latter, and this may be the key for us as readers to determine how radical his critique and vision are. Still, I do not see this as telling the whole tale, and I concur with Balfour's and Turner's suggestions that we should allow for Baldwin's radicalism as neither positing a fixed end in advance nor being fearful of demanding significant material, social, political, and personal transformation. In order to do so, however, there needs to be a stronger foundation upon which to stand, one that pushes Baldwin's views to their limits and does not disavow the tensions. One foundation for a more radical Baldwin resides in his views on the relationship of white Americans to history and memory.

On American Memory:
"We've Made a Legend out of a Massacre"

To begin, I return to the 1963 speech Baldwin made in Los Angeles in which he told the joke about Tonto and the Lone Ranger. As noted, prior to telling the joke he talked about the conquest and colonial genocide of Indigenous people. Here is the full passage:

> Part of the dilemma of this country is that it has managed to believe the myths it has created about its past, which is another way of saying that it has entirely denied its past. . . . We did several things in order to conquer the country. There existed, at the time we reached these shores, a group of people who had never heard of machines, or, as far as I know of money, I think we would call them now a backward nation, and we promptly eliminated them. We killed them. I'm talking about the Indians in case you don't know what I'm talking about. . . . I'll bet you . . . that there are not many American children being taught American history who have any real sense of what that collision was like or what we really did, how we really achieved the extermination of the Indians, or what that meant. And it is interesting to consider that there are very few social critics, none to my knowledge but I say very few, who have begun even to analyze the hidden reasons why the cowboy-Indian legend is still one of the most popular legends in American life, so popular that still in 1963 it dominates the television screen. And I suppose, to finish off that particular item or to pose it for the moment that all those cowboy-Indian stories are designed to reassure us that no crime was committed. We've made a legend out of a massacre.[47]

As noted early, Baldwin incorporates himself into the "we" of the American nation in this political memory of the nation. This passage also makes clearer why Baldwin so often returned to the figures and myths of "cowboys and Indians." For him, they were popular components of a powerful collective memory that Americans, himself included, need to come to terms with to refuse the disavowal of genocidal violence against Indigenous peoples as constitutive of the nation's foundation. To this end, he took careful note of how Indians live on in U.S. popular culture in cowboy and Indian shows to help "make" a legend of the cowboy as the embodiment of noble American frontier masculinity in contrast to the Indigenous person who stands as the archaic, long-defeated enemy, who is "massacred." In his critique and condemnation of

Euro-American foundational violence, Baldwin draws upon settler memory in constructing Indigeneity as a simultaneous absence and presence in American political life. However, in stating that "we've made a legend out of a massacre" to "reassure us that no crime was committed" in the genocidal violence against Indigenous peoples he also refuses settler memory to the degree that he connects this history to the creation of the political and cultural context of his time. In so doing, Baldwin conveys to his audience a key dynamic of settler colonialism, astutely set out by Mishuana Goeman: "Settler colonial structures must imagine a homogenous stable present space developed for the good of the majority, even while they rely on forgetting the violence it took to produce the nation-state and the violence and fear it takes to sustain the sociopolitical order, which necessitates a lack of acknowledging the ongoing structures of the colonial moment."[48] Baldwin is not quite pointing to a forgetting per se but rather to the role of national collective memory that can turn historical facts into the mythologies that construct, legitimate, and reproduce a white settler sense of national belonging on these lands.

I place Baldwin's long exposition about the role of American myth-making and collective memory into the wider arc of his nonfiction work in which we can see him negotiating the tension between reproducing and refusing settler memory. It is in the midst of this tension that he is working out some of the radical potentiality of his thought and possibly coming up against its limits. This is the case especially as it concerns Baldwin's consistent diagnosis of the American condition, which focuses on the white American relationship to history. A conceptual focal point in this regard comes in Baldwin's defining insight about the notion of whiteness as *innocence*, by which he means the relationship of white Americans to history as being a relationship of disavowal that produces the dangerous and "paralytically infantile" racial, gender, and sexuality norms composing white settler masculinity.

In "My Dungeon Shook," the first letter in *The Fire Next Time*, Baldwin repeatedly refers to white people as "innocent." As he states, "It is the innocence which constitutes the crime."[49] This innocence is defined through disavowal, for as he puts it in another essay, written in 1961, "The effort not to know what one knows is the most corrupting effort one can make."[50] George Shulman draws out the roots and implications of Baldwin's claim about white innocence:

> "Innocence" thus denotes, partly, a denial of the Dionysian that he links to carnal mortality and the "tragic" nature of life; partly, a denial of the reality of others and a disclaiming of this refusal; and, partly, a denial of

the past that constitutes our situated particularity . . . for we undergo "life" through another subjection: to social categories, ascribed hierarchy, domination, and violence. For Baldwin, innocence also means denying this social reality and positioning in it. In his critique of white supremacy, therefore, disavowal creates the blackness that enables whiteness as a form of innocence. One is a specter of what is disclaimed in life and humanity; the other is a purified identity he depicts as idolatry.[51]

The white American disavowal of acknowledging what one knows to be true is about denying the reality of life and death itself, of mortality, of tragedy, of danger, and of precarity. Much of what represents the danger and threat of and to life for white Americans is projected on to the Black body, the policing, demonization, and oppression of which serve to perpetuate the racist heteronorm of Black threat, the white dream of safety, and the infantile white fantasy of immortality; thus, the logic behind Baldwin's stark statement that "white Americans do not believe in death, and this is why the darkness of my skin so intimidates them."[52] Or as Vine Deloria Jr. puts it, "What the white cannot understand he destroys lest it prove harmful."[53] With Deloria's words in mind it is worth then asking what happens to the Indigenous body in Baldwin's schema? This is a question of no minor importance. In fact, it is critical to Baldwin's persistent claim about the white American hostility to history, especially since challenging and shaking white Americans out of this antihistorical posture of political disavowal was a consistent imperative for him. Baldwin addresses this urgently, here in 1965: "White man, hear me! History, as nearly no one seems to know, is not merely something to be read. And it does not refer merely, or principally, to the past. On the contrary, the great force of history comes from the fact that we carry it within us, as unconsciously controlled by it in many ways, and history is literally *present* in all that we do."[54] As much as he refers to history here, I argue that Baldwin is offering a political theory of memory, in which contemporary racial injustices are the practices of the past embodied, reproduced, and lived in the present form, not merely reflections or echoes of the past.

The past on its own was not really the point for Baldwin, as we see in a July 1968 interview he did for *Esquire* magazine only months after the assassination of Martin Luther King Jr. The interviewer, a white man, asked: "You would say, then, that we have a lot to answer for?" In his answer, Baldwin began with "I am not trying to accuse you, you know. That is not the point," and he eventually offered his advice, or warning: "All that can save you now is your confrontation with your own history . . . which is not your past, but your present. Nobody cares what happened in the past. One can't afford to care what happened in the past. But your history has led you to this moment, and you can only begin to change yourself by looking at what you are doing in the name of your history, in the name of your gods, in the name of your language."[55]

Baldwin was a theorist of the racial politics of memory, about what is done in the present "in the name of your history . . . gods . . . language" and the shaping force memory has on how we interpret and act in the political present. As Shulman argues in his analysis of Baldwin's prophetic inclinations, "American culture is resolutely antihistorical: Each must escape the past or annul its power, to achieve the status of subject, of freedom as self-determination. But, for Baldwin, freedom begins only in recognizing that the past is not past or dead: We trap ourselves if we deny its power; we repeat it by efforts to escape."[56] Shulman's reference to American culture being *antihistorical* rather than *ahistorical* is vital, for he points not to the absence of historical awareness but rather to an opposition or resistance to it. As Baldwin puts it in "Stranger in the Village" from 1954: "People are trapped in history and history is trapped in them."[57] I suggest this is about a politics of memory rather than of history strictly defined because it is not about active efforts to resist knowing history but rather the work of disavowal that shapes political meaning in the here and now. Similarly, for Deloria, resolving the racial question in the United States is not about "either blacks or Indians. It involves the white man himself. He must examine his past. . . . The white must learn to stop viewing history as a plot against himself."[58] Deloria speaks here to how history seems to haunt white Americans as a hostile force, and thus the inclination is to disavow and distance from it. Baldwin and Deloria converge here in arguing that the white American disavowal of the political relevance of the nation's history comes at the expense of those who are compelled to live with this history, Black and Indigenous people in particular, every day.

Baldwin conveys this point during his 1965 debate with Buckley. Here, Baldwin argues that the history and memory of chattel slavery in the United States constructs his being such that there is no meaningful distinction between the past of slavery and his living present as a Black American in the 1960s. This is how he puts it: "From a very literal point of view, the harbors and the ports and the railroads of the country—the economy, especially in the South—could not conceivably be what they are if it had not been (and this is still so) for cheap labor. I am speaking very seriously and this is not an overstatement: I picked cotton, I carried it to the market, I built the railroads under someone else's whip. For nothing."[59] Baldwin connects the materiality and brutality of the history of slavery to that of his own body in the 1960s. The history of racial capitalism through the centuries of chattel slavery and into the afterlife of slavery shapes Baldwin's subjectivity and the political and economic status and experience of a Black man in the 1960s. Thus, when he states that he was among those who "picked cotton" and "built the railroads" under the "whip," Baldwin's claim is phenomenological in terms of the habitual practices and experiences of racial oppression and also political and socioeconomic regarding how little has changed in the structural inequalities between white and Black people. White Americans, to Baldwin, "are dimly, or vividly, aware that the history they have fed themselves is mainly a lie, but they do not know how to release themselves from it." Instead, when confronted with the history of slavery, they disavow its relationship to their present status with the familiar response, "Do not blame *me*, I was not there."[60] Because white Americans refuse to accept this past as their own, Black Americans are not allowed to forget and gain distance from it.

In a 1973 interview, Baldwin spoke to this point after granting to his interviewer that "nobody wants to suffer, and you do everything you can to forget it. . . . On the other hand you can't, because the situation of being a black American is not past or present. If you want to forget it, you can't forget it— you know, some cop will certainly remind you. Some landlord will remind you, a bank will remind you. Your kid will remind you, you know. It's not a question of forgetting; you can't forget. I have another point of view. From my point of view, it's a very great error to try to forget."[61] What we discern in Baldwin's words in 1973 and in the 1965 debate with Buckley is the way in which, as P. J. Brendese puts it: "For Baldwin, the past is not merely an object of active recollection that memory can conjure or set aside at will. Rather it lives and breathes beneath the surface of human interactions, rhythms, and aversions that shape our lived experiences of race."[62] In so doing, Baldwin "illuminates . . . the complex legacy of segregated memory in American politics in general" and "offers a window into an understanding of how power shapes memory and thereby perpetuates a collective inability to confront [racial] inequalities."[63] Brendese calls this the "*habituated disavowal of segregated memory*" whereby white people deem themselves innocent of this history through their disavowal of it, while Black people are not allowed to forget, even if they try, because they live this past every day in the material, institutional, cultural, and sociopolitical conditions of racial subjection by the cops, landlords, and banks.[64] The framing of memory as segregated speaks to the deeper truth of a nation divided along racial lines, and it makes sense as far as it goes. At the same time, this framing constrains how we grasp Baldwin's politics of memory to the parameters of the Black-white binary. In taking closer account of Indigeneity and settler colonial resonance in Baldwin's words, both in his disavowal and acknowledgment of them, the politics we end up with is a more radical critique of white innocence, of white settler masculinity, and of the American nation's prospects.

This more radical posture emerges in the same 1973 interview in which he discusses how Black Americans cannot forget. Baldwin follows that discussion by digging deeper into the American historical and mnemonic sensibility:

> Most Americans have no attitude toward history at all. Because, in fact, the whole achievement of being American is the attempt to destroy history. It does not exist. It is a *concept*. Americans don't know what Wounded Knee is about, for example. They don't know what happened. And white Americans don't know what it means to represent a people who have never had a single treaty with the Indians, what that means. What Americans mean by "history" is something they can forget. They don't know they have to pay for their history, because the Indians have paid for it every inch and every hour. That's why they're at Wounded Knee; that's why they took over Alcatraz. That's how you got Cassius Clay; that's how you got Malcolm X.[65]

Here, Baldwin does more than simply replicate the pattern of beginning with the genocidal logic of elimination of Indigenous peoples and ending with the Black political condition. He is opening up a vision of contemporary radical politics and coinhabitative connections among Indigenous and Black peoples based upon distinguishing between the "they" of white settler colonial rule and a potential "we" of Black-Indigenous solidarity. The white American disavowal of Indigenous people's history and settler colonial history he refers to here is not the same as the disavowal that white people offer when faced with the "disagreeable mirror" of the Black American.[66] Where the white American response to Black Americans regarding the nation's history of slavery is to say, "Do not blame *me*, I was not there" when it comes to being accountable for the nation's history of Indigenous genocide and territorial dispossession, the white settler response to Indigenous people's claims is some version of "You cannot blame *me, you're* not here." This is the necro-Indigenous response, in which disavowal is premised on the view that Indigenous peoples no longer exist; there is no one left with the political and legal standing to make demands. The anti-Black and necro-Indigenous responses speak to the constitutive relationship between segregated memory and settler memory in the white settler American imagination. One without the other leaves much out of the picture. In this sense, it is not a coincidence that after referring to radical Indigenous resistance by the Lakota people and the American Indian Movement (AIM) at Wounded Knee on the Pine Ridge Reservation and the occupation of Alcatraz Island by Indigenous activists of Indians of All Tribes in the early 1970s, Baldwin transitioned to Malcolm X and to the radicalization of boxer Cassius Clay into the Black Muslim Nationalist and Vietnam War resister Muhammad Ali. Here, I do not read Baldwin as separating these forms of radical expression, the former concerning Indigenous radical politics as, say, merely a platform to discuss Black radicalism. I read him as pointing to the connection between radical Indigenous and Black struggles of his time. What the political struggles he mentions have in common is direct expression of or support for revolutionary resistance to U.S. colonialism and empire at home and abroad. This quote is indicative of the manner in which out of the tension between how Baldwin reproduces and refuses settler memory he implicitly produces a critique that places settler colonialism as inescapably bound up with how to understand and oppose U.S. white supremacy and imperialism on these lands.

Indigenous peoples are not the exterminated people of the past in Baldwin's words in the 1973 interview, as he incorporates the urgency of radical Indigenous politics into his portrait of the contemporary U.S. context. With this passage, Baldwin calls out the settler colonial foundation at the heart of white America, just as he acknowledges the persistence of Indigenous political struggle. Baldwin's words point to forms of Indigenous political activism and protest across these lands in his time. In referring directly to the seizure and occupation of the federally abandoned prison and island of Alcatraz in San Francisco Bay from 1969 to 1971 and the armed conflict at Wounded Knee, he notes the power and presence of radical Indigenous politics and that this activism calls out the United States as an imperial nation, here and abroad.[67] In this regard, Baldwin's words echo and resonate with the following words by Deloria: "Until America begins to build a moral record in her dealings with the Indian people she should not try to fool the rest of the world about her intentions on other continents. America has always been a militantly imperialistic world power eagerly grasping for economic control over weaker nations."[68] Baldwin's words from the 1973 interview are in solidarity with Deloria's from 1968, as Baldwin centers Indigenous people as those who directly pay the price for the history that white Americans seek to "destroy" as any sort of living, breathing force that shapes the present. In his phrasing of the price that Indigenous peoples pay, Baldwin allocates this cost in terms of land and life. I read this as a cost of land and life in the phrasing of "every inch" (of land) and "every hour" (of lives) that have been taken from Indigenous peoples by settler colonization. I place this 1973 quote into the context of Baldwin's responses in two other interviews—one from 1970 and one from 1980—that reveal him to be making a case that one cannot grasp U.S. white supremacy and racial capitalism without accounting for the history and present of settler colonialism.

In a 1970 interview with David Frost, Baldwin gave the following answer to Frost's question "What is the greatest problem we now face?"

> Someone told me that in California in 1848 or '49, there were something like a hundred and fifty thousand Indians, and at the turn of that particular century, there were ten thousand, and I was really astounded by this.
>
> Martin Luther King was right when he said this nation was one of the few nations, but not the only one, which had to destroy the indigenous population in order to become a nation. But we're not a nation yet. And if you're a black cat living in this place and in this time, though you may spend your entire life knocking on the radiator, knocking on the steam pipes to get heat, trying to get protection from the rats and the roaches, and all the horrible details one lives with in the ghetto and gets used to it, you also know that if oil was discovered beneath the tenement in which you are living and dying, that wealth would not belong to you.
>
> When the Indians were driven out of wherever they were into Oklahoma, and oil was found in Oklahoma, it did not belong to the Indians.
>
> I am saying that to be a black person in this century, and to be relatively conscious, is to recognize to what extent the wealth and the power of the western world depend on your condition, that your condition is in some sense indispensable to that wealth and power.[69]

To recall Mays's critique, one can defensibly claim that Baldwin's response is another example of the use of settler colonization and the history of Indigenous genocide as a "prophetic tool" for Black Americans. Settler memory is at work here, but I argue that it exists in the context of a wider message Baldwin is conveying that goes beyond the rudimentary imaginary of him or Black people being Indian. Rather, here he is tracing out two distinct but deeply interconnected narratives. The first, built out of the words of Dr. King, is the explicit assertion that settler colonial violence against Indigenous people is fundamental to the story of the birth and life of the white American nation. Second, Baldwin's narrative of Black Americans being potentially dispossessed from their homes should valuable natural resources ever be discovered in the ghetto, as happened to Indigenous peoples dispossessed from the

Southeast and then in parts of Oklahoma and across the Americas, connects the dots between settler colonialism and racial capitalism. He is offering a modern example of the layers of dispossession I discussed in chapter 2 regarding Indigenous and Black dispossession from their lands and homes. Baldwin is making a structural argument about the political economy of the white settler nation that requires continual accumulation of resources at the expense most often of colonized nonwhite others. Additionally, within his response to Frost, Baldwin offers a form of refusal in his claim that "we're not a nation yet." But what exactly is he refusing, and what sort of political vision is both implied as possible but also contained by the "we" and the "yet" in Baldwin's phrasing? What if the most radical version of the "we" Baldwin is offering here is one in which there is no "yet" to the American nation but rather a *never* or a *no longer*?

With these questions in mind, I return to Baldwin's conversation with Audre Lorde in 1984, in particular as it concerns Lorde's refusal of incorporation into Baldwin's narrative of the relationship of Black people to the American nation. The following exchange occurs after Baldwin refers to W. E. B. Du Bois's effort—an ill-advised effort, Baldwin grants—to encourage Black Americans to enlist in the U.S. military during World War I to demonstrate their loyalty and worth as citizens:

> JB: Du Bois believed in the American dream. So did Martin. So did Malcolm. So do I. So do you. That's why we're sitting here.
>
> AL: I don't, honey. I'm sorry, I just can't let that go past. Deep, deep, deep down I know that dream was never mine. And I wept and I cried and I fought and I stormed, but I just knew it. I was Black. I was female. And I was out—out—by any construct wherever the power lay. So if I had to claw myself insane, if I lived I was going to have to do it alone. Nobody was dreaming about me. Nobody was even studying me except as something to wipe out.
>
> JB: You are saying you do not exist in the American dream except as a nightmare.
>
> AL: That's right. And I knew it every time I opened *Jet*, too. I knew that every time I opened a Kotex box. I knew that every time I went to school. I knew that every time I opened a prayer book. I knew it, I just knew it.[70]

Apart from the question of to what degree and consistency Du Bois and Malcolm X believed in the American dream, Lorde offers a more fundamental refusal of Baldwin's claim. For her, it is less that she is not a believer in the

American dream than that this dream was never a believer in her because it was built upon Black women's othering, denigration, and disappearance. Here, I return to Maracle for her insights on and connection with Lorde. In her fundamental work, *I Am Woman: Native Perspectives on Sociology and Feminism*, Maracle writes: "For me, Audre Lorde most properly represents the women's movement in North America. The women's movement is all about the liberation of humanity from the yoke of domination." Maracle then sets out her connection to and compatibility with Lorde in terms of how their radical Indigenous and Black feminist politics, respectively, speak to the nexus of colonialism and racial capitalism as central pillars of white settler, heteropatriarchal rule: "Audre Lorde and I were destined to be close. The combined knowledge of African ex-slaves and colonized Natives in North America is going to tear asunder the holy citadel of patriarchy. Who can understand the pain of this land better than a Native woman? Who can understand the oppression that capitalism metes out to working people better than a Black woman?"[71] In their own ways, Maracle and Lorde speak to the role of patriarchy and heteronormativity in the logics of genocidal elimination undergirding white supremacy and colonialism in settler states such as the United States and Canada; the latter being Maracle's main focus. Neither of these radical feminists has a longing or a vision of redemption for these white settler nations. Their approaches are abolitionist and decolonial and as such require the dismantlement of heteropatriarchy and capitalism. Lorde chastens Baldwin's redemptive imaginary for the American nation—and his assertion of some fealty to the American dream—and does it from the perspective of a Black woman who sees herself as having no place in this imaginary, as she experiences every time she "opens a Kotex box." To the contrary, the country is built on her exploitation and elimination. Maracle reinforces this view while bringing critical attention to the intertwined functioning of racial capitalism with heteropatriarchy, white supremacy, and colonialism, premised on Indigenous elimination. I draw attention to Lorde's exchange with Baldwin and Maracle's explicit assertion of solidarity with Lorde to show not only that Baldwin's engagement with radical Black feminism meaningfully provokes his view of the redemptive (im)possibilities of the American nation but also that it connects him in a coinhabitative web of critique of white settler heteropatriarchal rule along with the likes of Lorde and Maracle, as well as Vine Deloria Jr. This is not to say they all agree or, in the case of Deloria and Baldwin, actually conversed or that this connective relationship defuses Jung's critique of Baldwin's attachment to the American nation. Rather, I want to suggest that when considered in light of those moments when he implicitly refuses the settler memory of colonialism in and of the United States, we can read Baldwin in productive conversation with these thinkers.

With this in mind, I turn now to Baldwin's words in the 1980s to offer evidence not of the end point in the development of his thoughts on the matter, for any such construction is an unfair imposition of a singular narrative on a wide-ranging, complex thinker. Rather, what we can discern is that settler resonance and colonial distinctions persist in how Baldwin assesses and reveals to us the rotting core of the incomplete, and even impossible, American nation. In 1980, Baldwin did a wide-ranging interview with Wolfgang Binder, conducted in Cannes, France. The location of the interview is relevant because at one point Baldwin and Binder have an exchange over the contrast between how Europeans and Americans relate to history:

> JB: And in terms of America, the Americans are even more abject than
> the Europeans who are stifling among their artefacts, their icons,
> which they call history. The Americans have never even heard of
> history, they still believe that legend created about the Far West, and
> cowboys and Indians, and cops and robbers, and black and white, and
> good and evil. There is a reason that the most simple-minded men,
> Mr. Carter and Mr. Reagan, who might be considered to run a post
> office, are the only candidates America can find to run the world.
> If the Europeans are afflicted by history, Americans are afflicted by
> innocence.
> WB: Are they innocent?
> JB: The Americans would like to be. Go back to the beginning of the
> country, go back to the last of the Mohicans. It was poisoned from
> the beginning, and no one has been able to admit it.[72]

As he often did, Baldwin returns to the claim that nothing so fundamentally defines white American identity as its antihistorical outlook. There is, to be sure, an American exceptionalist tone and theme to Baldwin's assessment here, positioning the United States as somehow unique or special when it comes to the erasure or disavowal of ugly historical truths.[73] I posit that one can refuse to follow him down this path of reproducing such exceptionalism while still taking up the core and power of his critique of American political memory. The innocence he refers to here is constituted by the unwillingness to engage with how the dominant political memory of the nation reproduces paralytically infantile cowboy figures, the "simple-minded men"—the Gary Coopers of their time, Jimmy Carter and Ronald Reagan—whom white Americans keep turning to as their representatives. This inclination may even have reached its apogee with the 2016 election of Donald Trump as the unparalleled embodiment of paralytically infantile masculinity. The binaries Baldwin sets out in the 1980 interview conjure a Manichaean worldview premised upon the defense of white American innocence, with cowboys versus Indians, cops versus robbers, white versus black, and good versus evil. The chain of equivalences at work here link together the cowboys, cops, whiteness, and goodness that protect white settler society from Indians, Black people, robbers, and all the evil they represent.[74] Baldwin then points to the colonial roots of it all: the fantasy of cowboys confronting the "last of the Mohicans," which is the violent conquest and settler colonialism that "poisoned" the nation at its founding. This is the nation that never was and maybe never could nor should be, as it is diseased from the start. Speaking in 1980, the year of Ronald Reagan's election, Baldwin connects this foundational poison to the politics of his specific time. For Baldwin, to understand why the United States has the leaders it does one must examine the political role and function of memory, which shapes the political present in defining and toxic ways.

A little later in the 1980 interview, Baldwin sets out in even starker terms the relationship between settler colonialism and white supremacy in the United States. Here is Baldwin's response to a question from Binder about race: "Race is a concept, which has no validity whatever. It is cowardly—all racists are cowards. It is a word which arose with the rise of the western nations, with the justification of slaughter. 'Manifest Destiny' in the United States is simply a way of saying, we have the right to slaughter everything in our path, because it is obvious that we will control this part of the world, so that I became a thing, my father became a thing, and the Indian became a corpse."[75] While Baldwin's view of Indigenous people and settler colonialism is fraught, complicated, and at times even contradictory, what the direct imagery of this quotation places before us to acknowledge is that Baldwin did read settler colonialism into the political memory of the story of U.S. white supremacy. Baldwin speaks here not of a racialized logic by itself but a colonialist one justified through racialization—genocidal slaughter in the cause of land dispossession and settler expansion under the ideological, nationalistic, and imperialistic guise of manifest destiny. His final sentence paints an unflinching portrait of the consequences for Black people—he and his father as "things," objects and property to be owned and exploited—and Indigenous people as "corpses," the massacred. I do not see this claim by Baldwin as the articulation of necro-Indigeneity in a settler memory form as he is far from disavowing the political importance of this logic of elimination. Nor, given his statements about the resistances at Wounded Knee and Alcatraz, does he view Indigenous political life as consigned to the past. Baldwin is unraveling the political life of race in the United States in a manner that may well be unfamiliar to many of his readers. He does so by grounding it in colonization, the condition of the possibility of chattel slavery, just as the expansion of slavery served as a key impetus for greater land dispossession from Indigenous nations. Baldwin did not often connect these two as explicitly as he does in the 1980 interview, and he constantly struggled with his own pull toward settler memory. However, when we pay serious heed to his own grappling with the settler resonance of white supremacy, it becomes difficult to ignore that when we turn to Baldwin for insights on the United States we find him directing us to acknowledge the "poison" of settler colonialism as a central source of the nation's racial ills.

Conclusion

James Baldwin struggled and dealt with, and even reproduced, the constraining parameters of U.S. race discourse that does not have much room for Indigenous peoples or settler colonialism. Still, out of the tensions of his grappling with the settler resonance of U.S. white supremacy, Baldwin offered us words that cut to the core of how the violent settler colonial foundation of the United States maintains a shaping force on the present. In his own way and in fits and starts, Baldwin saw that settler colonialism is a structure and a process and that to understand race, gender, and sexuality in the United States one must attend to it. But attending to it is easier said than done. Baldwin was never hesitant to speak truths about the rot at the core of the American nation, and his struggles to maintain a consistent approach in acknowledging the role of settler colonialism and Indigenous politics is reflective of a wider struggle of radical political actors and thinkers to do the same. For those of us who continue to turn to Baldwin to shed light on our world, my hope is that this chapter may offer, as a start, an alternative pathway for thinking through a more capacious Baldwin by theorizing the limitations and expansive potential of his critique and insights, possibly in conversation with a few of his vital contemporaries, such as Lorde, Maracle, and Deloria. This sort of approach to Baldwin might offer a model for how a critical engagement can be carried out among students, writers, and activists in and across U.S. race studies, Indigenous studies, settler colonial studies, and political theory. The complex terrain of contemporary politics in the United States and beyond demands it. In the final two chapters of the book, I examine the contemporary U.S. political context. Next, in chapter 4, I discuss the matter of Indian-themed sports team names and mascots and their relationship to U.S. race politics and discourse. Baldwin's words provide a fitting transition to this topic. For when team owners and corporations profit from and fans cheer for and pledge furious fealty to teams with names such as the Washington Redsk*ns, Baldwin's words from 1963 ring just as true today: "We've made a legend out of a massacre."

CHAPTER FOUR

The Free Pass

The Racial Politics of Indian Team Names and Mascots

Introduction

In July 2014, the Center for American Progress released a research study titled "Missing the Point: The Real Impact of Mascots and Team Names on American Indian and Alaska Native Youth." Written by Erik Stegman and Victoria Phillips, the study further substantiated that the use of Indian team names and mascots has a negative social and psychological impact on Indigenous people, especially young people.[1] To introduce and publicize the report, the center invited guest speakers and a panel to address the topic. The keynote speaker was Congresswoman Betty McCollum (D-MN). In discussing the controversy over the name of the Washington, D.C.-based National Football League (NFL) team, McCollum said that if a derogatory word for people who are Jewish, African American, or Chinese were proposed as a team name, it "wouldn't be allowed, no one would stand for it, but for some reason, the term 'Redsk*n' gets a free pass."[2] McCollum was here speaking as an advocate for ending the use of these names and mascots for sports teams at the high school, college, and professional levels in the United States. However, her "for some reason" statement reveals an underlying confusion about why this was even an issue at all and why there had been no comprehensive indignation and swift action to end this practice. McCollum was not alone in her confusion, as it was and still is articulated often by those who oppose such names and mascots. The source of this confusion is the inability to grasp the manner in which settler colonialism and Indigenous peoples are both ubiquitous and, for most people, relatively invisible in contemporary U.S. political life. The history and present of settler colonial violence toward and the dispossession and appropriation of Indigenous people's bodies, territory, and identity is the historical and political context of the sports names and mascots issue. The appropriation of Indigenous people's identities by settlers is coexistent with the appropriation of territory and efforts to absorb and eliminate Indigenous presence through violence and assimilation. One cannot grasp the team names and mascot issue adequately without attending to settler colonialism, past and present. However, what most political actors and observers see and discuss in this debate is not settler colonialism but rather race and racism, specifically through a liberal framework in which the focus is on redressing offensive representations and exclusions through greater inclusiveness into the society as it is presently constituted. To deem as racist names such as the Redsk*ns is not so much wrong as analytically incomplete and politically limited for grasping why these names and mascots get a "free pass"—why so many were created in the first place, persist, and are vehemently defended today by those who seek to maintain the status quo.[3]

The work of settler memory is one of the primary reasons why Indian-themed sports team names and mascots persist as popular representations into the twenty-first century. These names and mascots are mnemonic devices, which tell us that Indigenous people are both everywhere in symbolic form and absent as active, contemporary political subjects. This disavowal thus also applies to settler colonial practices of dispossession, violence, and forced assimilation. People who have spent decades defending such names as the Redsk*ns deny and disavow the historical and political meaning of the term by utilizing the popular settler justifications that these representations are traditions that must be preserved and that they honor Indigenous people. These sorts of justifications, accepted by many in the U.S. population, are a few of the reasons why Indian-themed representations in U.S. sports culture have become the most prevalent example of "legends" that are made "out of a massacre."

Understanding why the name of the Washington football team existed for decades up until the summer of 2020 while hundreds of other names/mascots continue to get what McCollum called the "free pass," requires analyzing the racial politics here, with attention to the work of settler memory. In so doing, what we end up seeing is how racial liberalism predominates in twenty-first century U.S. race politics at the direct expense of radical antiracist and anticolonial perspectives. After decades of protest and resistance by Indigenous activists, Washington football team owner Dan Snyder was finally compelled to change the team's name due to escalating pressure and public criticism, in the immediate moment, provoked by the nationwide antiracist political movement led by the Movement for Black Lives (M4BL) following the murder of George Floyd by Minneapolis police in May 2020. This movement has demanded radical transformation, such as defunding police departments, centering the terms of their contention on abolishing systemic racism. The M4BL also stands in solidarity with the political struggles and claims of Indigenous peoples, such as in the coinhabitative actions of toppling Confederate statues and those of Christopher Columbus. While the M4BL was an important short-term factor leading to the change in the Washington team as well as that of the Cleveland baseball team, as announced in December 2020,[4] the long-term causal force behind this change was the political work done by Indigenous activists over many decades to build a political movement to raise awareness about, contest against, and demand an end to these and other such names and representations. In particular, Suzan Shown Harjo (Cheyenne and Hodulgee Muscogee), Amanda Blackhorse (Diné), Jacqueline Keeler (Diné and Yankton Dakota), and Jody TallBear (Cheyenne-Arapaho and Sisseton Wahpeton Oyate) led the way through political lobbying, direct action, movement organizing, and court petitions that reached as far as the U.S. Supreme Court.[5] It speaks to the power of the "free pass" that the Washington team enjoyed for decades that it took such a historic antiracist political movement, one that did not constrain itself to liberal parameters, to finally force the NFL and the Washington team owner to retire the name.

The welcome demise of these particular names does not mean this issue is over, as the National Congress of American Indians (NCAI) found that in 2020 there remain hundreds of such forms of Indigenous appropriation, caricaturing, and stereotyping at the professional, college, and K–12 school levels.[6] In contrast to the radical, movement-based, and intersectional approach of the M4BL and that of radical Indigenous activism, the terms and discourse of racial liberalism still predominate in shaping the debate on this matter through a framework centered on the ideals of multiculturalism, diversity, and inclusion within the U.S. economic and political system.[7] The work of settler memory reinforces the boundaries defined by racial liberalism, which we can discern in much of the discussion around this issue across the political spectrum, from those who are critics of it to those who defend these representations.

I focus on the history of the Washington NFL team name as representative not only of the hundreds of such examples of this specific name/mascot phenomenon—what Jacqueline Keeler calls *mascotry*, a term I will utilize in this chapter—but also of a wider dynamic not contained to the sports realm. While it was a welcome and positive development to see an end to the Washington name as the most infamous example of mascotry, this team's history and the battle over its name offer lessons going forward. As I noted in the book's preface, one can find such Indigenous representations in topographical markers and names, consumer products, and military nomenclature. As to the latter, I will conclude the chapter by connecting the role of these representations on the football field to those on the U.S. imperial battlefield—all sites of aggressive, violent settler masculinity. I turn first to set out the history of the issue. Upon this basis, I then examine the role of race in the contemporary debate over team names and mascots. I argue that the issue of Indian mascotry points us in two directions: (1) to the constraining dynamics of contemporary racial liberalism as generally understood and (2) to the practices of U.S. settler colonialism that are so meagerly understood.

The Historical and Political Context

The history of the Washington football team's name reveals this naming practice to be a product of settler colonial history, practices, and governance that exist in an intertwined relationship with the history, practices, and governance of white supremacy in the United States. In 1933, George Preston Marshall renamed his Boston-based NFL team the Redsk*ns; the name had been the Braves in 1932, the team's inaugural season. The etymology of the name can be traced back to the late eighteenth and early nineteenth centuries when, according to one historian, it was not a derogatory term. By the late nineteenth century, one could no longer make such a case.[8] For example, in the wake of the U.S.-Dakota War of 1862 an ad in the September 24, 1863, edition of the *Winona Daily Republican* in Minnesota offered the following: "The State reward for dead Indians has been increased to $200 for every red-skin sent to Purgatory. This sum is more than the dead bodies of all the Indians east of the Red River are worth."[9] The genocidal tone and aims for which "red-skin" is utilized in this public forum show that the word is meant to evoke and encourage violence against Indigenous peoples as a central practice of settler colonialism and to do so in a way that commodifies their deaths. The origin of the term places necro-Indigeneity at the heart of the signification of the team's name. Putting the team name in historical and political context also reveals that the naming of the Washington team in 1933 marked the end, or close to the end, of a defining era in U.S. Indian policy.

In his study of the history of this topic, J. Gordon Hylton discovered that "the practice of identifying professional teams by Indian names most likely began in 1886."[10] Prior to that there were no such names for professional teams, but soon after they began to proliferate, and most of the team names with which we are now familiar emerged between 1886 and 1933. The Boston Braves (eventually relocated to Milwaukee and then to Atlanta) got its name in 1912, the Cleveland Indians in 1915, the Chicago Blackhawks in 1926, and then the Washington football team in 1933. After 1933, one still sees intermittent cases of such naming—the Kansas City Chiefs in 1960, for example— but there is a clear decline and no new professional team names of this sort after

1963. Hylton's study, however, does not point out the relevance of this period from the 1880s to the 1930s. This is the time period of the Allotment era.

As discussed in chapter 2, the General Allotment Act became federal law in 1887 and stands as one of the most notorious and damaging legislative acts in the history of U.S. Indian policy. President Theodore Roosevelt's words in 1901 only further underscored that the aim of this legislation was to destroy Indigenous nations as collective entities, as communities: "In my judgment the time has arrived when we should definitely make up our minds to recognize the Indian as an individual and not as a member of a tribe. The General Allotment Act is a mighty pulverizing engine to break up the tribal mass."[11] As a result of such policies and also the direct violence against Indigenous peoples that I discussed in chapter 2, this late nineteenth and early twentieth-century period marked the low point in the recorded population of Indigenous people in the U.S. context, at 248,000 people in 1890.[12] One can also count the 1924 Indian Citizenship Act as a settler state measure of this era that sought to assimilate Indigenous peoples to the United States, as it unilaterally made Indigenous people U.S. citizens, regardless of whether they consented or not, and many Indigenous nations and citizens did not consent.[13] In sum, during the decades that span the Allotment era, U.S. state actors and white settlers forced Indigenous peoples even more to the margins through policies and practices of displacement, violence, commodification, and assimilation. This *massacre* thus slowly turned into consumable *legends* as symbolic Indigeneity moved increasingly to the center of the white American settler imaginary.[14]

This mutually constitutive dynamic reflects the relationship among the three pillars of settler colonialism focusing on territory, people, and identity. The mascotry phenomenon is an appropriative settler practice that helps to constitute and acculturate a sense of settler belonging on this land through the production of a settler tradition that both acknowledges the presence of Indigenous peoples as historical beings while disavowing their presence as contemporaneous beings. As C. Richard King argues, through the naming practices of this era, white Americans found, and continue to find, a psychic-libidinal way to "absorb indigeneity, laying claim to indigenous people's rightful inheritance while lamenting nostalgically their passing."[15] The settler practice of creating such team names and mascots, as with other forms of stereotypical representation of Indigenous peoples in U.S. culture, is not a peripheral or superficial matter compared to other settler actions against Indigenous peoples and territory. Rather, it is critical to the legitimation and disavowal of settler colonial violence, displacement, and appropriation. Also, the emergence of Indian mascotry during this time period fostered the development of modern forms of white settler masculinity in the wake of the decline of the so-called frontier through which such white masculine fantasies were imagined and enacted. As Jennifer Guiliano demonstrates in her studies of the gendered discourse of Indigenous sports names and mascots, the growth of college and professional sports during this period was an important vehicle for the expression and production of modern white middle-class masculinity by means of male participation in and support for an emergent, popular sports culture.[16] The realm of modern sports, especially but not solely that of football, is already defined in many ways by toxic forms of white settler masculinity, further evidenced in mascotry and the contemporary defense of it.

To conclude this section, I return to the specific history of the Washington football team. George Preston Marshall's motivation for giving the team this name derived from his "long time fascination with Native Americans" and in honor of the identity of his coach William Henry "Lone Star" Dietz, who was "believed to be a Native American" from the Sioux Nation, although in all likelihood he was not.[17] Dietz's previous positions included coaching at the Haskell Indian School, and he recruited six Indigenous men, a number from Haskell, to play for the 1933 Boston team.[18] As well as introducing the new name, that year Marshall also required Coach Dietz to "walk the sidelines wearing a Sioux headdress," and he had the players, white and Indigenous, "wear war paint when they took the field."[19] In this way, the white settler owner imposed not only the name but an entire performance of stereotypical Indigeneity, one reflecting not actual Indigenous practices but the owner's settler imaginary. Marshall's views and actions after he moved the team to Washington, D.C., in 1938 also exemplify the fact that the settler imaginary in the United States is deeply shaped by anti-Blackness as well as an eliminatory view of and relationship toward Indigenous peoples.

By 1961, the Washington football team stood as the only NFL team to have never had a Black player on its roster. Under the new John F. Kennedy administration and with the presence of an increasingly powerful civil rights movement, Kennedy's secretary of the interior, Stewart Udall, pressured Marshall to sign a Black player so that the team residing in the nation's capital would no longer be, in Udall's words, "lily-white," or "paleskins," as he called them. Marshall resisted, cementing his reputation as an open white supremacist, stating at one point that "we'll start signing Negroes when the Harlem Globetrotters start signing whites." Marshall had supporters in his effort to resist the Kennedy administration's pressure to integrate the team. Notably, the American

Nazi Party marched in support, and one photo shows two distinct signs carried by the uniformed Nazis. The first is a banner stating "America Awake," with a swastika positioned between these two words. The second is a sign held up by a Marshall supporter that says, "Mr. Marshall: Keep Redskins White!"[20]

Udall eventually forced Marshall to cede on this issue and integrate his team because the secretary had valuable leverage. Marshall had recently signed a thirty-year lease on the stadium in which his team would play, and that stadium—at the time called D.C. Stadium and then Robert F. Kennedy Memorial Stadium—resided on federal lands. As such, Marshall's landlord was the Department of the Interior, and Udall threatened to deny use of these lands if the team persisted in its discriminatory practices.[21] Here settler colonial invisibility and its modern functionality and material presence came into play. This land is part of "the ancestral lands of the Anacostans (also documented as Nacotchtank), and over time neighboring the Piscataway and Pamunkey peoples."[22] British colonizers and settlers seized this land in the late seventeenth and early eighteenth centuries. In the late eighteenth century, ten square miles of the land was turned over to the federal government in order to locate and build the nation's new Capitol in Washington, D.C. Here we see the constitutive relationship between settler colonialism and white supremacy in the history of Marshall's ownership of the team, and it foreshadows the contemporary debate over the team's name.

To start, take note of the American Nazi claim to "Keep Redsk*ns White," which echoed Marshall's effort to keep Black players off his team. Here, the preservation of whiteness in this settler imaginary is maintained through direct anti-Blackness and Indigenous erasure. We see here the working of settler colonialism as a structure and process in which an overt claim to an identification with and appropriation of Indigeneity does not upset the notion of white racial purity—if anything it reaffirms it, as I discussed in the book's introduction—because in settler memory Indigenous peoples have been made functionally absent, a safe part of the past, through genocidal elimination and absorption into whiteness as a settler identity. This is also an example of how anti-Blackness stands as a key pillar of white settlerness, as this explicit defense of the team name makes clear. The team's name and history is part of a white settler tradition that deploys settler colonial practices of appropriation to affirm settler belonging and anti-Blackness to affirm white racial superiority. As I will discuss later when deconstructing the contemporary efforts to defend the team's name, the notion that anti-Blackness shapes the history of the team and its name along with the more evident function of necro-Indigeneity is not simply a consequence of Marshall's open white supremacy as an individual. The practice of Indian mascotry exists in the context of the wider racial topography of the United States, where Indigenous peoples are rendered "honorable" because they are deemed long dead, a necro-Indigenous presumption, whereas other nonwhite groups are not deemed honorable but rather are abject, degraded, and exploitable contemporaneous others to the white settler norm. This part of the story of the Washington team is brought to a close with the Kennedy administration succeeding with regard to ending Marshall's practice of a particular form of anti-Black racism, the exclusion of Black people from the marketplace—in this case that of professional athletics—due to racial discrimination. Marshall was violating a key tenet of racial liberalism, which is access to the marketplace, and in the nation's capital no less. The settler government's claim over this land proved the leverage needed for Marshall to eventually and reluctantly include Black players on his team. This was a victory for racial liberalism won through the deployment of settler colonial governing power over land dispossessed from Indigenous peoples. Well into the twenty-first century, the constitutive relationship of settler colonialism to white supremacy and of Indigeneity to race continues to resonate in the controversy over the team's name and the practice of mascotry more generally.

The Contemporary Debate:
The Anti-naming Claim of Racism

Just as in the early 1960s, when the Washington football team was at the center of a storm over a violation of racial liberalism and the owner's anti-Blackness, in the contemporary era this same franchise in the most profitable professional sports league in the United States was under intense scrutiny over the team's name until the summer of 2020. For many years, a wide range of Indigenous and non-Indigenous political actors voiced their opposition to the name, demanding that present team owner Dan Snyder change it. They include, but are not limited to, the aforementioned Suzan Shown Harjo, Amanda Blackhorse, Jacqueline Keeler, and Jody TallBear, as well as the Oneida Nation under the leadership of Ray Halbritter, the NCAI, and the Leadership Council on Civil and Human Rights, which is a coalition that includes the National Association for the Advancement of Colored People (NAACP), the American Civil Liberties Union, the Human Rights Campaign, the National Council of La Raza, and the American-Arab Anti-Discrimination Committee. Additionally, in 2014 then president Barack Obama stated that if he were the owner of a team with a name "that was offending a sizeable group of people,

I'd think about changing it."[23] Halbritter, while leading the Oneida Nation's public campaign against the name, also wrote a 2014 editorial critiquing what he saw to be hypocrisy in the NFL pondering a plan to penalize players for saying the word "n*gger" on the field while the Redsk*ns remained the name of one of its franchises. Comparing the *N-word* and the *R-word*, Halbritter argued that the latter is like the former in that it is a well-recognized racial slur.[24] And in the wake of the National Basketball Association (NBA) banning Los Angeles Clippers' owner Donald Sterling in April 2014 for making racist statements in the private realm, a number of public figures used this moment as an opportunity to demand the NFL take action on the Washington team name, seeing the two situations as analogous. Football player Richard Sherman, when asked if he believed the NFL would have taken the same stance on racist statements as the NBA, stated: "No, I don't. Because we have an NFL team called the Redskins." Then Senate majority leader Harry Reid (D-NV) implored the NFL to follow the NBA's lead, mocking those who defended the Washington team name as a matter of tradition, stating, "What tradition, a tradition of racism." At this time, Representative Henry Waxman (D-CA) also called for a congressional hearing on the team's name, stating that the committee "could play a constructive role in challenging racism" by calling NFL commissioner Roger Goodell and Snyder to testify and defend the name. And on May 21, 2014, fifty U.S. senators, all Democrats, signed on to a letter to Commissioner Goodell calling for a change to the Washington team's name. The letter also builds on the NBA example and includes the following claims and statements

> that racism and bigotry have no place in professional sports;
>
> What message does it send to punish slurs against African Americans while endorsing slurs against Native Americans?
>
> This is a matter of tribal sovereignty—and Indian Country has spoken clearly on this issue.
>
> At the heart of sovereignty for tribes is their identity. Tribes have worked for generations to preserve the right to speak their languages and perform their sacred ceremonies. . . . Yet every Sunday during football season, the Washington, D.C. football team mocks their culture.
>
> The NFL can no longer ignore this and perpetuate the use of this name as anything but what it is: a racial slur.[25]

While these Democratic senators supported changing the name, a 2013 poll found that 79 percent of Americans thought the Washington team should not have to change its name.[26] Thus, while the issue gained momentum to the degree that mainstream political and public figures became comfortable speaking out against the name and there were successes in ending some mascotry, a significant portion of the public still did not view it as a serious problem. To make sense of this, we need to take a close look at the politics and discourse of race deployed here.

The predominant claim made by those opposing the Washington team name was that the name is racist, a slur upon Indigenous peoples. The claim that this practice is racist, or a racist slur, is clearly defensible in that the Washington football team name in use until 2020 is a dictionary-defined slur and a dehumanization of Indigenous people. The problem here is not the charge of racism itself but the fact that it has become hegemonic in the debate. In so doing, this discourse marginalizes the idea and claim that these team names and mascots are persistent practices of settler colonialism that exist in a constitutive relationship with white supremacy. The relative invisibility of settler colonialism in this debate is as much a product of disavowal as a consequence of a lack of knowledge or a mere by-product of the predominant focus on race. For example, the letter from the U.S. senators asserts that the issue is a matter of tribal sovereignty, which thus conveys their knowledge that Indigenous nations stand in a distinct nation-to-nation relationship to the United States. This assertion might have opened a path to defining this naming practice as a settler colonial one—one of appropriation built upon genocidal and dispossessive practices against peoples who assert their status as sovereign nations, which could then connect this matter to settler injustices against Indigenous nations in the areas of land appropriation and violence. But the senators' letter focuses on matters of "identity" with no mention of land and also closes with the presumptive assertion that the team's name is "what it is, a racial slur." This is unsurprising, as U.S. senators—specifically Democratic senators—can comfortably stand against racism in this particular form while also standing, if implicitly, for the maintenance and reproduction of American settler colonialism in the form of liberal colonialism. By liberal colonialism, I mean polities comprising institutions, norms, and practices that reflect a compatible relationship between liberal democracy and colonialism in the political development and contemporary formation of nations such as the United States. Within a liberal colonial context, there is no tension between an open opposition to practices that explicitly violate racial liberal principles and the simultaneous disavowal and reproduction of settler colonialism. They go hand in hand.

Robert Nichols sheds light on the tensions that emerge when antiracist efforts presume the persistence of settler colonialism and the settler state. He notes, "Antiracist critique may inadvertently reproduce the official state narrative of the settler colony. . . . In fact, it is often through the removal of so-called race-based barriers to integration and subsequent enclosure and incorporation of previously self-governing Indigenous polities that settler colonialism has operated."[27] As a consequence: "Insofar as this form of antiracist critique enables settler colonial sovereignty to structure the terms of its own contestation, it is classically, hegemonic."[28] It is this hegemony that is in play in the liberal critique of team names and mascots in which race-based discriminations and barriers become the primary focal point of the discourse such that settler colonialism is, at best, placed into the background while the resolution to this racial violation follows the logic of inclusion and thus affirms settler colonial governance. The resolution to the exclusion of Black players from the Washington football team in the early 1960s came by means of settler state actors and institutions using as leverage against a white supremacist team owner the fact that said team owner sought to profit from long-term access to lands dispossessed from Indigenous peoples. Racial inclusion was achieved and settler colonial governance was the means to achieving this aim. When settler colonial governance shapes the "terms of its own contestation" in this way, the historical, territorial, and political sources and meaning of the appropriation of Indigenous identity and imagery get subsumed and disavowed. With this perspective in mind, I see racial liberal discourse at work in the 2014 letter from the fifty U.S. senators as well as other forms of opposition to the Washington name and similar sports names. This discursive work is evident in the popular rhetorical trope referenced by Representative McCollum positing a hypothetical in which there is an appropriation of the identities and imagery of non-Indigenous racial and ethnic others to the white Christian norm. A visual example of this device is an image widely shared across social media showing three baseball caps side by side: those of the hypothetical New York Jews and San Francisco Chinamen and the actual team, the Cleveland Indians, each with its own derogatory caricature of an individual from these respective groups.

The image was the centerpiece of a poster and social media campaign produced and disseminated by the NCAI. The image includes the following tag line: "No race, creed or religion should endure the ridicule faced by the Native Americans today. Please help us put an end to this mockery and racism by visiting www.ncai.org."[29] The point made here is that if one finds unacceptable the hypothetical New York and San Francisco team names and mascots, then one should by racial liberal analogy find the third, that being the Cleveland Indians and their logo/mascot Chief Wahoo, also unacceptable. In terms of short-term political tactics, it makes sense for activists to utilize this form of race-based discourse to generate public attention to the issue in a context in which racial liberalism is hegemonic. In fact, as of 2019 the Cleveland team no longer uses the logo of Chief Wahoo on team uniforms, and as noted in late 2020, the Cleveland organization also decided to stop using the team name during games and in public advertising. Thus, we see a victory here, and it is a meaningful and positive step to be sure, but it is also contained in its critique and aims within a particular racial framing and set of presumptions. We see this in two respects.

First, here are Major League Baseball (MLB) commissioner Rob Manfred's words in a press release about this decision regarding the Chief Wahoo logo: "Major League Baseball is committed to building a culture of diversity and inclusion throughout the game."[30] "Diversity and inclusion" is a fine sentiment as far as it goes, but it can only go so far due to the fact that its framing emphasizes *inclusion* and therefore assimilation to and affirmation of the settler colonial context. We see the limitations of this framework also in a second respect, whereby even after declaring that the Cleveland baseball team would no longer use the "Indians" name, the team is continuing to offer for sale to its fans team merchandise with both the Wahoo logo and team name. Here is the statement made by the team, posted on the MLB website: "We will continue to sell selected merchandise featuring our historic names and logos, including Chief Wahoo as a way to acknowledge our history. As part of our ongoing commitment to promote diversity, equity, and inclusion, it is our intention to donate profits from the sale of Chief Wahoo merchandise to Native American-focused organizations and causes."[31] Here, then, we see a prime example of racial liberalism and settler colonial hegemony. For while the Cleveland team may not be directly profiting off the sale of such items, by removing these offensive representations from active public viewing but still reproducing the name and logo at fans' request the organization and MLB are abiding by the norms of racial liberalism while leaving in place and even reaffirming the legitimacy of mascotry as a form of settler colonial appropriation and settler belonging for their fans.

Racial liberalism may have won here, but settler colonial processes remain relatively undisturbed. It is thus fair to question what this approach means in the long-term effort to generate anticolonial resistance to the massacres and dispossessions that mascotry turns into consumable legends when these legends continue to be consumed, in some form, even if out of the public eye.[32] In this light, the problems with a discursive move such as the example of the three-baseball-cap campaign, as effective as it may have been in one sense, are that, first, it is premised upon the idea that the experiences and resolutions to the injustices perpetuated upon these groups are analogous, and second, it undermines the effort to grasp why Indian mascotry persists at all. The baseball cap analogy does not answer the question of why Indian team names and mascots get the "free pass." Instead, it unintentionally further inscribes this pass. This is because the question that the hypothetical poses—how can we tolerate the Cleveland Indians when we would not tolerate the New York Jews or San Francisco Chinamen?—portends to be exposing the hypocrisy or inconsistency in the application of racial liberalism but really masks the deeper, disavowed problem. The problem is that colonial relations define the production and persistence of names like the Redsk*ns and the Indians, which exist in a constitutive relationship to race but cannot be collapsed as a matter of race, and race alone.

My effort to deconstruct the baseball cap analogy to focus on the settler dynamics at work is not to challenge the point that in contemporary life most people would not tolerate the New York Jews or San Francisco Chinamen as team names and mascots. That is clearly true. Instead, I mean to shed light on the fact that in U.S. history there is no point in which the creation of such team names and mascots would have made sense as a popular, sustaining phenomenon in the first place. This is not to say that Jewish and Chinese people did and do not experience structural discrimination in the United States but rather that there is a distinct, constitutive role for Indigenous identity and settler colonialism in relation to American settler identity and U.S. political and economic development. Without such a shift of registers from racial liberalism to a systemic racial analysis and politics in tandem with a critique that centers settler colonialism, the issue as popularly debated is more likely to reproduce than disrupt the hegemony of settler governance. I turn now to address a couple of the main arguments made in defense of mascotry to reveal the theoretical and political benefit of directly refusing settler memory in the debate and politics around this issue.

Two Defenses of Mascotry and Anticolonial Responses

There are two prevalent contemporary arguments made to defend the practice of Indian mascotry: (1) for the team and its fans, the name or mascot is an important tradition worthy of respect and preservation, and (2) these names and mascots are meant to honor Indigenous people, culture, and traditions, and in that spirit they are utilized to reflect and enhance team pride. Washington team officials and supporters made these two arguments in their defense of the team's name. I analyze each in turn as a prime example of the popular defenses one usually finds in the debate and fight over the hundreds of other forms of mascotry that persist.

It's a Tradition

In an October 9, 2013, letter to the season ticket holders of the Washington football team, team owner Dan Snyder addressed the controversy over the team's name. While stating that he "respects the feelings of those who are offended by the team name," Snyder invoked a number of common defenses of the name, in particular that of it being a tradition and an honoring. I start with the way he concludes the letter:

> So when I consider the Washington Redskins name, I think of what it stands for. I think of the Washington Redskins traditions and pride I want to share with my three children, just as my father shared with me—and just as you have shared with your family and friends.
>
> I respect the opinions of those who disagree. I want them to know that I do hear them, and I will continue to listen and learn. But we cannot ignore our 81 year history, or the strong feelings of most of our fans as well as Native Americans throughout the country. After 81 years, the team name "Redskins" continues to hold the memories and meaning of where we came from, who we are, and who we want to be in the years to come.
>
> We are Redskins Nation and we owe it to our fans and coaches and players, past and present, to preserve that heritage.[33]

I take Dan Snyder's claim that the team's name is a meaningful tradition to be sincere. He is right; it is a tradition—a settler colonial tradition. In no small part, a settler colonial tradition is one that supplants and replaces Indigenous people's history and presence with a settler history that seeks to establish settler belonging in the territory. Historian Jean O'Brien refers to this as a *replacement narrative* that effects a "stark break from the past, with non-Indians replacing Indians on the landscape."[34] O'Brien's focus is on the replacement narrative in nineteenth-century New England, and she finds "five locations" in which it can be read: "The erection of monuments to Indians and non-Indians, the celebration of historical commemorations of various sorts, the enterprise of excavating Indians sites, the selective retention of Indian place-names, and claims Non-Indians made to Indian homelands."[35] Working with O'Brien's categories, Indian sports names and mascots can be understood as a popular form of a monument and historical commemoration that serve the purpose of establishing settler belonging at the expense of Indigenous presence, as Snyder's words concede.

In response to criticism and protests, Snyder counters with a claim premised upon the weight and meaning of the over eighty-year history of the Washington team's name. It is his team's history, what he refers to as that of a "nation," that he positions as under threat from those who seek to change the name. For Snyder, this eighty-year historical span has generated collective identification and belonging, explicitly avowed in his assertion that the name "continues to hold the memories and meaning of where we come from, who we are, and who we want to be in the years to come." These are settler memories built upon the appropriation, representation, and replacement of Indigenous identity and presence by an emergent settler tradition and identity. Snyder constructs a "we" comprising non-Indigenous people, settlers, who find in the Washington team a mnemonic bond that links together fans and players of the "past and present." Snyder's construction of the "we" in this way is demonstrated by the fact that he starts his mnemonic tale with the meaning the name has for his own family and extends that feeling out to "your family and friends" and finally to "most of our fans as well as Native Americans." The latter phrase is a telling construction in that it splits off a settler fan base from Indigenous people. Even if Snyder included settlers and Indigenous people in his "we" of the Redsk*ns nation, the tradition he is defending is a settler tradition in its creation, development, and purposes. This is a tradition built upon locating active Indigenous peoples in the past, which settlers then *honor* via appropriation in the present day. In this way, the Washington team name and mascotry in general are active components of a contemporary replacement narrative that constitutes, and with each articulation reconstitutes, the story of settler belonging as a tradition unto itself.

To take at face value the claim to tradition and then consider the meaning of such a claim is to engage in an anticolonial critique by marking mascotry and the defense of it as an appropriative practice that serves in the constitution of settler identity. This approach goes further politically and critically than the claim that the name is racist on racial liberal terms, as it refuses to allow settler colonial governance to set the terms of this debate. It does so by putting the team name's into historical and mnemonic perspective as part of a persistent, deeply rooted settler colonial logic and set of practices traceable from the past to the present and thereby tying it to, rather than cleaving it off from, the history and present of settler colonial governance. This approach places settler colonialism at the center of this debate such that it can facilitate racial critique that goes beyond the parameters of racial liberalism. I draw this relationship out in the next section regarding the claim that these names and mascots honor Indigenous people.

It's an Honor

The claim that this naming practice is not a slur but is, to the contrary, an honoring of Indigenous peoples is bound up with the view that Indian team names and mascots are a tradition. The claim to be honoring Indigenous peoples is also one of the most prevalent defenses of mascotry and other consumer, militaristic, and topographical signifiers. Here are three examples of its deployment in reference to the Washington team name. First, this is an excerpt from NFL commissioner Roger Goodell's June 2013 letter to two congressional representatives: "Neither in intent nor use was the name ever meant to denigrate Native Americans or offend any group. The Washington Redskins name has thus from its origin represented a positive meaning distinct from any disparagement that could be viewed in some other context. For the team's millions of fans and customers, who represent one of America's most ethnically and geographically diverse fan bases, the name is a unifying force that stands for strength, courage, pride and respect."[36] Second, in an August 2014 interview with the television sports network ESPN, Dan Snyder offered the following in response to the question: What is a Redsk*n? "A Redskin is a football player. A Redskin is our fans. The Washington Redskin fan base represents honor, represents respect, represents pride. Hopefully winning. And it's a positive."[37] Finally, the website Redskinsfacts, a team alumni website funded by Dan Snyder with the listed support of such former players as Joe Theismann, Billy Kilmer, Mark Moseley, and Clinton Portis, made the following claim: "We believe the Redskins name deserves to stay. It epitomizes all the noble qualities we admire about Native Americans—the same intangibles we expect from Washington's gridiron heroes on game day. Honor. Loyalty. Unity. Respect. Courage. And more."[38]

Just as original team owner Marshall saw the name as an honorific that would stand as a positive symbol for his team in 1933, the parties supporting the name in the early twenty-first century are likely being sincere when they say that the name speaks to the "noble qualities" they admire about Indigenous people. In the conclusion to his book *Playing Indian*, Philip J. Deloria (Standing Rock Sioux) explained the role "playing Indian" serves for Americans in the production and meaning of their national identity, stating: "The self-defining pairing of American truth with American freedom rests on the ability to wield power against Indians—social, military, economic, and political—

while simultaneously drawing power from them. Indianness may have existed primarily as a cultural artifact in American society, but it has helped *create* these other forms of power, which have then been turned back on native people."[39] The key word here is "power." The comments of Goodell, Snyder, and those on the team alumni website articulate a vital, constitutive relationship between the honor that the name purports to convey to and about Indigenous peoples and the power that the team and its fans get from the name as a "unifying force," signifying "intangibles" they "expect from Washington's gridiron heroes on game day. Honor. Loyalty. Unity. Respect. Courage." The components and purpose of honoring as defined here by significant figures of the NFL and the Washington team invoke a process of drawing power from Indigeneity as a cultural artifact for the sake of enhancing the power of the collective identity of the team and its fans. The purpose here is to constitute settler identity, as the claim to honoring is an appropriative practice for which the Washington team name is a metonym for the wider dynamic constitutive of American settler identity itself. This appropriative practice of honoring is also a form of replacement narrative, in which settler collective identity—the American nation, the Redsk*ns nation—draws power from Indigeneity conceived as a cultural artifact that in its *noblest* form is ubiquitous in the past and invisible in the present. The replacement narrative here asserts that noble Indigenous people have tragically disappeared, and we, the settlers, honor them by taking up their name as our own in contemporary settler form.

In referring to honoring as a practice of appropriating Indigenous identity, I mean this as both building upon and occurring alongside the dispossession and appropriation of Indigenous peoples' territory and the effort to eliminate and undermine Indigenous peoples as distinct nations. Regarding this latter point, in their study of the psychological impact of mascotry, psychologist Stephanie Fryberg of the Tulalip Nation and her colleagues discovered that there are negative impacts to such names and mascots, especially for Indigenous youth, and these "effects are not due to negative associations with mascots." They found that even when Indigenous youth have, in Dan Snyder's terms, "a positive" association with an Indian team name or mascot there was still a negative impact on the self-esteem of these young Indigenous people. These researchers conclude:

> Although pro-mascot advocates suggest that American Indian mascots are complimentary and honorific and should enhance well-being, the research presented runs contrary to this position. American Indian

mascots do not have negative consequences because their content or meaning is inherently negative. Rather, American Indian mascots have negative consequences because, in the contexts in which they appear, there are relatively few alternate characterizations of American Indians. The current American Indian mascot representations function as inordinately powerful communicators, to natives and nonnatives alike, of how American Indians should look and behave. American Indian mascots thus remind American Indians of the limited ways in which others see them.

In sum, this appropriation diminishes and confines the ways in which many young Indigenous people understand and enact their sense of identity. This is a colonialist practice premised upon the enforced invisibility of Indigenous peoples as contemporary agents and the ubiquity of stereotypical representations of Indigenous identity and existence in such forms as mascotry. This colonial practice also simultaneously emboldens settler identity, as Fryberg et al. establish by referring to two studies that "revealed that after exposure to various American Indian representations, European Americans reported higher self-esteem compared to the control condition and to a nonnative mascot, namely, the University of Notre Dame Fighting Irish."[40] Just as the appropriation of Indigenous territory reduces the territory of Indigenous peoples in the process of enhancing the territorial holdings of the settler population, the appropriation of Indigenous identity through mascotry undermines the self-esteem and sense of identity of many young Indigenous people while enhancing the self-esteem and thus standing of white settlers, of "European Americans." Both practices are pillars of the structure and processes of settler colonialism.

The relationship between appropriation of territory and of identity is indicative of the wider colonialist dynamics at work here. That which I marked out as a constitutive relationship during the Allotment era continues to this day. As with the response to the tradition defense, an anticolonial response to the honoring defense does not need to challenge the idea of it being a positive representation, an honor, or a sign of admiration. Whether an image is meant as an honor or to be derogatory is not the fundamental point, as the psychological studies themselves show. Rather, the point to be made is that these names and mascots are created by the colonizer to represent the identity and existence of the colonized, drawing power to the former from the latter at a symbolic and cultural level that is tightly tied to the appropriations and violence directed against Indigenous peoples. Building upon this thought, an anticolonial response to the honoring defense should refuse to allow this debate to be reduced to race alone in racial liberal terms but instead can and should seek to draw out the often underattended relationship between colonialism and white supremacy in the mascotry issue.

While the U.S. Indian policy period from the 1880s to the 1930s is known infamously as the Allotment era, in the history of formalized U.S. white supremacy this is the period of the Jim Crow era that did not formally end until the mid-1960s. During the Allotment/Jim Crow eras, sports teams turned to Indigenous identity to draw power in order to generate their honorable, noble, and courageous team identities, but they did not turn to African American identity for this same purpose. The production of white American settler identity did involve the appropriation and drawing of power from African American identity, but in different form and with distinct meaning. As Eric Lott explains in *Love and Theft*, since well before the American Civil War the wearing of *blackface* by white Americans emerged out of their desire for and repulsion for African Americans. These minstrel performances helped to shore up the identity and standing of white working-class American males, in particular, who during this period faced uncertainty regarding the stability of racial status, meaning, and hierarchy.[41] There is an important difference between these forms of appropriation, which speaks to why a debate over team names and mascots that is reduced to the terms of racial liberalism does not recognize the persistent role of anti-Blackness at work here. Blackface minstrelsy presumed and continues to presume the presence of African Americans in an abject state at the bottom of the racial hierarchy of U.S. white supremacy, whereas Indian mascotry presumes the disappearance of Indigenous people who are honored as a cultural artifact.[42] In American settler memory, these two distinct yet constitutive imaginaries are, on the one hand, the abject Black American who is mocked and desired through blackface minstrelsy and, on the other hand, the Indigenous person made tragically invisible by U.S. settler colonial practices and then seemingly honored through mascotry. In the white settler imaginary, the abject presence of Blackness stabilizes white superiority in the U.S. racial hierarchy, while noble, disappearing Indigeneity stabilizes the settler replacement narrative of and claim to settler belonging.[43] When looked at in this way, one can safely posit that to white settlers in the early twentieth century the idea of looking to draw power from Black American identity so as to create an honorable team name was unimaginable, whereas utilizing Indigenous identity was readily imaginable, ubiquitously so. In this regard, original Washington team owner George Marshall's views and actions exemplify the manner in which anti-Blackness and the claim to honoring while replacing Indigeneity go hand in hand.

While present-day fans of the team would likely disavow previous owner Marshall's open white supremacy, as well as the assertion of the American Nazi Party to "Keep Redskins White," the team's public history on this account is not an exception to the rule of settler memory and tradition. Rather, it speaks to a collaborative relationship between settler colonialism and white supremacy in the U.S. context. This collaborative dynamic matters when attending politically to the likes of Goodell, Snyder, and so many others who do not view the N-word and the R-word as both problematic, because while they concede the former is a slur they insisted up until 2020 that the latter was an honor. That the likes of Goodell and others could not see the two words to be unacceptable was evident in 2014 when, as noted, the NFL seriously considered instituting a new on-field penalty for the use of the N-word by one player toward another, a situation that occurred almost solely among Black players.[44] To those opposed to the Washington team name, this further demonstrated that the Redsk*ns name was getting a free pass.[45] For example, C. Richard King in his excellent book *Redskins: Insult and Brand* deems the difference between American views of the N- and R-words as indicative of a "double standard. It is black and white. One word is read as a racial slur, and only a racial slur, and must not be uttered, even as the structures of violence, degradation, and inequality remain entrenched in society; the other word, despite linguistic, historic, and psychological evidence, is framed as anything but a racial slur and can be used in marketing, media, and fan cheers."[46] While this assessment is acute and understandable and goes beyond collapsing the discussion back to a simple framework of racial liberalism, it also relies on a presumption that the standard of assessment is defined through a racial logic—about whether it is a slur or not—and that there is thus a contradiction, a double standard at work here, as it concerns what counts and does not count as an actionable racial slur. However, this notion of the double standard leaves the discussion in a framework centered on race. Instead, a perspective that attends to the colonial dynamics in relation to racial ones sees less a double standard than a mutually compatible logic. An anticolonial analytical perspective highlights the constitutive relationship between settler colonialism and white supremacy at work in the manner in which a profound anti-Blackness is subtly woven into the honoring defense—for who is worthy of such an honor, and who is not in this logic and why, after all?—especially in light of the potential N-word ban. In the context of the NFL's proposed policy regarding the N-word, the claim by defenders of the team name that the Washington name was an honor implies that one particular group, Indigenous peoples (of a noble past), are worthy of the "honor" of white settler admiration, while another group, African Americans (of an ignoble present), are worthy of only white liberal paternalism.

An anticolonial and radically antiracist approach in this debate should make clear that the disappearing, noble, and honorable Indian that Dan Snyder and his supporters spent decades defending relies historically and logically upon the coconstitutive dishonor, exploitability, and ever presence of African Americans. In so doing, this approach maintains the focus on settler colonialism and anti-Blackness as deeply interrelated structures. It does so by taking the honoring defense at face value and reposing it as one that relies upon both Indigenous invisibility and elimination and Black American denigration and exploitation. This approach does not appeal to the inclusive, assimilatory framework of racial liberalism. In response to the honoring defense, an anticolonialist argument does not say we would never tolerate a derogatory name such as, say, the New York "N-words" so we should not have the Washington team name or others like it but instead asks the question: Why would the former have never entered the white settler imaginary in the first place, whereas the latter was ubiquitous in its formative period and persisted into the twenty-first century? This question speaks to the history and present of settler colonialism and white supremacy through a disruptive response to mascotry as a practice of white settler colonial rule.

Conclusion: Settler Memory from the Playing Field to the Battlefield

The "free pass" enjoyed by the Washington football team until 2020 and that persists to this day for hundreds of other team names and mascots exists because settler colonialism remains a trace in this political debate. In making this case, the purpose of this chapter is not to discredit the efforts of those seeking to do the important work of bringing an end to these names and mascots, as they have succeeded in important ways. Rather, the point is to consider the implications of the arguments deployed and to suggest even more historically attentive and radical ways to intervene in the debate and politics of this issue—to recompose the role of political memory in this debate. By refusing the work of settler memory, political efforts to oppose names and mascots can upset the mnemonic loop that reproduces settler colonial logic. However, if these efforts heed to the logic of racial liberalism in a post–civil rights paradigm that defines the mascot issue as a matter of offensiveness, exclusion, and discrimination rather than an anticolonial focus on appropriation, dispossession, and violence, they are more likely to reproduce, even if unintentionally, settler memory as a practice that sustains, or at least does not trouble, liberal colonialism. The politics of Indian mascotry can bring settler colonialism to the center of public debate in a way that does not exclude questions of race but rather pushes this discussion in even more radical directions. At the least, it is imperative to engage in a politics that works to refuse the invisibility of settler colonialism and Indigenous peoples. While this may complicate the argument a bit more than it is at present, the benefit would be to compel a widening of the discourse to account for Indigeneity and settler colonialism on their own and not as domesticated to the U.S. racial framework. As I transition to chapter 5 on the wider contemporary U.S. political context, it is worth noting that the dynamic that occurs across sports playing fields in the United States reaches into the battlefields of U.S. imperialism. This includes one of the most notable actions by the U.S. military in the twenty-first century.

On May 1, 2011, from Abbottabad, Pakistan, U.S. military forces counted out the steps of their mission, one letter-coded word at a time, in alphabetical order, and relayed them to President Barack Obama and his National Security team in the Situation Room of the White House. Then they got to the letter G in their mission, signified by the code word "Geronimo." When Central Intelligence Agency director Leon Panetta told Obama that "we have a visual on Geronimo," this indicated that the forces had arrived at the seventh stage of their mission.[47] They had found Osama bin Laden—the mastermind behind the attacks on September 11, 2001, that killed over three thousand people. Then the following communication came in from a U.S. admiral: "Geronimo EKIA"—that is, "Geronimo, Enemy Killed in Action." With that, the United States' most-wanted man was dead, killed after U.S. forces violated the sovereignty of another country by flying Black Hawk helicopters into Pakistani airspace without giving the Pakistan government advance warning, invading bin Laden's compound, and shooting him in the head and chest in front of his wife, who was wounded, and another woman. That evening, Obama evoked the "images of 9/11" that "are seared into our national memory" as he announced to the nation that bin Laden had been killed and that "justice has been done" for the "worst attack on the American people in our history."[48] A nationalistic fervor ensued, as an orgiastic celebration of this state assassination swept the country. Crowds filled the streets in massive numbers, waving American flags. A day that started with code words beginning with A, B, C, D, E, F, and then G for "Geronimo" went deep into the next morning with chants of "USA! USA! USA!"

Obama's authorization of a state assassination placed him in the company of many U.S. presidents, including Abraham Lincoln, whose memory and words Obama invoked most often and the president with whom he most identifies. As Obama wrote in December 2011, mere months after the assassination of bin Laden: "Lincoln is a President I turn to often. From time to time, I'll walk over to the Lincoln Bedroom and reread the handwritten Gettysburg Address encased in glass, or reflect on the Emancipation Proclamation, which hangs in the Oval Office, or pull a volume of his writings from the library in search of lessons to draw."[49] Almost 150 years before Obama heard the words "Geronimo EKIA" and then announced to a vengefully joyous nation the execution of a state enemy, it was President Lincoln who, in December 1862, selected and authorized the execution of 39 Dakota men out of the 303 men convicted by a military tribunal of killing civilian settlers during the U.S.-Dakota War of 1862. One man received a reprieve, and thus on December 26, 1862, in Mankato, Minnesota, 38 Dakota men were hung by the neck. As David Martínez (Akimel O'odham/Hia Ced O'odham/Mexican) argues, while Lincoln is remembered and credited by some for intervening to reduce the number of men executed, the deeper truth is that he "willfully ordered this mass hanging in order to appease a Minnesota settler populace threatening riots and anarchy, perhaps even secession, if he did not do as they demanded."[50] A mere six days after this historic mass state execution, Lincoln signed the Emancipation Proclamation on January 1, 1863, which declared as free all slaves held in the Confederate states and opened the Union army and navy to Black Americans. On December 31, 2012, President Obama signed a proclamation granting official state recognition of the 150th anniversary of the Emancipation Proclamation, about which Obama stated: "With that document, President Lincoln lent new moral force to the war by making it a fight not just to preserve, but also to empower. He sought to reunite our people not only in government but also in freedom that knew no bounds of color or creed. Every battle became a battle for liberty itself. Every struggle became a struggle for equality."[51] On December 26, 2012, 150 years after the execution of the Dakota thirty-eight, there was no statement at all from Obama regarding this anniversary. There was silence. Contemporaneously, as Layli Long Soldier points out in her poem "38": "There was a movie titled *Lincoln* about the presidency of Abraham Lincoln. The signing of the Emancipation Proclamation was included in the film *Lincoln*; the hanging of the Dakota 38 was not."[52] These silences are productive absences. They mark the presence of the work of settler memory in the service of U.S. imperialism and liberal colonialism.

It was not a mere matter of political incorrectness that the name of Geronimo, the legendary Chiricahua Apache leader whose Chiricahua name roughly translates in English as "Goyathlay," became military code for identifying bin Laden. Nor was it just a coincidence that the Emancipation Proclamation was signed only six days after the mass execution of the Dakota thirty-eight. Nor was it mere happenstance that the original owner who gave the Washington football team the name "Redsk*ns" was also an openly anti-Black white supremacist. It was also not a case of amnesia that led President Obama to ask the nation to remember the actions of President Lincoln as they concerned liberating enslaved Black Americans while staying silent on Lincoln's role in the execution of the Dakota thirty-eight,. What links all of these is that they are examples of the persistent and ubiquitous function of settler memory in the political life of race in the United States.

In particular, the utilization of Goyathlay/Geronimo for the bin Laden mission may well have been more a product of the work of habit memory than recollection memory. It may not have been an intentional effort to link Goyathlay to bin Laden, which only further underscores the rootedness of settler memory. As deployed in this case, settler memory habitually reminds the U.S. citizenry that the cold, violent state of today is the modern version of the vengeful defender of yore that fought Indigenous political and military leaders and anticolonial resisters, such as the actual Goyathlay, and that this work of settler state dispossession—of land, of life, of identity—goes on.[53] "Geronimo EKIA" is a prime example of a settler mnemonic that turns violent statist practices into unifying gestures linking past conquests to those of the present, and back again. In many ways, the Washington football team and other such names and mascots serve the same function. It was primarily in the words of radical Indigenous political actors that one heard any critical mention of this imperial-colonial linkage in the aftermath of the bin Laden assassination. The critiques made by Indigenous political actors did not speak in a normative language of multiculturalism or racial liberalism, of diversity and inclusion, but rather through an analytic framework premised around opposing the structure and processes of colonialism and reaffirming a politics of anticolonialism.

On the show *Democracy Now*, Anishinaabe writer and activist Winona LaDuke offered her analysis: "The reality is that the military is full of native nomenclature. You've got Black Hawk helicopters, Apache Longbow helicopters. You've got Tomahawk missiles. The term used when you leave a military base in a foreign country is to go 'off the reservation, into Indian Country.' So what is that messaging that is passed on? It is basically the continuation of the wars against Indigenous people."[54] Suzan Shown Harjo offered a similar reading to LaDuke's, arguing that the use of Goyathlay/Geronimo shows "how deeply embedded the 'Indian as enemy' is in the collective mind of America."[55] I would add to LaDuke's and Harjo's insights that, as we can see with the many examples of these forms of identity appropriation by white settler society, the work of settler memory is fundamental to the reproduction and legitimation of settler belonging through a relationship to the past that is not about forgetting but rather about a powerful form of remembering. As evident in sports stadiums, military ventures, contemporary political campaigns, social movements, and presidential actions and rhetoric, settler memory continues to shape, fuel, and also constrain political discourse and imaginaries in the United States. Looking next to chapter 5, we see this dynamic at work in the white settler nationalism articulated and enacted in the candidacy and administration of Donald Trump and in Trumpism as a movement more generally.

CHAPTER FIVE

Mocking Disavowal and Cruel Celebration
Trump's White Settler Nationalism

Introduction

On May 25, 2018, during his commencement address at the United States Naval Academy in Annapolis, Maryland, President Donald Trump said that too many Americans had forgotten the "truth" of their nation: "They have forgotten that our ancestors trounced an empire, tamed a continent, and triumphed over the worst evils in history." Shortly thereafter, he stated, "We are not going to apologize for America. We are going to stand up for America. No more apologies. . . . Because we know that a nation must have pride in its history to have confidence in its future."[1] Trump's boastful claim that the nation's ancestors "tamed a continent" came under immediate criticism. Black activist and policy analyst Samuel Sinyangwe summed it up in a concise tweet: "Genocide. He's celebrating genocide."[2] Indeed, Trump offered up a politics of memory here that embraced the genocidal violence against and dispossession of Indigenous peoples as one of the "things" done to "conquer the country," to recall James Baldwin's words from chapter 3. What Baldwin articulated as a lament, Trump claimed as a matter of pride and, as Sinyangwe put it, a cause for celebration.

This celebration of conquest was in evidence again two years later in Trump's acceptance speech for the Republican Party's presidential nomination at the 2020 Republican National Convention (RNC). By the end of the summer of 2020, the devastating effects of a nationwide COVID-19 pandemic included a death toll of almost two hundred thousand people in the United States alone, made much worse by the malignant neglect of the Trump administration. As well, the Movement for Black Lives led the largest nationwide political movement for racial justice in decades, if not in the nation's history, which continued well through the summer of 2020. Thus, in the context of these two historic developments, Donald Trump took to the podium at the 2020 RNC and defended his idea of American greatness as shaped by a history of conquest and settler colonial expansion—of settlers overcoming all challenges. His language in this regard was, unsurprisingly, not subtle:

> Our American ancestors sailed across the perilous ocean to build a new life on a new continent. They braved the freezing winters, crossed the

raging rivers, scaled the rocky peaks, trekked the dangerous forests, and worked from dawn till dusk. . . . These pioneers didn't have money. . . . When opportunity beckoned, they picked up their bibles, packed up their belongings, climbed into their covered wagons, and set out West for the next adventure.

Ranchers and miners, cowboys and sheriffs, farmers and settlers. They pressed on past the Mississippi to stake a claim in the wild frontier. Legends were born. Wyatt Earp, Annie Oakley, Davy Crockett, and Buffalo Bill. Americans built their beautiful homesteads on the open range. Soon, they had churches and communities, then towns, and with time, great centers of industry and commerce.[3]

To invoke Baldwin again, Trump speaks to how settler "legends were born" out of the inevitable massacre created by the "pioneers"—"ranchers and miners, cowboys and sheriffs, farmers and settlers"—staking their "claim in the wild frontier." Trump's overt appeal to the political memory of U.S. settler conquest and expansion to define American identity is not original, but in 2020 it was nevertheless striking in its celebratory tone and it did not include any mention of Indigenous peoples. These are just a couple of examples that point to how the politics of memory is a central part of Donald Trump's rhetoric and appeal, and settler memory is a critical feature of it, but in a slightly different way from that which I have discussed thus far.

While I argue that settler memory pervades across the political spectrum, I do not collapse all forms of political relationships to and memories of colonialism as identical. Not all settler memories take the same form, even if they reinforce and reproduce underlying structural consistencies. This brings us to the election of Donald Trump to the U.S. presidency in November 2016. In the book's conclusion, I will consider the liberal response to Trump's election. For this chapter, I attend to the settler dynamics of white nationalism that Trump and Trumpism represents, animates, and fuels but did not create. While it is increasingly commonplace in the political and scholarly sphere to deem Trump a white nationalist, I argue that we need to take the next step to read him and the movement he represents as that of white *settler* nationalism. This is a white nationalism deeply rooted and maintained through colonialism, through white settler claims over lands and life. Trump's candidacy and presidency, and the intense devotion of his supporters to him, are driven by white settler imperatives, grievances, identifications, and policies that manifest in implicit and explicit assertions of racial superiority, settler masculinity, and the often violent desire for territorial, bodily, and political domination. These imperatives include an even more enhanced commitment than that of his modern predecessors to settler colonial extractive policies such as oil pipeline development, a persistent and open hostility to the political movements, concerns, and lives of Indigenous and Black people, violent surveillance at the U.S–Mexico border and brutal treatment of migrating peoples, the support for Israel's occupation of Palestine, and the general effort to fight to reclaim or maintain the United States as a white settler nation. By definition in the United States, white nationalism is inherently a settler nationalism, and no U.S. president in the nation's history is exempt from this. However, there is something distinctly and overtly settler about Trump's white nationalism, as his words from 2018 and 2020 signal. Trump and Trumpism (the term I use for a movement that preceded and has been mobilized and shaped by him) celebrates aggressive, violent settler masculinity that serves the cause of emboldening white standing through fears of invasion, dependence, and national decline in a way that shapes a more complex assemblage of supporters than that which can be mobilized through the assertion of white supremacy alone.[4] In other words, claiming that Trump's appeal to his base is that he is racist, or that he appeals to white racism, gets us a good deal of the way there but still does not fully explain the expanse, and in some regards the diversity, of those who compose his fervent base of supporters. The imperatives, fears, longings, and violence of settler colonialism and settler masculinity help fill out our grasp of his appeal and the depth, breadth, and meaning of the U.S. white nationalism he has fueled so publicly. The lack of attention to the settler colonial imperatives of Trump and Trumpism limits the effort to better understand his presidency and the movement that supports him, one that he provoked into a violent, insurrectionary attack by thousands of his supporters, the vast majority of whom were white, in particular white men, against the U.S. Congress on January 6, 2021. At the time of this writing, the political and legal fallout, implications, and long-term meaning of what happened on that day are still to be determined. That will take time, as it will be a product of politics and political struggle. That said, the white settler nationalist grievances that drove this historic event, based on Trump's contriving and stoking the idea, now believed by millions of U.S. citizens, that the 2020 election and thus the country as they know and remember it is being "stolen" from them, is likely to persist well past the end of his administration. Thus, to understand the white settler nationalism of Trump and Trumpism before, during, and beyond his administration, it is important to keep an eye on the work of settler memory.

The settler memory at work in Trump's white nationalism is slightly different from that which I have drawn out concerning liberal and left articulations

of it. While they all have consistent and notable tendencies toward disavowing Indigeneity, they do not do so in the same way and for the same reason.
Liberals and leftists—in their distinct ways as noted thus far in the book—
often acknowledge the history of Indigenous peoples and anti-Indigenous actions by white settlers and the U.S. state but then refuse or do not know how
precisely to attend to the contemporary politics and persistence of Indigenous political life and of settler colonialism. On the other hand, the views of
white nationalists are shaped by their righteous settler claims to authority over
territory in order to define who belongs on these lands and who does not,
and what can and should be the proper uses of the land as a secure site of settler domesticity and as a resource. This imperative leads white nationalists to
disavow contemporary Indigeneity in terms that mock and dismiss Indigenous agency and genocide in order to affirm the positionality and impunity
of violent, possessive settler masculinity. In contrast to viewing settler colonialism as either a mistake or sin of the past, white nationalists led by Trump
embrace colonialism and the violence of conquest as a defining and positive
feature of the history of the American nation. They celebrate the cruelty of its
historical and contemporary manifestations as proof of the righteousness of
their domination over land, life, and people. Across the range of policy realms,
cruelty is a persistent tool and payoff of Trumpism. As journalist Adam Sewer
put it, the cruelty is "the point . . . in shared scorn for those they hate and
fear."[5] While true, I also argue that it goes deeper than a dynamic solely unique
to Trump, for settler colonial conquest and white settler nationalism have always been cruel, and the myths of the United States have found ways to celebrate this cruelty by transforming these actions, these massacres, into legends.
Thus, it is not the cruelty of settler colonialism itself that is unique but the
politics of memory deployed around it by Trump that is worthy of a distinct
analysis for its underlying consistency and implications. I argue that there is a
logic at work here linking Trump's policy statements and directives that may,
on the surface, seem chaotic and disordered. In Trump and his supporters,
I discern less the disavowal of settler colonialism than a willful, and even a pleas-
urable and profitable, celebration of the nation's settler colonial history—of
how "our ancestors . . . tamed a continent" and "pioneers . . . settlers" staked "a
claim in the wild frontier." In all, I argue that white nationalist settler memory
comprises the mocking disavowal of Indigeneity and the cruel celebration of
settler colonization.

To demonstrate my point, I weave a discussion of Trump's white settler
nationalist policies in with an analysis of his habitual references to Senator
Elizabeth Warren as "Pocahontas," his way to allude to Warren's problematic

claims to some form of Indigenous ancestry, her faint trace. My concern in this chapter is not Warren herself, although I will discuss her claim in the book's conclusion. My immediate focus is on how Trump's repeated use of this type of attack on Warren habitually expresses his own knowledge of a rudimentary history of settler colonial conquest and of Indigenous peoples, through which he embraces the former in all its cruelty and mockingly disavows the contemporary agency of the latter. In analyzing the work of settler memory here, I draw out the fundamental role of settler masculinity in Trumpism and link it to policy developments during his one term as president. These policy directives and aims under Trump build upon and reinforce the settler imperatives of American nationalism, which avowedly recenters and affirms the ground upon which the nation stands in order to defend it against ostensible invasion. Trumpism is premised on *standing the ground* of the white settler colonial nation and of settler domesticity—defending it with violent impunity against perceived attacks from internal and external threats. This violence and impunity were in stark evidence during the insurrection in Washington, D.C., in early 2021 when thousands of, for the most part, white people stormed Congress. In the end a handful of people were arrested on that day for their actions inside the Capitol. It was obvious to even mainstream media and political observers that police preparation for and response to this resistance was much less than it was against protests by the Movement for Black Lives, Indigenous activists such as those at the Standing Rock/NoDAPL resistance, Muslim rights advocates, Antifa activists, or any group not allied or identified with a white settler nationalist politics.[6] It was another indication that the concept of *law and order* so popular with the likes of Trump, as with prior presidents such as Richard Nixon, applies most forcefully and consistently to those deemed outsiders or threats to the white settler nation, to be. enforced by the citizen-deputies of the white settler state, be they the official state police or settler masculine militias such as the Proud Boys. For white settlers, freedom itself is a celebrated form of lawlessness involving the domination of racial and colonial others experienced, imagined, and remembered as representing the lawless frontier of the continent that was *tamed* in Trumpian settler memory. As Cristina Beltrán puts it, this "frontier freedom represented an ongoing opportunity for white citizens to engage in practices of invasion, war, removal, and settlement. . . . The American desire to claim freedom and resist tyranny was constituted through the imposition of tyranny and unfreedom on others."[7]

Thus, while Trump's candidacy has had its unique qualities, to be sure, the deeper roots of violent racism and misogyny he has drawn upon and cultivated are not unique to him. The same is true regarding the meaning of his candidacy and presidency for Indigenous people's lives and for the settler relationship to land. In this regard, I concur with and expand upon Leigh Patel's argument that Trump's popularity can be apprehended "through the lens of settler colonialism, which relies on various technologies, including racism and heteropatriarchy, to accomplish its aims." As Patel explains:

> The occupation of land is never finished, Indigenous people must always be disappearing, and there can never be enough property, land and chattel, in the hands of a few. Since contact invasion, the structure of settler colonialism has been maintained by eradicating and punishing Indigenous, Black and brown peoples. The constant running fear of those peoples transgressing their labor and property functions within the settler structure is animated through many lurid attacks conducted in the name of the United States. Donald Trump's political rise and traction is one stanza in how these fears and practices have been bundled together by a settler colonial logic.[8]

Recall Rita Dhamoon's definition of settler colonialism as "not only a structure but also a process, an activity for assigning political meanings, and organizing material structures driven by forces of power."[9] In considering this process in the Trump era, with its material, structural, and human implications, Patel's notion of Trump as "one stanza" in the long political history of settler colonialism speaks to Trump's own contributions and to the legacy upon which he builds. Patel also offers an imaginative and telling site of intervention, as the stanza—a grouped set of written lines set off from others—aptly captures the mode of discourse favored by Trump in social media tweets, public statements, and in the defining catchphrase of his white settler nationalist movement, "Make America Great Again."[10] Trump's slogan is an open appeal to a reactionary white settler nationalist politics of memory. In this spirit, I begin this analysis by comparing the distinct presidential memories invoked by Trump and his predecessor, Barack Obama.

"Trump and Jackson, Jackson and Trump"

While Barack Obama's presidential role model is Abraham Lincoln, Donald Trump's is Andrew Jackson. There are differences between Obama and Trump at the level of policy and personality. However, these differences do not include either of them challenging settler colonial governance. Rather, they represent different ways to reproduce settler colonial structure and the processes and events that maintain it. Obama's version takes the form of the racial liberalism analyzed in chapter 4. For Obama, we saw this in his deployment of the popular memory of Lincoln as a liberator of the slaves and a unifier of the nation. This is a memory that disavows Lincoln's actions toward the Dakota thirty-eight and also, as W. E. B. Du Bois would remind us, the role of Black Americans in freeing themselves from slavery. Obama's recommendation that Washington football team owner Dan Snyder consider changing the team name since it is "offending a sizeable group of people" captures the limits produced by racial liberalism and settler memory. Obama's words affirm the popular neoliberal multicultural concern with mobilizing against offensive acts in an individual sense and advocating for diversity and inclusiveness within liberal capitalist institutions and settler civil society. Trump, on the other hand, explicitly advocates a politics that celebrates offensiveness and rejects racial liberalism's aims of diversity and inclusion. As Jodi Dean puts it, Trump revels in the "freedom from civility, the privilege of enjoying superiority."[11] As it concerns the Washington football team, in October 2015 as a candidate for the Republican presidential nomination, Trump stated: "Honestly, I don't think they should change the name. . . . Unless the owner wanted to."[12] Soon after his inauguration in 2017, Trump's decision to place Andrew Jackson's portrait in the Oval Office of the White House symbolically signaled a clear shift from Obama's racial liberalism to overt white settler nationalism as the framing discourse, politics, and policies stemming from the office of the U.S. presidency.[13]

The connection between Trump and the legacy of Jackson goes beyond just the portrait in the Oval Office. In his work on Trump's populist presidency, Joseph Lowndes explains the historical and political affinities between the two U.S. presidents:

Jackson's coalition of poor frontier farmers, white urban workers, and southern slave-owners anticipates in some ways Trump's own coalition, just as Trump's singular obsession with removing millions of undocumented people from the country echoes Jackson's campaign of Indian Removal. Indeed Jackson's combative stance toward the Supreme Court on Indian Removal has become the stuff of popular myth in the United States, and one on which the Trump administration draws.

One of the first things Trump did upon moving into the White House was to hang a portrait of Jackson in the Oval Office. Soon after, he made a pilgrimage to Jackson's grave in Nashville, Tennessee, where he laid a wreath and said, "It was during the Revolution that Jackson first confronted and defied an arrogant elite. Does that sound familiar? I wonder why they keep talking about Trump and Jackson, Jackson and Trump."[14]

In contrast to Obama's disavowal of Lincoln's role in the execution of the Dakota thirty-eight that reinforced the image of both as racial liberals, Trump's attachment to the political memory of Jackson is indicative of the white settler nationalist imperatives of his presidency and of Trumpism in general. Andrew Jackson built his fortune and career on financial investments in and political and military actions to perpetuate chattel slavery and settler colonization. The website that sells tours of his museum and home, the Hermitage in Tennessee, affirms that "in all reality, slavery was the source of Andrew Jackson's wealth."[15] As well, the most infamous element in the collective political memory of Jackson concerns the manner in which his successful military and political careers were built, like no other president before him or afterward, on his earned reputation for fighting and killing Indigenous people and forcibly removing them from their ancestral territories.[16] As Adrienne Keene, a scholar and a citizen of the Cherokee Nation, points out:

> Jackson's military and political career were built upon Indian killing and removal: Prior to his presidency, Jackson had been deeply involved in battles with southeastern tribes. From 1813 to 1814 he led troops against the Creek Nation in the Creek War, and in 1818 he waged campaigns against the Seminole in Florida. In these battles, he and his men wiped out entire villages, physically slaughtering Native men, women, and children, and gained millions of acres of Native lands for the U.S. through treaties signed, often under duress, afterward. He used this military experience to gain political trust and influence, and vowed that once elected president he would begin the process of moving Native peoples west—freeing land for the development by and use of white settlers.[17]

It was Jackson's actions as U.S. president from 1829 to 1837 that prompted, among other forms of devastation to Indigenous peoples, the murderous Trail of Tears removals and forced marches of many Indigenous nations, including the Cherokee, to Indian Territory out West, which became the state of Oklahoma in 1907.[18] Evoking the power of intergenerational memory, Keene's observation about Trump's celebration and attachment to Jackson's memory leads her to "think about my ancestors on that march. I think about how that's actually not that long ago, and my great-grandma grew up hearing stories from her grandparents about their experiences on the trail."[19] In light of Keene's words, one gets a sense of how Trump's eager embrace of Jackson's political memory represents a mocking disavowal of Indigenous people and a cruel celebration of settler colonization.

Trump's words later in his presidency further confirm his celebratory attachment to the political memory of the Indian removal era of the Jacksonian period, which he deployed in a familiar stanza. Here he is in a tweet from February 9, 2019, after Elizabeth Warren announced that she was running to be the Democratic Party's 2020 presidential candidate: "Today Elizabeth Warren, sometimes referred to by me as Pocahontas, joined the race for President. Will she run as our first Native American presidential candidate, or has she decided that after 32 years, this is not playing so well anymore? See you on the campaign TRAIL, Liz!" The capitalization of the word "trail" is the central signifier here, indicating the intentionality behind the reference that links Trump's views to the legacy of Jacksonian-era white settler nationalist expansionary violence. Trump ridicules Warren for her problematic claims to Native ancestry and cruelly deploys the history of Indigenous removal to generate a barely veiled threat about seeing her on the "campaign TRAIL," a threat seeped in the history of genocidal violence. In this regard, both Patel's reminder that "Indigenous people must always be disappearing" and Keene's point about the meaning for her people of Trump's identification with Jackson's political memory underscore the need to take serious account of the settler colonial policy directives and the positioning of Indigeneity in the political worldview of Trump and Trumpism.

The policy-level manifestations of Trump's unrestrained commitment to settler colonial invasion and predation were evident in the first few weeks of his administration and persisted through Trump's term in office. Upon Trump's urging, in February 2017 the deputy secretary of the army, who oversees the Army Corps of Engineers, moved to grant the permit to approve the Dakota Access Pipeline. The Dakota Access Pipeline, owned by Energy Transfer Partners, is the target of the #NoDAPL/Water Protectors resistance at Standing Rock. This pipeline threatens the water of the Missouri River located above the Standing Rock Sioux reservation and the land, water, and human and nonhuman life residing throughout the expanse of Oceti Sakowin territory and the four states that the 1,170-mile oil pipeline would traverse.[20] In early December 2016, the Water Protectors succeeded in getting the Obama administration to agree to a substantial environmental review, with the hope of a permanent halt to the pipeline project. However, Trump's election a month earlier was a direct threat to this victory. The Trump administration's approval of the pipeline was soon followed by the forceful removal of occupants of the Standing Rock camps, as Nick Estes notes: "On February 22, 2017, the Army Corps, Morton County deputies, and North Dakota Highway Patrol forcefully evicted the remaining campers at Oceti Sakowin."[21] This settler colonial capitalist imperative was again evident in March 2017 when the Trump administration approved the Keystone XL pipeline targeted to travel and threaten the land and bodies of territory along a path from the United States into and through Canada. In 2015, the Obama administration had vetoed and thus stopped further construction of the Keystone XL pipeline.[22] These pipelines remain under political and legal contention, and in 2018 a federal judge halted the Keystone project due to insufficient environmental review. However, the Trump administration remained committed to circumventing and forestalling all environmental reviews and political protests that blocked their path.[23] Another policy directive that reinforced the settler colonial logic and structure at work here arose when Trump signed two executive orders removing from protected status two million acres of the Bears Ears National Monument in Southeastern Utah. As a result, not long "after five tribes (Navajo, Hopi, Zuni, Ute Mountain Ute and Unitah Ouray Ute) with a history of conflict came together to successfully petition the federal government to create Bears Ears to protect significant cultural resources, Trump has reneged on a previous president's pledge to preserve the land."[24] Furthermore, as the COVID-19 pandemic first started to take real hold on the nation in March 2020, shutting down most of the country, the Bureau of Indian Affairs (BIA) of the U.S. Department of the Interior declared that the Mashpee Wampanoag Tribe's "reservation will be 'disestablished' and its land taken out of trust, per an order from Secretary of the Interior David Bernhardt."[25] In 2015, the Obama administration put the 321 acres of the Mashpee reservation into trust, and it became federally recognized tribal sovereign land under the defined jurisdiction of the Mashpee Wampanoag tribal government, not subject to federal and state taxation. The Trump administration argued that since the Mashpee Wampanoag were not under federal jurisdiction at the time of the passage of the Indian Reorganization Act in 1934 (the tribe gained federal recognition in 2007), when the concept of trust land was enacted, they were not eligible to have their land placed into trust in 2015. Mashpee Wampanoag tribal chairman Cedric Cromwell framed this action by the Trump administration in terms that spoke directly to the settler colonial imperatives at work: "Taking our land is a direct attack on our culture and our way of living. . . . This is an unconscionable act that's ushered in a new termination era, and it is the latest evidence of the erosion of the Department's willingness to act consistent with its trust duties to protect tribal lands."[26] In July 2020, the U.S.

House of Representatives passed an amendment to an appropriations bill to protect this Mashpee territory and set a one-year moratorium on the Department of the Interior expending funds to seek to remove the land from trust. The matter continues to be subject to legislative and judicial contention by the Mashpee Wampanoag Tribe.[27] With respect for the fact that this is but a sample of the anti-Indigenous actions by the Trump administration, these policy decisions have in common the effort to further enhance settler colonial rule over the territories of Indigenous peoples so as to open up even more lands for predatory capitalist practices and diminish or eliminate Indigenous sovereignty and nationhood. While the Obama administration's neoliberal multicultural approach also led to the approval of extractive projects of colonial capitalism that served the interests of the fossil fuel industry, upon taking office the Trump administration showed that the new order of the day would be even more aggressive white settler nationalism and unrestrained capitalist development. Anyone or anything standing in the way of these projects would be, as they were under Andrew Jackson, forcibly removed. I have set out these policy efforts and decisions before I transition to assess Trump's references to Indigeneity in his social media and public stanzas because the libidinal, symbolic, and political economies of the white settler nationalism of Trumpism are mutually reinforcing components that need to be read together to gain a sense of the full picture.

"Pocahontas" and the White Settler Masculinity of Trumpism

A scene at the White House in the fall of 2017 underscored the need to be attentive to the role of settler memory in the white settler nationalism that Trump represents and propagates. In the Oval Office on November 27, 2017, President Trump hosted a ceremony to honor three of the remaining Navajo code-talker veterans from World War II. They were Peter MacDonald, Thomas Begay, and Fleming Begaye, who was at the time ninety-seven years old and the oldest living U.S. forces veteran from that war. The year 2017 marked the seventy-fifth anniversary of the code-talker program, in which Navajo (Diné) men were recruited into the U.S. Army to utilize their native language to pass coded messages—constructed through a language indecipherable to Japanese military intelligence—to help win the war in the Pacific for the United States and its allies. One commentator pointed to the "bitter irony" that the Navajo code talkers were recruited and deployed for the strategic advantage their Diné language provided the U.S. military, whereas during this time period Indigenous children who had been stolen from their communities and taken to boarding schools were, among other things, forbidden from and punished for speaking their native language.[28] The podium in the Oval Office for this gathering was positioned directly in front of the portrait of Andrew Jackson, with the flags of the U.S Army and the U.S. Marines on either side. There was no flag of the Navajo Nation in sight. As well, a small bronze statue of a cowboy on a bucking horse sat on the table right below Jackson's portrait and between the two U.S. military flags. The statue cowboy's right arm was raised, whip in hand, ready to strike the wild horse. The statue was Frederic Remington's *The Bronco Buster*. According to the White House Historical Association, "Remington became well known for his ability to capture the frontier spirit of Americans settling the west."[29] He created the statue in 1895 and gave it to his friend Theodore (Teddy) Roosevelt when the latter became president in 1901. *The Bronco Buster* was the most popular small statue in the United States in the late nineteenth century; duplications continue to be sold, and it has been a consistent feature in the Oval Office since Roosevelt's presidency.

While the positioning of Jackson's portrait indicates Trump's express desire to place the presidential symbol of settler nationalism in the Oval Office, *The Bronco Buster* symbolizes the long-term commitment of the office, its occupants, and the federal government to the dispossession of and settlement upon Indigenous peoples' lands. It is also indicative in another sense, for while Trump openly seeks comparison with Jackson, and there are many reasons to concur with him on this account, he was also, I argue, the most anti-Indian president since Theodore Roosevelt. It was Teddy Roosevelt who stated in an 1886 speech in New York: "I suppose I should be ashamed to say that I take the western view of the Indian. . . . I don't go so far as to think that the only good Indians are the dead Indians, but I believe nine out of every ten are, and I shouldn't like to inquire too closely into the case of the tenth. The most vicious cowboy has more moral principle than the average Indian."[30] In this historical light, Roosevelt's placement of *The Bronco Buster* in the Oval Office comes to have more distinct settler colonial meaning. As president, Roosevelt built a reputation for his commitment to conservation and national parks, which might seem to contravene Trump's antienvironmental inclinations. However, Diné scholar Majerle Lister notes that the premise of Roosevelt's conservationist vision was the removal and elimination of Indigenous peoples from these "public lands." Lister concludes, "Trump, a violent racist and nationalist, has more in common with Teddy Roosevelt than most conservationists care to admit."[31] With this historical background in mind, we can also see the similarity between Teddy Roosevelt and Trump in two political moments, one in Trump's role as a private citizen and one as president.

As a private citizen in 1993, Trump's settler colonial imperative to erase Indigenous presence was evident at a House subcommittee hearing on tribal casinos when he challenged the tribal sovereign status of the Mashantucket Pequot Nation, his competition in the casino business, stating, "They don't look like Indians to me, and they don't look like Indians to Indians. . . . Why is it that the Indians don't pay tax, but everyone else does, I do?"[32] Here, through his white settler gaze that racializes who Indigenous people are supposed to be and how they should look, often phenotypically, Trump offers far from his last declaration about who in his eyes is or is not an Indigenous person. Trump's claim that "Indians don't pay tax, but everyone else does, I do" also posits an imaginary of white settler victimization and invasion that would manifest overtly in his presidential campaign and administration. It resonates with Roosevelt's hope, as noted in chapter 4, that the General Allotment Act of 1887 would prove a "mighty pulverizing engine to break up the tribal mass" by compelling Indigenous people to become assimilated, tax-paying citizens rather than remaining as citizens of Indigenous nations. As president, Trump's Roosevelt-like inclinations toward eliminating Indigenous nations through forced assimilation took policy form with his administration's 2018 directive from the U.S. Department of Health and Human Services to deny Indigenous people exemption status in relation to Medicaid work-requirement rules. The move to deny exemption, as first reported in April 2018, was based on the Trump administration's contention that "tribes are a race rather than separate governments, and exempting them from Medicaid work rules— which have been approved in three states and are being sought by at least 10 others—would be illegal preferential treatment."[33] Researchers and historians have referred to this initiative as an effort at eliminating Indigenous peoples through *paper genocide*: "'Paper genocide' is used when a culture is wiped from mass consciousness and visible autonomy through tactics such as removing their ethnic designations from a national census—or in this case, having their sovereignty dismantled by the notion that Native American is a 'race' and not a diverse sum of distinct cultures and subcultures of sovereign Nations, tribes, and Peoples."[34] This form of racialization is a way to make Indigenous peoples disappear into the U.S. racial framework, which as critical theorist Jodi Byrd of the Chickasaw Nation explains, is a "transformation that equates the distinctions of indigenous nations as sovereign and independent with that of every other racialized and diasporic arrival to be mediated within U.S. citizenry."[35] This particular policy change received significant pushback from Indigenous nations and supportive members of the U.S. Congress, and the Trump administration relented a bit, for some Indigenous nations, although it left room to allow states to impose work requirements in the future.[36] This effort by the Trump administration to potentially terminate Indigenous tribal sovereignty as a federal status and destroy Indigenous nations and citizenship as political entities was not an isolated incident for Trump and those on the political Right who supported him. Prior to and during his administration, those on the political Right continued to seek to destroy such policies as that of the Indian Child Welfare Act (ICWA) passed in 1978 to keep Indigenous children with their communities.[37] The Trump administration supported these efforts. Trump's racializing, erasing, and assimilatory views from the early 1990s on up to his presidency and the settler eliminatory political legacies of Jackson and Roosevelt that echoed in his presidential vision are important to keep in mind as we return to the scene in the Oval Office with Trump and the Diné code talkers. This is because the outrageous words Trump speaks and tweets are neither a mere distraction from nor epiphenomenal features of his administration's white settler imperatives; they are constitutive of it. They are a feature, not a bug, of his settler nationalism.

After code-talker veteran Peter MacDonald spoke at the ceremony, Trump took to the podium. He acknowledged in glowing terms the role of the code talkers generally and the three veterans before him and then said the following directly to the Diné men:

> You're very, very special people. You were here long before any of us were here, although we have a representative in Congress who they say was here a long time ago. They call her "Pocahontas." But you know what, I like you, because you are special, you are special people, you are really incredible people, and from the heart, from the absolute heart, we appreciate what you've done, how you've done it, the bravery that you displayed, and the love that you have for your country, Tom I would say that's as good as it gets, wouldn't you say? That's as good as you get.[38]

While this was neither the first nor the last time Trump utilized the myth and legacy of the historical figure of Pocahontas to attack Elizabeth Warren, his effort to do so given the already problematic presence of the Jackson portrait led to swift public criticism from, among others, commentators in the press, elected officials from both major political parties, and the families of the code talkers.[39] It was not lost on any reasonable observer that there was something fundamentally discordant politically, historically, and morally about the whole scene such as to render it almost universally condemnable. To most observers this was another example of Trump's aberrant, boorish, self-absorbed, and racist behavior. While true, the entire scene and the particular words he spoke offered a clear window on that which is central to Trump, Trumpism, and white settler nationalism. This is the persistent place and function of the disavowal of Indigeneity and the celebration of the nation's settler colonial history. The disavowal Trump engaged in here was more egregious and more overly white settler nationalist in that respect because of how he framed the deeper meaning of the presence of MacDonald, Begay, and Begaye and that he used this moment to make another Pocahontas remark.

To begin, Trump set out a basic fact of settler colonial contexts from a settler perspective, which is that Indigenous people were "here before any of us were here." In this case, he turned the three Diné men into representatives of Indigenous peoples of the Americas generally, in which their contemporary presence was as a metaphor for Indigenous peoples located in the precontact past. On the one hand, this was an expression of knowledge of Indigenous people's history while, on the other hand, it was a disavowal of Indigenous presence because at no time did Trump mention the Navajo Nation or Indigenous sovereignty as contemporary political presences. Trump then engaged in another disavowal when he shifted registers by mobilizing the myth of Pocahontas as a form of attack against an opponent and critic. At that moment, Trump disavowed the political relevance and agency of the three men standing right before him as Indigenous people from the sovereign Diné Nation. They became props in what Trump turned into settler nationalist theater, under the watchful eyes of Jackson, in which he declared who is a real Indian and who is not, as he did in 1993 to the House subcommittee. To be clear, this is not a defense of Warren's claims but rather a critique of Trump's settler declaration of who is and is not Indigenous, which in Warren's case is not up to Trump but rather up to Indigenous peoples themselves, especially the Cherokee. In a final disavowal, Trump turned the meaning of the action of these men as code talkers into a statement about their love for "your country," by which he meant the United States, which is "as good as you get." This is not to say MacDonald, Begaye, and Begay would or would not object to Trump's words, although their families did, but rather that what Trump did here is position these Diné men as representing the long-distant Indigenous past and the patriotic American present but not the Indigenous political present. While the target of Trump's attacks was Warren explicitly, the scene was implicitly a mocking disavowal of any Indigenous presence in the contemporary context as sovereign Indigenous nations not assimilated to or primarily loyal to the United States. As Darren R. Reid sums it up well: "Trump's view of Indian Country demands assimilation and surrender to federal (or presidential) will; and it demands something very much like racial purity. It rewards Native

American identities that contribute to the United States but do not require special treatment, privilege, or exception. To compound matters, many of Trump's supporters likewise view Native Americans through a highly colonialist lens."[40] In all, then, this scene at the White House epitomizes and reproduces the absence and presence of Indigeneity—absent as contemporary figures, present as historical ones. It was also an open and celebratory embrace of white settler masculine aggression by the use of the Pocahontas myth. We can draw out this expressly gendered dynamic by taking a closer examination of the myth that Trump habitually deploys in his settler stanzas. To do this, I look back to Trump's words in the months before the presidential election of 2016.

Here is one of the earliest examples of Trump's attack upon Warren, during a presidential campaign rally in Virginia in June 2016: "Pocahontas is not happy, she's not happy. She's the worst. You know, Pocahontas—I'm doing such a disservice to Pocahontas, it's so unfair to Pocahontas—but this Elizabeth Warren, I call her 'goofy,' Elizabeth Warren, she's one of the worst senators in the entire United States Senate."[41] This particular verbal/social media attack by Trump against Warren needs to be read through the prism of the history and present of sexual violence against Indigenous women and girls. Trump's deployment of "Pocahontas" is an example of his intentionally offensive racial *illiberalism* that draws upon and reaffirms white settler masculine domination of the United States. In stating that he is being "so unfair" and "doing such a disservice to Pocahontas" (by attaching her name to Warren), Trump speaks an unintentional truth about the historical and mnemonic place of Indigeneity in the history of white settler supremacy in the United States. As historian Honor Sachs explains,

> Trump's choice of "Pocahontas" reflects a deeply complicated history of ancestry and white racial fantasy. . . . Long before Disney, white American popular culture mobilized myths about Pocahontas to serve purposes ranging from colonial conquest to Civil War, and from racial segregation to white supremacy. Each usage promoted an unequal society that benefited whites at the expense of indigenous peoples and African Americans. Trump's use of the name "Pocahontas" to serve his politics of racial division fits right into this historical trajectory. His cooptation of her name is just the latest example of how those in power manipulate indigenous history and how white people historically have claimed the right to define what it means to be Native American.[42]

To be precise, building upon Sachs's insights here, Pocahontas is a white *settler* fantasy. The racial element is already implicated as a "white" fantasy, and it is the settler imperative and desires that are doing significant work in this myth as it concerns colonial heteropatriarchy, violence, and conquest.

While Trump's references to Pocahontas to attack Warren usually receive criticism for being offensive for refusing to abide by certain basic parameters of racial liberal discourse, he is also habitually drawing upon and updating a long tradition of deploying Indigeneity in the service of American settler nationalism, to the "disservice" of Indigenous peoples. It is here where we see the settler colonial roots of Trump's racism and misogyny. The Pocahontas myth is a form of American settler memory that disavows the role of gender, sexuality, and sexual violence in the foundation and functioning of settler colonialism—*of the taming of the continent.* Cherokee citizen and journalist Rebecca Nagle speaks to how Trump's words in this regard reproduce and erase the history and present of sexual violence in the service of settler colonialism: "Trump casually throws around the word 'Pocahontas,' but few are aware of the traumatic history it evokes—one that mirrors the grim reality that Native women face everyday. The fictional Disney character Pocahontas is based on a real Powhatan teenager named Matoaka, who was actually kidnapped and held hostage by White settlers. She died in England at the age of 21. Today, four in five Native women will be raped, stalked or abused in our lifetime and nine out of 10 of the perpetrators are non-Native."[43] In her work on the history of Pocahontas and the politics of Trump, Ellen Gorsevski claims that "Pocahontas was likely raped multiple times by different Englishmen. The rapes of Pocahontas resulted in her birthing at least one child."[44] Nagle and Gorsevski insightfully speak to how the story of the actual historical figure Matoaka is known or available to be known, especially as regards her kidnapping and likelihood of being subject to sexual assault, but is disavowed and subsumed within the myth produced by American settler memory.

This settler disavowal also occurs at a different level in the analysis of Trump's campaign, for Gorsevski argues that Trump is turning "Pocahontas" into an "object of ridicule to silence a vocal woman, Senator Warren as a political opponent" and a "means to ridicule progressive women in politics."[45] To be sure, this is a valid point as it concerns the immediate purpose in the presidential campaign, but it also elides the deeper drive of white settler masculinity regarding the violent claim to gendered bodies, as Trump himself confessed in his own, secretly taped, words. Through an analysis that refuses settler memory, the white settler masculine imperatives at play in Trump's political stanzas indicate less an effort to silence white progressive women such as Warren than they do a cruel celebration and legitimation of the sexual violence that Trump discussed in a tape revealed to the public in October 2016.

In that tape, he admitted to kissing women without their consent—"I moved on her like a bitch"—and much more: "I don't even wait. And when you're a star, they let you do it. You can do anything. Grab them by the pussy. You can do anything."[46] The libidinal, symbolic, and material implication here is not about Elizabeth Warren first and foremost; it is about violence against women and girls generally. What we see here is the working of settler colonial logic that "bundles together" Trump's words about Pocahontas—a historical person who was kidnapped and likely assaulted as a young girl—and his bragging about sexually assaulting women. Thus, Trump's own words underscore the need to include the function of sexual violence for how one understands his place and role in, as Isabel Altamirano-Jiménez (Zapotec) puts it, "the long-standing structure of dispossession and invasion that has characterized this country."[47] His habitual "Pocahontas" references guide us to the settler colonial roots of his infamous assertion that he can "grab" women. Separating these elements due to the work of settler memory disavows Indigenous presence to the detriment of fully analyzing how the persistence of such colonial violence in the twenty-first century shapes mainstream U.S. political life and is a key element of Trump's avid and loyal following from his base. Rebecca Nagle's words direct us to the unattended role of colonial heteropatriarchy and sexual violence that continues to be perpetuated against Indigenous women and girls and how Trump's eager use of Pocahontas's name serves to, at once, cruelly celebrate and mockingly disavow this violence through a powerful myth in U.S. collective memory.

One must also put Trump's open celebration of sexual violence and the violence and predation of settler colonization into the context of the contemporary crisis of missing and murdered Indigenous women and girls (MMIWG) and the movement and media campaign to raise awareness about it that emerged years before the 2016 U.S. presidential campaign. While the MMIWG movement to raise awareness and action emerged in Canada, there are efforts to develop such campaigns in the United States as well.[48] In this light, we witness the power of liberal settler memory when Trump's references to Pocahontas are criticized as racist and a silencing of progressive, usually privileged white women, but fewer commentators (and mostly Indigenous feminists in this regard) make the connection to the history of the kidnapping and sexual assault of Indigenous women that is a well-substantiated part of the historical record concerning Matoaka/Pocahontas. This history of colonial sexual violence is constitutively intertwined with the dispossession of Indigenous people's lands as well. In short, *grabbing* women and *grabbing* land go together in the past and present of settler colonialism. Given the context of

Trump's habitual references, consider the argument made by Chris Finley (Confederated Tribes of the Colville Indian Reservation), building upon Cherokee scholar Rayna Green's notion of the *Pocahontas Perplex*. Finley argues that resonant settler myths such as the story of Pocahontas depend upon the manner in which "the conflation of Native women's bodies with racialized and sexualized narratives of the land constructs it as penetrable and open to ownership through heteropatriarchal domination."[49] The myth of Pocahontas, as Finley makes clear, produces these sexual relations as consensual—such as the mythology of a consensual relationship and marriage between the teenager Pocahontas and the full adult Englishman John Rolfe—instead of as a story of invasion, plunder, kidnapping, rape, violence, and conquering. In this way, as Joanne Barker argues, "stripped of any vestiges of her own political agenda and her own cultural and affiliation and identity, Pocahontas is made to speak to that new world, to that America, as heroine and ancestor. . . . Such inventions render her insignificant outside her heterosexualized relationships to men and erase her affiliation as a Powhatan."[50] This mythology of sexual consent in the myth of Pocahontas is intertwined with the mythology that Indigenous peoples do not exist on the land, or do not exist properly, and thus the land is empty, terra nullius, and free to take—to "grab." In sum, the Pocahontas myth is a constitutive allegory for how violence and the urge to dominate land and bodies is an embedded, deeply gendered, and disavowed component of settler colonialism, of white settler masculinity.

Trump's references to Pocahontas thus reveal structural insights about white settler possessive violence against gendered bodies and land, providing we refuse settler memory and acknowledge the settler colonial imperatives at work here. The imbrication of sexual violence and the plunder of land that Finley points to is evident in the sexual violence and trafficking perpetrated, with virtual impunity, in the so-called man camps that are the name for the temporary, transient facilities that house workers, usually all men, along the development path of extractive industries such as fracking sites and oil pipelines. For example, as Muscogee (Creek) scholar Sarah Deer notes, "There has been a significant increase in crime committed against Native people in North Dakota since 2008, likely attributable at least in part to the man camps associated with the oil boom. . . . The crime that Native women are experiencing as a result of the exploding fracking business has parallels with the harm being done to the planet."[51] Furthermore, the June 2019 report of the Canadian National Inquiry into Missing and Murdered Indigenous Women and Girls underscored "the 'urgent need' to consider the safety of Indigenous women in all stages of resource-extraction projects," as the inquiry "found 'substantial evidence of a serious problem' in a link between resource extraction and violence against Indigenous women, girls, and LGBTQ and two-spirit people."[52] While this report addresses the Canadian context, its findings directly concern the U.S. context in at least two respects: first, it further substantiates the connection between sexual violence and pipeline development and, second, it points out that multinational settler colonial pipeline projects such as the Keystone XL are not meant to respect national borders. Similarly, Trump's much-touted southern border wall is not meant to keep pipelines or capital in or out; its target is racialized peoples constructed as threats to white settler territory and domesticity. Oil pipelines, extractive industries, and the settler violence against human and nonhuman life and land that they generate far precede the rise of Trump and Trumpism. Still, the Trump administration's intensified commitment to oil pipeline development and Trump's habitual celebration of the tropes and practices of sexual violence are further perpetuated by the building of these pipelines and reveal settler colonial imperatives as even more fundamental to the white nationalism of Trumpism than to the neoliberal multiculturalism of the Obama administration.

To the Border and Beyond

Examining the relationship of human and nonhuman bodies to land through a settler colonial analysis of Trumpism leads us then from pipelines to the most defining political symbol and obsession for Trump and his supporters during and beyond his 2016 presidential campaign. This is the border between the United States and Mexico. Trump's loud claim, and his supporters' roaring approval, about building a "big, beautiful wall" on the U.S. southern border is not only about xenophobic racism against, in particular, Mexican people and any people deemed outsiders to the white American nation, including Indigenous peoples from Central and South America migrating north away from violence and poverty.[53] The symbolic role of the wall for Trump is more important than its practical function. As Greg Grandin argues, "Whether the wall gets built or not, it is America's new symbol. It stands for a nation that still thinks 'freedom' means freedom from restraint, but no longer pretends, in a world of limits, that everyone can be free—and enforces that reality through cruelty, domination, and racism."[54] While I concur with Grandin's claim about the wall's symbolic role and its constitutive relationship to a politics of "cruelty, domination, and racism," Trump's focus on it is less a *new* symbol than it is a provocation and fueling of a historically persistent one. Assertions about the status of a border wall in the United States necessarily are—not *were*—claims premised in an assertion of settler sovereignty over the land and the claim to authority over who gets to reside on this land. In the United States, as is the case with any nation built upon the dispossession of Indigenous peoples from their territories, such an imperative is necessarily and inherently a settler colonial one.

To elaborate, I turn to a Trump tweet/stanza about Elizabeth Warren one final time. On January 13, 2019, he posted the following comment regarding Warren's Instagram video to promote her presidential candidacy: "If Elizabeth Warren, often referred to by me as Pocahontas, did this commercial from Bighorn or Wounded Knee instead of her kitchen, with her husband dressed in full Indian garb, it would have been a smash!" Before getting in to the implications of this particular Trump tweet, I take a moment here to underscore a major point I have set out thus far. That is, if you take account of Trump's adoring memory of Jackson, his repeated attacks on Warren as Pocahontas, and the policies his administration has proposed and enacted, one can see that Trump and by correlation his avid supporters persistently and cruelly celebrate the history of violence and removal against Indigenous peoples and advocate policies that follow suit. This is neither coded nor tangential messaging, and it is in some sense even more open and persistent than that concerning white supremacy and racism on their own. As chaotic as Trump, along with his former administration, appears at times, there is an underlying logic at work here, and his supporters get it.

For example, the clarity of Trump's message was evident in the actions of his supporters during a well-documented and publicized scene on the National Mall in Washington, D.C., in January 2019. On this day, Nathan Phillips of the Omaha Nation and a few of his Indigenous and non-Native allies were surrounded by boys from the Covington Catholic High School in Kentucky, most of whom were wearing the iconic MAGA hats. The school bused the students to Washington, D.C., to support an antichoice March for Life event. Phillips and his colleagues were at the National Mall for an Indigenous People's March that had a specific focus on raising awareness about the issue of missing and murdered Indigenous women and girls. As the two parties intersected, Phillips was singing and chanting while playing his drum. However, as he sought to walk forward he was stopped by the mob of young boys, who circled him, laughing at him and at Indigenous people generally by mocking his singing and chanting, doing "tomahawk chops," and making such statements as "Land gets stolen, that's how it works."[55] Notably, one MAGA-hat-wearing student, sixteen-year-old Nick Sandmann, stood directly in front of Phillips. Sandmann smirked at Phillips while blocking his path for an extended

period. This confrontation eventually led to a right-wing meme with a picture of Sandmann above the phrase "Stand Your Ground." Sandmann's "stance"
against Indigenous peoples received further affirmation when the Trump
campaign invited him to speak at the RNC in August 2020. Alyosha Goldstein
deftly assesses the intertwined dynamics at work here: "'Land gets stolen,
that's how it works' expresses a casual and categorical dismissal of Indigenous
land claims. . . . The idea that 'land gets stolen, that's how it works' presumes
irrevocability. It provides the presupposition that settlers possess the ground
upon which they stand and that 'stand your ground' is an unequivocal relation of white settler belonging and rightful ownership of the land."[56] In this
emblematic scene and its aftermath, the mocking disavowal and cruel celebration that is central to Trump's white settler nationalism was on full display
by his youthful supporters, and its manifestation was constitutively linked to
the signifier of the border wall. As Phillips tells it: "I heard them saying, 'Build
that wall, build that wall.' . . . You know, this is indigenous lands. We're not
supposed to have walls here—we never did for millennia, before anybody else
came here."[57] With this scene in mind of young settler citizen-deputies surrounding a small group of peacefully assembling Indigenous people and allies, behaving in a mocking and threatening manner while declaring "Land
gets stolen, that's how it works," I take a look at the politics of memory invoked by Trump's tweet about Warren that referred to Wounded Knee. I do
so with the assistance of the analysis and historical context provided by historians Alyssa Mt. Pleasant (Tuscarora) and David Chang (Kanaka Maoli).

As Mt. Pleasant and Chang remind us, "On December 29, 1890, the U.S.
7th Cavalry massacred hundreds of Lakota near Wounded Knee Creek in
South Dakota. It was hardly the largest settler massacre of Native peoples, but
it is the most infamous." They expand on the reasons for its infamy:

> Wounded Knee was the culmination of decades of tension and conflict
> on the Plains as Native peoples resisted American efforts to expropriate
> their lands and confine them to reservations. The U.S. government forced
> unfair treaties on tribal nations, wrenched away their land, failed to live
> up to its own treaty obligations, and failed to stop settler squatters from
> invading Native lands. In the late 1880s, a politically potent spiritual
> movement that Americans called the Ghost Dance grew from the
> teachings of the Paiute prophet Wovoka and caught fire among the
> Native peoples of the Plains.[58]

President Benjamin Harrison feared an "Indian uprising" from the Ghost
Dance and ordered the movement suppressed and Indigenous leaders arrested,

which led to the killing of Lakota holy man Sitting Bull and made refugees of hundreds of Lakota men, women, and children. Eventually, the U.S. Seventh Calvary caught up to and surrounded the Lakota refugees at Wounded Knee Creek and forced them to disarm. In the midst of this process, a small confrontation led to a gun firing off. In response, the Seventh Calvary unleashed its firepower on the four hundred Lakota refugees, killing around three hundred of them. "The slaughter was relentless," Mt. Pleasant and Chang chillingly note. They then speak to the politics of memory invoked by Trump: "So when Trump made light of Wounded Knee, he invoked an episode that still remains raw and powerful in Native memory today. . . . To Trump, real Indians are clearly a defeated remnant of the past, frozen in time at Bighorn and Wounded Knee, wearing 'Indian garb.'"[59] Trump's overt use of Wounded Knee is another example of the cruel celebration of settler colonial violence and mocking disavowal of Indigenous presence. Furthermore, Trump's stanzas are in line with his administration's policy decisions that had a negative impact on Indigenous peoples and any people deemed "other" to the idea of the United States as a white, Christian settler nation. In light of the violence, family separations, and suffering caused by the intensification of the policing of the border under the Trump administration—in which cruelty was key to the administration's strategy for deterring migration, as Trump granted in stating, "If they feel there will be separation, they don't come. . . . You know, if they feel there's separation, it's a—it's a terrible situation"—the southern border of the United States has become the site of Trump's "Wounded Knee."[60] I mean this analogy not to disavow Indigenous presence but rather to illustrate the violence that comes with the policing of settler state borders that are imposed upon migrant and Indigenous peoples.

To be sure, the border between the United States and Mexico far precedes Donald Trump, but the creation and perpetuation of it continues to come at the direct expense of the lands and communities of Indigenous nations and migrating peoples. To recall Leigh Patel's discussion of settler colonial imperatives, "The occupation of land is never finished. . . . Settler colonialism has been maintained by eradicating and punishing Indigenous, Black and brown peoples." This particular occupation on the Southern border can be traced to the mid-nineteenth century, in the wake of the U.S.-Mexico War from 1846 to 1848, when "the traditional homelands of 36 federally recognized tribes—including the Kumeyaay, Pai, Cocopah, O'odham, Yaqui, Apache and Kickapoo peoples—were split in two by the 1848 Treaty of Guadalupe Hidalgo and 1853 Gadsden Purchase, which carved modern-day California, Arizona, New Mexico, and Texas out of northern Mexico."[61] A major portion of the U.S.–

Mexico border also divides the territory of Tohono O'odham Nation. To-hono O'odham people have been engaged in resistance against the border for decades and have had to increase their efforts due to the Trump administration's move to escalate the construction and policing of the border. Altamirano-Jiménez explains the contemporary situation:

> The Tohono O'odham, a nation whose reservation spans 75 miles of the US Mexico border, announced it will oppose the construction. They accused President Trump of signing an executive order without consulting their tribe. The Tohono O'odham have long struggled with the militarization of a border that divides their traditional lands, which stretches south to Sonora, Mexico. Similarly, the Kumeyaay and the Kickapoo, among others, occupy land along the US-Mexico border and are discussing tactics to oppose border security. Narratives supporting the proposed wall not only erases the border as a product of the US invasion but also disregards its effects on real people and communities.[62]

The opposition by the Tohono O'odham, Kumeyaay, and Kickapoo Nations is part of the wider movement of Indigenous resistance to the colonial border that has been going on since well before as well as during Trump's presidency.

For example, in 2007 Margo Tamez cofounded the Lipan Apache Indian Women Defense/Strength with her mother, Eloisa Tamez. The political aims of the group are "to protect sacred sites, burial grounds, archeological re-sources, ecological biodiversity, and way of life of Indigenous people of the Lower Rio Grande, North America . . . in response to the attempt by the U.S. Department of Homeland Security (DHS) to force their surrender of heredi-tary lands in El Calaboz, Texas, for the U.S.-Mexico Border Wall."[63] Their organization's activism and leadership are "centered in Indigenous women and Ndé-ness [to reflect the diversity of intersocietal kinship among lower Rio Grande River peoples], which works on restoring hereditary title through women. . . . This is really an act of resistance to the colonization of women and of our culture."[64] In other words, this Indigenous organization represents a simultaneous resistance to grabbing land and women. The Lipan Apache Indian Women Defense/Strength mobilized through media awareness, po-litical appeals, and court petitions against such U.S. federal departments as the U.S. Army, Customs and Border Protection, and the Department of Home-land Security, putting forth the claim that the border violated the idea of "In-digenous communities protected under international human rights law. The law directly impacts the lands of Apache, Kickapoo, Tigua Isleta, and numer-ous other tribes on the border."[65] Through this approach, the Lipan Apache

Indian Women Defense/Strength succeeded in slowing, and in some areas stopping, the development of the border wall across Indigenous lands in 2006 and 2007, which allowed for further review on such matters as the sacred sites threatened by border construction. By halting the construction, these activists forestalled for the time being the perpetuation of an even harsher impact of the border on Indigenous nations and migrating peoples.

However, the Trump administration's publicly stated priority of building the wall presented a clear threat to the efforts of the Indigenous women of Lipan Apache Indian Women Defense/Strength. Thus, on April 30, 2017, after President Trump signed an executive order to further construct the U.S.–Mexico border wall—in the context also of the administration's effort to ban immigration from seven predominantly Islamic countries—the Apache Ndé Nneé Working Group conveyed an "Urgent Action/Early Warning" letter to the Committee on the Elimination of Racial Discrimination (CERD) at the Office of the United Nations High Commissioner for Human Rights (OHCHR). The letter requested that the CERD and OHCHR endorse the appeals of the Lipan Apache Women Defense organization in their effort to gain international support and backing to oppose and address the crises of colonial imposition, dispossession, and violence that the Trump administration was intensifying. The letter concluded with a request for the "acknowledgment" of both the historically rooted and contemporary forms of colonial rule over Indigenous peoples as that which must be addressed, resisted, and brought to an end. The letter asked the CERD to "acknowledge that a United States Government's policy/mandate-induced expansion of a United States-Mexico border wall, and without the Free, Prior and Informed Consent (FPIC) of the affected Indigenous Peoples, including the Lipan Apache Band (Ndé), is a continued colonial and genocidal territorial alien domination of the traditional Indigenous Peoples and lands and in direct violation of international law as per the *ending of all forms of colonialism*."[66] As of March 2018, there had been no response from the United Nations nor a relenting of the efforts of the Trump administration, as became more evident in early 2019 when the administration declared a "state of emergency" to be able to garner the funds to further build the wall, even without authorization from Congress. As of 2019, "Congress has already sent nearly $3 billion to Trump for a border barrier, including up to 37 miles in Hidalgo and Starr counties. Almost half of that, $1.34 billion, was allocated for the Rio Grande Valley, the compromise outcome of the longest government shutdown in history."[67] While the precise outcome of the contemporary political and human struggles at the U.S. southern border is still to be determined, the violent escalation at the border remains a settler nationalist form of "stand-your-ground" politics, done through Indigenous territories, with violent consequences for racialized peoples who represent the "threat" of invasion to the white settler nation.

These violent consequences were made brutally evident on August 3, 2019, at a Walmart store in El Paso, Texas. On that day, Patrick Crusius murdered over twenty people, with a stated intention of targeting Latinx people he deemed to represent the threat of "invasion" against and replacement of the white settler population of the United States, a theme he picked up from the repeated references to invasion made by Trump, his supporters, and right-wing media.[68] Tellingly, Crusius began his manifesto by invoking the genocide of Indigenous people as a cautionary tale for the white American population faced with the *great replacement* by nonwhite people, stating that "the natives didn't take the invasion of Europeans seriously, and now what's left is a shadow of what was."[69] Inspired by and interpellated through the political discourse of Trumpism, Crusius deployed a distinct form of settler memory—Indigenous people as the naive dead of the past and the disavowed part of the present, "a shadow"—to justify his murderous effort to stand the ground of the white settler nation.

This settler stand-your-ground dynamic was evident during the highly public occupation of the Malheur National Wildlife Refuge in Oregon that began in early 2016, led by Ammon Bundy, in response to the arrest and conviction of two local ranchers, Dwight Hammond Jr. and his son Stephen, for starting fires on their property that led to wildfires on federal land. As Daniel Martinez HoSang and Joseph Lowndes analyze it, the occupation that "drew right-wing activists from militia and patriot groups from across the western United States" needs to "be understood through the commitments and histories of a highly masculinized white-producerist and settler-colonial worldview."[70] In many ways, producerism is an inherently settler colonial perspective in societies built on the dispossession of Indigenous peoples from their lands. This is because producerism is a cohering form of identification for a cross-class coalition of white settlers who imagine themselves as the true builders of the nation pitted against people they deem parasitical upon the nation and all the work these settlers ostensibly did to build it. Financiers and politicians from above and Black people, migrants, and Indigenous people from below stand as those constructed in this producerist, settler imaginary as those who undermine freedom and take advantage of the labor and efforts of these ennobled, and now victimized, white masculine producers. Thus, as HoSang and Lowndes put it, the Malheur occupation was an "effort to regenerate social, political, and economic life through a re-creation of settler occupation and violence" on the ancestral lands of the Paiute Nation, who were dispossessed and removed from their lands after the 1878 Bannock War.[71] While this occupation preceded Trump's presidency, there is a clear symmetry with the themes of his campaign and administration, in particular the centrality of white settler masculinity that poses itself as under siege and threat of invasion from domestic and foreign racialized entities. This connection became explicit in July 2018, when President Trump pardoned Dwight and Steve Hammond, thereby indicating his support for the people and the cause of the Malheur occupation and enforcing a "strong link between Trumpism and the militia movement," as HoSang and Lowndes put it.[72] The Malheur occupation that occurred before Trump's rise and his subsequent 2018 endorsement of it show both how white settler nationalist imperatives preceded Trump and also that the imperatives of his campaign and presidency drew from and emboldened an overt commitment to maintaining and securing white settler colonial governance. Trump's 2018 support for a white settler militia's violent occupation of land in Oregon was also an ominous foreshadowing of his explicit inciting of an insurrectionary settler nationalist mob—comprising various white nationalist, neo-Nazi, and Western chauvinist militia groups—that invaded and occupied the U.S. Capitol building in early January 2021 to take *their* country back from those they deemed invaders and usurpers.[73]

We can locate more evidence of Trump's commitment to settler colonial invasion and occupation by looking beyond the boundaries of the U.S. settler state to the support he has provided to other settler states, in particular that of Israel in its colonization and occupation of Palestine and continued dispossession of the Palestinian people from their lands. There are two distinct directives through which Trump broke with the decades-long policy stances of Democratic and Republican administrations as they concern Israel and Palestine. On December 6, 2017, the Trump administration announced that it would formally recognize Jerusalem as the capital of Israel and in that spirit move the U.S. Embassy to Jerusalem from Tel Aviv. In so doing, Trump went further than had any U.S. president in seventy years, since the founding of Israel, in naming the Holy City as Israel's capital. The administration claimed it was supporting the idea that "Israel is a sovereign nation and, like every other sovereign nation, has the right to choose its own capital." Or, in Trump's own words, "Today, we finally acknowledge the obvious: that Jerusalem is Israel's capital."[74] Then, on March 21, 2019, Trump announced in a tweet that "After 52 years it is time for the United States to fully recognize Israel's Sovereignty over the Golan Heights, which is of critical strategic and security importance to the State of Israel and Regional Stability!" While there are domestic political factors that influenced Trump's move to legitimate Israel's seizure and occupation of Palestinian and Arab lands,[75] including appealing to his white Christian evangelical supporters, these actions also fall in line with the words and deeds of a white settler regime that celebrates settler conquest, from pipelines to sexual predation, to the border and beyond. In this regard, Trump's actions regarding Israel echo Alyosha Goldstein's assessment of the Covington Catholic High School boy's assertion of the right to settler possession by conquest: "'Land gets stolen, that's how it works' . . . an unequivocal relation of white settler belonging and rightful ownership of the land."

One can trace this mutually supportive settler colonial relationship from Palestine back to the U.S. southern border as well, for it is an established fact that the United States and Israel share border-policing methods. President Trump has directly referenced Israel's border wall approach as the model for his vision of how to police the southern U.S. border.[76] This is because settler society border walls—their materiality and their imaginary—are not only xenophobic efforts to demonize and keep out racialized others but also persistent reassertions of settler colonial claims to define, bound, and rule over land seized through dispossession and maintained through occupation. Through an analytical and political lens that places settler colonial logic at the center, disavowing neither settler colonization nor the active presence and resistance of peoples under occupation, we can grasp in the U.S. context the logic behind the Red Nation collective's political slogan of #NoBanonStolenLand. This slogan and movement combines support for migrating peoples in their humanity with a rejection of the idea that the United States, as a country built upon stolen land, has legitimate authority to decide who does and does not reside here.[77] This is but one example of a well-known U.S. policy that can be theorized in a more expansive way, one that opens up the possibilities for coalitional activism and theorization of anticolonial and antiracist politics in the United States and other settler colonial contexts. We only get there, however, by refusing settler memory that disavows the settler colonial logic that "bundles together" the imperatives and predations of the white settler nationalism of Donald Trump and Trumpism, both of which have shown no signs of receding from U.S. political life in the wake of Trump's 2020 electoral defeat to Democratic candidate Joe Biden.

Conclusion

In April 2019, at the Politics and Prose bookstore in Washington, D.C., an audience gathered to hear author Jonathan Metzl read from his new book, *Dying of Whiteness: How the Politics of Racial Resentment Is Killing America's Heart-land.* Before he could start, ten white nationalist protestors interrupted and started chanting, "This is our land" while marching through and eventually out of the store.[78] These activists, like the president with whom they most identify and the Covington Catholic High School boy who said, "Land gets stolen, that's how it works," are loudly telling the world that settler claims to land are central to their white nationalist commitments and to the meaning of whiteness itself.

Paying close attention to this dynamic is not only important for analysts and scholars when seeking to understand Trumpism and Trump in the context of U.S. political history. It is also helpful to pinpoint targets of critique, challenge, and opposition to the wider imperatives of settler colonialism animating across the spectrum of U.S. political life. These imperatives speak to a significant mobilizing rationale of the right-wing settler nationalist violence evident in the attempted Trumpist insurrection on January 6, 2021, as well as the violent threats and actions by these groups at state capitols around the country. Next, I begin the conclusion of the book by examining the role of settler memory in the liberal #resistance to Trump that emerged after his election in 2016. I follow that by discussing contemporary solidarity practices and theories of radical anticolonial and antiracist resistance that has a long and underappreciated history. I will suggest that it is in the poetic stanzas of the voices that speak to the imperatives of these struggles that we find the imaginaries for countering, dismantling, and moving beyond white settler nationalism.

Conclusion
Refusing Settler Memory

The November 8, 2016, election of Donald Trump to the U.S. presidency came as a shock to most of the country. The vast majority of polls and pundits predicted that the racist, xenophobic, misogynistic, and, as I have argued, white settler nationalist Republican candidate who took pleasure in being "politically incorrect" could not garner the necessary electoral college votes to win a national election against Democratic nominee Hillary Clinton. Right after the election, starting the next day and continuing for months, massive demonstrations took place, as millions of people took to social media and to the streets to #Resist, with many asserting that Donald Trump was #NotMyPresident. On January 21, 2017, the day after Trump's inauguration, the Women's March on Washington, D.C., and in locales across the country turned into possibly the largest demonstration in U.S. history at that time, with estimates of over four million participating nationwide and over five million worldwide.[1] A random survey of attendees at the Washington, D.C., march, which had an estimated one-half million people in attendance, found that one-third of them were participating in their first-ever protest, and 56 percent had not been to a demonstration in five years. Ninety percent of those surveyed said they voted for Hillary Clinton.[2] Thus, in the wake of Trump's victory many Americans, especially white liberal Americans although not entirely or exclusively so, engaged in forms of political activism unlike anything they had ever done or had done in a number of years. Radical scholar and activist Angela Davis referred to the 2016 election as a "wake-up call for Americans."[3] By the morning of November 9, 2016, a new day seemed to have dawned for millions of Americans, marking a clear break between the past and present of their nation.

A new day for some, however, was a familiar one for others. In particular, given the rise of and significant public attention garnered by Indigenous and Black radical political movements in the preceding years, it is safe to say that the distinct past/present break experienced by millions of Americans after the 2016 election likely did not resonate quite as much with the organizers and activists of #NoDAPL/Standing Rock and Black Lives Matter (BLM). As Jonathan Rosa and Yarimar Bonilla put it, "For many, the election was felt not as a punch in the gut but as a forceful, sequential blow to an already-bruised political body."[4] This lived sense of the "past that is not past," to recall Christina Sharpe's words concerning the history and afterlife of slavery, speaks to the deeply woven sense of political memory that shapes how, notably, Indigenous and Black communities situate the contemporary political moment. As LaDonna Brave Bull Allard, Lakota activist and historian of the Standing Rock Sioux Tribe, stated in September 2016 in the midst of the standoff against the Dakota Access Pipeline: "We must remember we are part of a larger story. We are still here. We are still fighting for our lives, 153 years after my great-great-grandmother Mary watched as our people were senselessly murdered. We should not have to fight so hard to survive on our own lands."[5] Brave Bull Allard's words call forth the pain and political persistence shaped by a clear sense of history, "the larger story," within which she and her community exist and fight. Her words convey "a sense of place made strong through intergenerational memory," which to quote Mishuana Goeman's discussion of the memory work of Indigenous visual art, "avoids reaffirming notions of vanishing Indians or stagnant traditions."[6] This sense of strength that comes through a deeply embedded, intergenerational politics of collective memory stands in contrast with the wave of national mnemonic dysfunction and contestation that was provoked but not created by the Trump candidacy and election. I observed this dysfunction at a political event not long after Trump's inauguration, an event that included a liberal form of settler memory.

On February 4, 2017, I attended a pro-sanctuary city rally held at the city hall of Somerville, Massachusetts, the city in which I live. Politically, Somerville is a decidedly liberal-left city, where Hillary Clinton won 85 percent of the vote in the 2016 presidential election. This rally occurred in the wake of the Trump administration's proposed "Muslim bans" and general anti-immigrant rhetoric, policies, and state practices. The people who attended the rally, the city's mayor, Joe Curtatone, and the city's elected representatives are all strong advocates in support of Somerville being a sanctuary city, as it has been for over thirty years. In fact, Curtatone became a nationally famous mayor for his defiant stance in support of sanctuary cities well before the rise of Trump.[7] As I was walking home from the rally, I saw a sign held up amid the departing crowd.

Framed entirely by images of the U.S. flag, with the red, white, and blue reproduced in the color of the text situated on a white background, the sign's visual aesthetics offer an overtly positive evocation of the American nation. The sign's words then provide a liberal, and in some forms left, trope of national identification that asserts solidarity with immigrants and refugees on the assumption that "we"—that being American citizens—"are all immigrants,

Near city hall, Somerville, Massachusetts, February 4, 2017. Photo by Kevin Bruyneel.

literally.*" Then there is the smaller printed text, positioned in the lower right-hand corner, which offers an addition, an asterisk to the idea of the United States as a nation of immigrants—"*Except Native Americans." This sign is a metonym for how Indigenous peoples are often an afterthought in the political life of race in the United States, a product of settler memory that, at once, remembers and disavows Indigenous people and settler colonialism. As if ripped from the pages of Indigenous critical theory, the * is an example, literally, of the idea of Indigenous peoples as asterisks who are simultaneously there and not there in the larger story being told. This is an astute metaphor set out by John Garland in his discussion of the "American Indian research asterisk" that one often finds in race and ethnicity research when "American Indian data are generally not reported or discussed within quantitative research findings" because such data are not deemed statistically significant in relation to the wider pool of results.[8] Eve Tuck and K. Wayne Yang speak to how this dynamic works in a more general sense to the degree that Indigenous peoples are often positioned as "asterisk peoples ... footnotes in the dominant paradigms" of the United States as a whole.[9] The sign's messaging not only positions Indigenous peoples as, at once, absent and present; it is also implicitly anti-Black by incorporating (without so much as a footnote *) Black Americans into the mythos of the nation's immigrant story in a manner that disavows the history of kidnapping from Africa, the terror of the Middle Passage, and enslavement in the Americas.[10] This sign is not an exception. It is representative of a dominant mode of liberal collective memory production—one that reinforces the status, logic, and boundaries of the white American settler nation as regenerative fuel for making political claims and shoring up alliances.

In the context of the #NotMyPresident slogan and the general inattention to the role of white settler nationalism in bringing Trump to power, a familiar liberal response to his election involved constructing an imaginary in which the America that voted for Trump was not really their America, not *literally*. For example, in response to Trump's mnemonic call to "Make America Great Again," during the election many liberals asserted that such greatness was not at all lost but rather quite present, just underappreciated. Most famously, Hillary Clinton voiced this perspective in her acceptance speech at the 2016 Democratic National Convention when she roused the delegates in the convention hall with the phrase: "America is great—because America is good."[11] In the years, months, and weeks leading up to the Democratic National Convention in late July 2016, highly public acts of police violence against Black Americans continued, as did the BLM mobilization to address this issue.[12] Additionally, during the exact days in which the Democratic National Convention took place the U.S. Army Corp of Engineers approved easements for the Dakota Access Pipeline, lawyers representing the Standing Rock Sioux Tribe filed injunctions against these decisions, and the #NoDAPL encampments and protests gained greater public attention.[13] In light of these events occurring just before and during the Democratic convention, Clinton's statement of American greatness/goodness reads as, at best, a thoughtless erasure and, at worst, a cruel disavowal of white settler violence. This is an all too familiar disavowal in U.S. liberal discourse, exemplified in the post-2016 election context by Senator Elizabeth Warren's political and personal relationship to Indigeneity.

The problematic nature of Elizabeth Warren's claim to first Cherokee and then a general Native American identity—through the discourse of oral history in her family and then through DNA testing—has been incisively analyzed by Indigenous feminist writers and scholars Kim TallBear, Jacqueline Keeler, and Rebecca Nagle. TallBear's work speaks to the racialization of Indigenous identity through genetic-based claims. In her statement about Warren's 2018 DNA test results, TallBear argues that Warren's turn to genetic science privileges the "voices of (mostly white) genome scientists and implicitly cede[s] to them the power to define Indigenous identity." To TallBear, this is another example that shows how "one of the privileges of whiteness is to define and control everyone else's identity."[14] Along these lines, Keeler argues that "if Sen. Warren is serious about helping Native peoples (much less being a Native person) she cannot slide into old colonial habits of appropriation of Indigenous identity which has gone hand in hand with assuming the rights to the land and resources of those Native nations and peoples." Keeler also points out the manner in which Warren's liberal and progressive supporters disavow settler colonial logic and history in their support for her: "When her supporters rail at Native Americans criticizing the senator and hold up her record on taking on Wall Street, they fail to see the connections between that fight and the fight for Indigenous sovereignty. Throughout American history, the spread of modern capitalism across this continent has been incumbent on the obliteration of Native nations."[15] Thus, Keeler calls forth the intricate role of settler colonialism in capitalist development and its centrality to U.S. racial capitalism. For her part, Rebecca Nagle refuses the idea of fractionated Indigenous identity in Warren's claim, asserting that "I am not *part* Cherokee. There is not *one* member of my family who *was* Cherokee. I *am* Cherokee." Nagle rejects the notion of genetic ancestry or blood descent as the basis for her claim, emphasizing that Cherokee is a political identity in which someone either is or is not a citizen, not *half* or *part* citizen, according to the community, not according to the U.S. government. She thus gets to the heart of the matter in terms of the relationship between one's claim to identity and one's political commitments, rejecting the idea of Warren as "a hero because, despite claiming to be the only Native woman in the U.S. Senate, she has done nothing to advance our rights."[16] Building upon the insights offered by these three writers, what I discern in the Warren case and in the defense made by her supporters is a clear example of the work of settler memory from liberal/progressive positionalities in U.S. politics.[17] From the white liberal-progressive perspective, Warren's claim is, at once, an innocent expression of her connection to Indigenous people's history while also being a matter that should not be politicized by those supportive of Indigenous political concerns. In fact, those of us who have criticized Warren's claim to Indigenous identity often stand accused by liberals of helping the cause and case of Donald Trump in his attacks on Warren. In all, Warren's claim is its own form of a liberal

"*Except Native Americans" footnote that seeks to demonstrate knowledge of Indigenous people's history but, as with Warren herself in her own political history, does not make an assertive effort to speak to and support Indigenous concerns from a position of power in the U.S. Senate. Settler memory shapes how liberal and progressive supporters of Warren, and Warren herself, explain and rationalize the meaning of her assertion of an ancestral identification with Indigenous people. This is an identification situated in the past and disavowed from political commitments in the present, which is a familiar construct for those engaged in the work of settler memory.

Across the arc of the book, my aim has been to locate and reveal the implications of the work of settler memory in how we grasp the meaning of Bacon's Rebellion and the Reconstruction era, interpret James Baldwin's work, make sense of the politics of Indian mascotry, and examine the meaning of Trump and Trumpism. I conclude the book with an eye to the words of those who offer a poetics and politics of refusing settler memory. I do so primarily through the stanzas and interventions of poet Layli Long Soldier and literary scholar Christina Sharpe. They each artfully and powerfully speak to the constraints of the past upon the present regarding settler colonialism, for Long Soldier, and slavery, for Sharpe. They each also generate their own radical refusals of the disavowals of white settler colonial societies, such as the United States, that are built through the violent practices and institutions of genocide, dispossession, enslavement, and heteropatriarchy.

As I noted in the preface, I read a resistance to and a refusal of the workings of settler memory in Long Soldier's poem *Whereas*, in which she recasts the meaning of that word utilized twenty times in the Native American apology resolution signed by President Obama in December 2009. This resolution seemed a possible step toward political acknowledgment and redressing these wrongs, but it concludes with a disclaimer that nothing in the resolution "authorizes or supports any claim against the United States" and instead merely urges the president to admit wrongs and bring "healing to this land," without authorizing any tangible action to achieve this end.[18] Thus, the resolution is a disavowal of the political implications and contemporary impact of U.S. settler colonialism. The term "whereas" is an example of a settler disavowal; a recognition or awareness of harm caused and a withdrawal or refusal to follow through on accountability for the damage done. As Long Soldier puts it: "Whereas the word *whereas* means it being the case that, or considering that, or while on the contrary; is a qualifying or introductory statement, a conjunction, a connector. Whereas sets the table."[19] "Whereas" sets a seemingly inviting table and then, as white settler/trader Andrew Myrick did in 1862 when learning that the Dakota were starving, says, "Let them eat grass."[20] In her poetry, Long Soldier resists and refuses the disavowal of the settler "whereas": "Whereas I have spent my life in unholding. *What do you mean by unholding?* Whereas asks and since Whereas rarely asks, I am moved to respond, Whereas, I have learned to exist and exist without your formality, saltshakers, plates, cloth. Without the slightest conjunctions to connect me. Without an exchange of questions, without the courtesy of answers. It is mine, this unholding, so that with or without the setup, I can see the dish being served. Whereas let us bow our heads in prayer now, just enough to eat."[21] Long Soldier sees the dish of disavowal being served and refuses the invitation, refuses to be held by—to be in the *hold* of—false promises. Instead, she ends the collection with her own disclaimer that poetically mocks, refuses, and recasts the disclaimer from the 2009 apology resolution:

Nothing in this book—
(1) authorizes or supports any claim against Layli Long Soldier by the United States; or
(2) serves as a settlement of any claim against Layli Long Soldier by the United States, here in   thegrassesgrassesgrasses.[22]

The space before thegrassesgrassesgrasses I take to be the space of her unholding. This being the effort "to loosen the hold" of the settler "whereas,"[23] that conjunction and qualifier of settler colonial discourse that sees and disavows, that which she tires "of understanding weary, weakened, exhausted, reduced in strength from labor. Bored."[24] In the space of unholding, meanings are not in the hold of the settler discourse. Thus, thegrassesgrassesgrasses can take on multiple meanings, representing her and her community's unceasing relationship to territorial homelands first and foremost and also the threat to these lands from settler colonialism and the threat made with them to starving Dakota by the likes of Myrick. It also represents a source of Indigenous resistance. As Long Soldier notes in her poem "38" about the Dakota thirty-eight, during the preceding Sioux uprising that arose in response to the starvation, predation, and sexual violence perpetuated by settlers, the Dakota killed Myrick and other settlers and traders:

When Myrick's body was found,
                    his mouth was stuffed with grass.
I am inclined to call this act by the Dakota warriors a poem.[25]

This is a stanza of radical resistance, and the space in the first and second lines marks, possibly, the unholding of refusal and resistance against settler colonialism—a space that suspends or reimagines what she refers to at one point as "the rules that writing dictate," or for that matter the rules that other structures, settler colonial structures, dictate.[26] In all, Long Soldier offers a model of the poetry of resistance, in that resistance itself is a form of poetry to the degree that it takes that with which we are familiar and turns its function on its head to reimagine social relations so as not to reproduce the disavowals that maintain their structural preconditions.

I find a coinhabitative traveling partner for Long Soldier's antagonistic refusal of the "whereas" from a place of unholding in Christina Sharpe's notion of *wake work*. Long Soldier's sense that she has "learned to exist and exist without your formality, saltshakers, plates, cloth" resonates with Sharpe's notion of the "mode of inhabiting *and* rupturing this episteme with our known lived and un/imaginable lives."[27] Brought together, they set out a model for refusing settler memory in a way that fosters wake work, which, among other things, I read as a politics of memory derived out of the lived resistances and "un/imaginable lives" of communities made other to the white settler society. We can discern this dynamic in the expressed and enacted solidarity voiced by people involved in contemporary Black and Indigenous radical movements.

Consider the words of Miski Noor, an "organizer with Black Lives Matter Minneapolis" who visited the encampments at Standing Rock in August 2016 with other BLM organizers. Here Noor offers her take on what connects these movements:

> This isn't just an Indigenous issue; water is life for all of us and we have a responsibility to the Earth and future generations to protect it. While at the camp, I heard over and over again from Native folks how they have shown up in their cities across the country for Black lives. As BLM, we have built power and we have a platform. And as a movement, we have a duty to uplift and amplify the stories and struggles of all marginalized folks, as our liberation is intertwined. The history of genocide and stolen land and stolen labor in America will forever link Black folks and Indigenous folks (and let us be clear that the two are not mutually exclusive), as there can be no Black liberation without Indigenous sovereignty.[28]

Noor emphasizes the importance of interconnection, intergenerational memory, and a refusal to abide "mutually exclusive" demarcations—such as land and labor or Indigenous and Black—as the basis of collaborations over time.[29] These sorts of claims build out of the coinhabitation of the white settler colonial system as a form of wake work whose disruptive threat to the dominant episteme comes in the critical practice of refusing to abide the containment of identities, movements, claims, and concerns into discrete rather than interconnected matters. When such containment succeeds, collaborations and disruptive coinhabitations that are at the heart of solidarity work are undermined or never get off the ground, as we saw in the political memory of the failed forms of cross-racial, class-based solidarities during Bacon's Rebellion and the Reconstruction era. The popular Left history and memory regarding what these solidarities were and might have been may foreclose more radical imaginaries going forward and at the time may well have doomed them to failure as they would doom future movements built upon such constrained political memories. Contrary to this tendency, Noor refuses the idea that environmental concerns are solely or primarily an Indigenous issue. These same sentiments can be found in BLM's official statement of solidarity with Standing Rock, posted in early September 2016: "Black Lives Matter stands with Standing Rock. As there are many diverse manifestations of Blackness, and Black people are also displaced Indigenous peoples, we are clear that there is no Black liberation without Indigenous sovereignty. Environmental racism is not limited to pipelines on Indigenous land, because we know that the chemicals used for fracking and the materials used to build pipelines are also used in water containment and sanitation plants in Black communities like Flint, Michigan."[30] Here we see, again, the refusal of contained categories and an embrace of coinhabitation without collapsing experiences, identities, and claims. This BLM statement refuses settler memory, which opens up the imaginary for political critique and activism built upon coalitional and coinhabitational connections. The claim of "no Black liberation without Indigenous sovereignty" does not deny possible tensions. For example, questions that will arise include: What forms do Black liberation and Indigenous sovereignty take in relation to each other, and what defines the key stakes and parameters of liberation and sovereignty in their respective visions, with due attention to the role of community, care, and land relations? One finds in contemporary Black radical theorizing efforts to address this question in ways that refuse the settler "whereas" and animate the coalitional possibilities of wake work—in a way to think and act collaboratively without collapsing and homogenizing subject positions and claims.

In their 2018 book, *As Black as Resistance: Finding the Conditions for Liberation*, Zoé Samudzi and William C. Anderson provide a rigorous articulation of the complexity and possibilities of Black-Indigenous solidarity in resistance to U.S. settler colonialism. Their argument about the conditions for the liberation of Black people in the United States is based upon a fundamental premise about political positionality, which, as noted earlier, is that "Black Americans are residents of a settler colony, not truly citizens of the United States."[31] Thus, for Samudzi and Anderson, the political life of white supremacy in the nation is coimplicated with the imposition, development, and maintenance of the United States as a settler colonial state and society. The authors make clear, in this regard, that there can be no true Black liberation within the confines of the U.S. settler colonial society. To the contrary, "The existence of free Black people necessitates a complete transformation and destruction of this settler state."[32] Samudzi and Anderson thus make the politics of decolonization a necessary component of the effort to abolish white supremacy.

Attention to decolonization means centering the role of land in the imaginaries of liberation. In particular, Samudzi and Anderson argue that "Black American land politics cannot simply be built on top of centuries-old exterminatory settler logic of Indigenous removal and genocide. Rather, the actualization of truly liberated land can only come about through dialogue and co-conspiratorial work with Native communities and a shared understanding of land use outside of capitalistic models of ownership."[33] They thus offer a coordinated response to what I have called the layers of dispossession experienced by Indigenous and Black communities historically and in our time. Samudzi and Anderson set out a model of the conditions for liberation in which solidarity among Black and Indigenous peoples, to start, is not an option; it is necessary for the freedom of both. In short, "The solution to white supremacy is the active rejection of it and the dual affirmation of Indigenous sovereignty and Black humanity. We must reject the violent machinations of the settler state (e.g., mass incarceration, treaty violations, transmisogyny, and so on)."[34] These authors build their sense of the importance of this solidarity on a premise that I have sought to come back to throughout *Settler Memory*, which is that anti-Blackness is fueled by settler colonialism, and thus the disavowal of the latter undermines efforts to address the former, and vice versa. For examples of this solidarity, Samudzi and Anderson turn to political memory: "The lessons of the past are here for us, should we choose to accept them and build what they have to offer."[35] Black-Indigenous forms of solidarity expressed by BLM and the Water Protectors of Standing Rock are not new. They are the legacy of forms of "Black and Native coalitions" that go back to before "the Revolutionary War."[36] For example, Cedric Robinson's study of the long history of Black radicalism, *Black Marxism: The Making of the Black Radical Tradition*, is peppered with references to Indigenous and Black political and social comingling, such as "in Hispaniola, Blacks had joined the native uprising of 1533," "several plots involving first Indians and Blacks, and then Blacks separately were reported discovered in 1709, 1722 and 1723. And in 1727, a maroon community of Indians and Blacks, which its inhabitants called des Natanpelle, was betrayed by a former resident."[37] In *Black Movements in America*, Robinson carries this historical narrative forward and with attention to the emergent U.S. context as he discusses the distinct yet also intertwined, coinhabitative radical struggles of Indigenous and Black peoples that can be traced to and beyond the American Revolutionary period:

> Like the Native American nations that sided with the British, the Black Loyalists sought to employ the British army to serve their own interests, for their own ends. Long after the defeated British had departed, their allies, the Native Americans and the Blacks, continued the struggle for liberty. For generations to come, Native Americans recognized America as a colonial power, and Blacks read the new nation as tyrannical. Their suspicion of and opposition toward American society survived in the political cultures of Blacks and Native Americans for the next two hundred years.[38]

As well, he notes that in the seventeenth, eighteenth, and nineteenth centuries, "in the Southeastern United States, Black Indians and Black-Indian alliances had pursued liberty through anticolonial struggle and under the authority of Indian nations."[39] The point here is that on their own and in tandem Black and Indigenous peoples have never not been resisting settler colonialism, enslavement, and the rippling consequences of both. In this regard, there is an urgent need to heed the lessons regarding the "past that is not past" of white settler rule, for as Samudzi and Anderson put it: "Finding liberation truly entails interrogating the past, understanding how that past has enabled the present, and then imagining and beginning to actualize a future in meaningful and material ways."[40] I have argued that the answer here is less a turn to history, on its own, as if knowledge and facts speak for themselves. Rather, what is required is a turn to political memory, in which knowledge, myth, and lessons are mobilized to political ends through narratives built out of intergenerational memories, un/imaginable lives, and coinhabitations that rewrite and reimagine the story of *the past that is not past* to open up possibilities for the future.[41]

The articulation of this collaboration in the contemporary form is further evident in Indigenous solidarity practices that seek to engage and support the movements and concerns most directly associated with and mobilized by Black Americans. For example, in April 2016, as the Standing Rock encampments and standoff against the Dakota Access Pipeline were just beginning and thus before #NoDAPL was in the public eye, Kyle Mays notes how "his Michigan

Native cousins, the Little Traverse Band of Ottawa Indians, gave $10,000 U.S. dollars to support the residents of Flint." A well as financial assistance, Mays observed solidarity practices in artistic expression, including by Christy Bieber, an Anishinaabe singer performing with the Dream Keepers Native American Youth Group in Detroit. One song, which includes the lyrics "let's meet up by the water/Nakweshkodaadiiidaa Ekobiiyag," Mays describes "as the sounds of drums and rattles—sacred sounds to Indigenous people—poetry, and rapping. It is a protest song, preparing people for a ceremony to bring healing to the residents of Flint, suffering under the yoke of Governor Rick Snyder's decision to deliberately poison its citizens with water from the Flint River."[42] While the urgency of this resistance stems from the crisis in a specific community, the effort here is to refuse the constraints of the dominant episteme cohered through the disavowals of the settler "whereas" so as to open up space for wake work as a practice of care and community action with potential collaborators.

In this regard, consider Miski Noor's earlier reference to "Native folks" showing up to BLM demonstrations in cities to support Black communities in their protest against police violence. Studies show that Indigenous people suffer proportionally higher rates of police violence and abuse than any other group, but as an article on this matter phrased it, "Nobody is talking about it" as an Indigenous issue too.[43] Leanne Betasamosake Simpson (Michi Saagiig Nishnaabeg) reminds us that police violence is not random. It is, rather, a product of historically rooted structural domination and exploitation that have shaped the contemporary context: "Indigenous and black people are disproportionately attacked and targeted by the state, and, in fact, policing in Turtle Island was born of the need to suppress and oppress black and indigenous resistance to colonialism and slavery."[44] In this spirit of solidarity and support, Simpson dedicates her poem "Caribou Ghosts and Untold Stories" to "the intelligence and commitment of BLM Toronto for halting the Pride parade in 2016."[45] BLM Toronto took this action to call out and protest the anti-Black racism and general mistreatment of Black LGBT people by the Pride Parade organization, particularly as it concerned Toronto Pride's work with and support for the police in the city.[46] Simpson concludes "Caribou Ghosts and Untold Stories" with these words:

> catharsis is still elusive
> so we'll save that
> for another day
> meet me at the underpass

rebellion is
on her way[47]

These stanzas of resistance express solidarity from an Indigenous writer and activist to Black queer radicals on Turtle Island. The rebellious meeting place "at the underpass" resonates with Long Soldier's "life in the unholding" and with Sharpe's wake work as "inhabiting *and* rupturing this episteme with our known lived and un/imaginable lives." The underpass, the unholding, and the un/imaginable lives signal that which settler memory keeps white settlers not so much from seeing or knowing—as any claim to such a right evokes the violent specter of white settler surveillance, be it from the left, center, or right politically—but acknowledging rather than disavowing stories and experiences that convey, among other things, the meaning of the past in the present, the terms and stakes of the struggle against racial, colonial, capitalist, and heteropatriarchal domination, and the possibilities for liberation. In this spirit, to conclude I briefly discuss two existing organizing models and one underattended crisis for thinking and positioning ourselves to deal with the fact that these are all of our problems and should define our major political commitments.

The first is We Are All Treaty People, which is a concept and emergent practice that emanates from the settler colonial context of Canada. The Ontario Institute for Studies in Education at the University of Toronto provides a We Are All Treaty People curriculum module for use by teachers. The overview description begins with the following statement to establish the premise of and need for such a course: "Many people think of treaty rights as 'special' indigenous rights however, all people living in Canada are treaty people with their own set of rights and responsibilities. Treaties are a foundational part of Canadian society. Every road, house, building or business that exists today in a treaty area was made possible because of a treaty."[48] To be sure, not all lands in Canada or the United States exist under the historical context of a treaty agreement and relationship, as a significant amount of territory that settlers dispossessed from Indigenous nations occurred without the pretense of any treaty agreement. Still, with that important stipulation in mind, the aim of We Are All Treaty People is to educate settlers, in particular, to understand that the fulfillment of treaty obligations and the government arrangements they set out are a matter of obligation for all of us who reside on treaty-defined lands. In other words, fulfilling treaty promises is our responsibility and co-governing commitments as settlers. The value here is of engaging and educating settlers as ourselves coimplicated and obligated in a way that can expand the imaginary of what citizenship and political community mean in relationship to these lands. Tara Williamson, Anishinaabekwe/Nehayowak and a member of the Opaskwayak Cree Nation, had her own revelatory response to and thoughts on this concept: "It wasn't until I became an adult that I first heard the expression 'We are ALL treaty people.' Quite frankly, it blew my mind. I mean, of course *I'm* a treaty Indian, but, it never occurred to me that my neighbours were Treaty Settlers. But, of course! Treaties and agreements require at least two parties. How did Settlers forget that? How did I forget that?" She notes the manner in which "colonization and settlement have been normalized," leading to a forgetting by her, and by settlers. In the context of the present climate crises, she also sees the notion of We Are All Treaty People as a possible avenue to which settlers might turn when they realize that settler governments will not address the issue due to their lack of care and respect for the land. In this regard, she concludes: "I mean, who are you going to trust when it comes to protecting the land for your children: Indigenous peoples or the Canadian government? And, when you answer that question for yourself, remember the treaties. After all, we are all treaty people."[49] Since climate change is a problem we all face—although to different degrees in the short term but in a more encompassing sense universal in the long term—the logical thing to do is support governments that are inclined toward addressing rather than denying and disavowing the problem. To be clear, as it concerns a politics committed to decolonization and the abolition of white supremacy, We Are All Treaty People does not expressly aim for the dismantlement of white settler governments. Rather, it asserts and defends the obligations of all in a context in which settler and Indigenous governance coexist according to treaty principles. Still, if taken seriously as a set of commitments across the entirety of Turtle Island, this model would represent a significant step toward an imaginary that refuses settler memory and the qualifying disavowals of the settler "whereas" and opens more coalition possibilities.

The second model provides a more radical politics, as it is based upon the claim that "no one is illegal." No One Is Illegal (NOII) is a movement composed of immigrants, refugees, and allies that advocates for the rights of migrants around the world and organizes around the principle that "granting citizenship to some who are privileged and denying it to others exploits migrants and perpetuates oppression." While the movement had its origins in Europe in the late 1990s, it has gained its most direct organizational traction in cities across Canada with "a focus on indigenous sovereignty, poverty and racism" in connection with the defense of and support for undocumented immigrants.[50] For example, the vision statement for the organization NOII-Vancouver Coast Salish Territories focuses on setting out "specific demands to address Border Militarization, Migrant Worker Programs, Undocumented People & Status for All, Conditions for Immigrant Workers, National Security Apparatus & Anti-Terror Legislation, and more."[51] This movement seeks the dismantlement of institutions of the settler colonial state as a fundamental requirement for ending the practice of privileging who gets to be the citizen of a community and who does not. To this end, the NOII movement connects migrant justice, gender and sexuality justice, racial justice, and justice for Indigenous peoples not as competing visions but as collaborative ones. Harsha Walia, an organizer and theorist of NOII-Vancouver Coast Salish Territories witnessed how the notion of no person being illegal morphed into a connected challenge to the legality of the settler state itself: "There was a march on the last day of the gathering and we heard the MC start chanting, 'No one is illegal. Canada is illegal.' This was an incredible moment— articulating a vision that the settler-colonial state and its laws are illegal and illegitimate, not displaced and migrating human beings. Also this chant was a genuine expression and gesture of relationship and solidarity."[52] The NOII movement was an important source for the radical stanza "No One Is Illegal on Stolen Land" that can be seen in statements and on banners and T-shirts at political rallies.[53] This stanza is in collaborative alignment with the claim of #NoBanOnStolenLand, devised and articulated by the Red Nation in the U.S. context, as noted in chapter 5. What one can see here, when settler memory is refused, is an alternative imaginary for collaborations, coalitions, and liberating visions. In contrast to liberal claims about being a "nation of immigrants" where "we are all immigrants, literally,*" *except Native Americans, which is a framework that presumes and reaffirms rather than problematizes the white settler state, NOII is a movement that mobilizes on the premise that supporting migrant rights necessarily means opposing and abolishing settler colonialism and white supremacy.

We Are All Treaty People and No One Is Illegal on Stolen Land are just two examples of what a politics of coalition, collaboration, and radical imaginaries can start to look like when settler memory is refused. To be clear, this is not to set out Canada as ideal in this regard, for it is a settler colonial state and society. If settler memory takes a slightly different hold there due to greater, though still grossly insufficient, awareness of Indigenous peoples' concerns than is the case in the United States, in the Canadian context there is a deep disavowal of that nation's white supremacy and its own history and afterlife of slavery.[54] Thus, I do not pose these examples in a naively optimistic way. Rather, in thinking about what politics in the United States might look like when settler memory is refused, the commitments implied by We Are All Treaty

People and NOII open up alternative models of coinhabitative wake work. Another urgent avenue of political intervention and collaboration concerns the historical and contemporary crisis of missing and murdered Indigenous women and girls (MMIWG) in Canada and the United States. The June 2019 Canadian report of the National Inquiry into Missing and Murdered Indigenous Women and Girls determined this to be a matter of genocide against Indigenous peoples, and as noted in chapter 5, extractive industries across North America are predictable contributing factors to this genocide.[55] Thus, when one opposes these extractive industries because of their contribution to climate change and the poisoning of life and land one is also engaged in the effort, whether one knows it or not, to abolish one contributing element to the violence against Indigenous women and girls. This connection needs to be made consistent and explicit as a critical and collaborative practice. Additionally, and in the spirit of Sharpe's wake work, attention to MMIWG as a problem produced and linked to the structural practices of colonial and racial capitalism must also call us to refuse any disavowal regarding the violence perpetuated against Black women and girls, immigrant women, and LGBTQIA+ peoples. In particular, a 2018 report by the National Organization for Women (NOW) revealed that "over 18% of African American women will be sexually assaulted in their lifetime," while an American Civil Liberties Union report including Black women, girls, and nonbinary people placed that figure at 22 percent.[56] This violence is the past that is not past in the afterlife of slavery, which contributes to what the NOW report refers to as a "sexual abuse to prison pipeline" that implicates white supremacist practices that can be traced from policing in schools to the functioning of mass incarceration.[57] These crises of sexual violence among different communities have their distinct dynamics but are also consistent features of the problem and crises of settler colonialism, white supremacy, capitalism, and heteropatriarchy.

With this in mind, I turn one final time to Sharpe and do so with regard to her discussion of the hold. As Sharpe reminds us, "the bottom of slave ships" were "the hold," which is the place on a ship where the cargo—here captured people transported across the Middle Passage—is stowed belowdecks. From the hold of a ship during enslavement to the holding cell of a prison in the afterlife of slavery, the role of "the hold repeats and repeats and repeats in and into the present."[58] The intergenerational repetition of these practices produces and reinforces dominant worldviews about racial hierarchy, which can become passively accepted as somehow the unchangeable work of history, as just the way things are. In this sense, "The hold is what is taken as given; it is the logic, it is the characterization of a relation in that moment."[59] I place

Sharpe's words here into constructive collaboration with Long Soldier's notion of spending one's "life in unholding." Long Soldier's unholding is a refusal to accept the settler "given," the "logic," or the "characterization of a relation in that moment," which does not mean she can wish it away but rather refuses to abide its false promises and contained sense of possibility—"it is mine, this unholding." Just as Long Soldier refuses the hold of the settler "whereas," Sharpe recasts the hold to ask about our obligations to, rather than our constraints upon, one another: "How are we beholden to and beholders of each other in ways that change across time and place and space and yet remain?"[60] The wake work of radical political movements and the work of settler memory end up with different answers to this question of our beholdenness, our obligations. Wake work provides the basis to shift and radically alter the frame of coinhabitation so as to imagine otherwise than is at present and thereby demand of collaborators a greater level of critical thinking, care, responsiveness, action, and beholdenness. This can take the form of We Are All Treaty People, No One Is Illegal, #NoBanonStolenLand, #MMIWG, #BlackLivesMatter, #SayHerName; demands by Indigenous nations for their #LandBack;[61] and the Red Nation's proposed Red Deal (a radical decolonial version of the Green New Deal); as well as the overt or implied expressions of solidarity among Indigenous, Black, migrant-supporting, feminist, queer, and working-class radical movements that defend and support the safety and health of life and land.[62] By contrast, the work of settler memory narrows the scope of one's sense of obligations to others and to the world around us, as it provides white settlers in particular the disavowal escape hatch of the "whereas" to avoid our responsibilities and accountability. This lack of beholdenness to humankind, other-than-human life, and the land and waters upon and through which we all exist diminishes the capacity to radically reimagine what the world might look like beyond this moment, and it thus puts our world into greater danger. This is a danger for all of us, and it will not just go away. Thus, for settlers who refuse to refuse settler memory, Layli Long Soldier's words offer food for thought: "Now/make room in the mouth/for grassesgrassesgrasses."[63]

Notes

Preface

1. Lee Maracle, *Memory Serves: Oratories*, ed. Smaro Kamboureli (Edmonton, AB: NeWest Press, 2015), 26, 27, 31.

2. Maracle, *Memory Serves*, 25.

3. Maracle, 37.

4. Maracle, 22.

5. A foundational article that set out and has shaped a great deal of the discourse around *white privilege* is Peggy McIntosh's "White Privilege and Male Privilege: A Personal Account of Coming to See Correspondences through Work in Women's Studies" (Working Paper 189, Wellesley College Center for Research on Women, MA, 1988).

6. For more on Canadian settler colonialism and white supremacy, see Glen Coulthard, *Red Skin, White Masks: Rejecting the Politics of Colonial Recognition* (Minneapolis: University of Minnesota Press, 2014); Audra Simpson, *Mohawk Interruptus: Political Life across the Borders of Settler States* (Durham, NC: Duke University Press, 2014); Iyko Day, *Alien Capital: Asian Racialization and the Logic of Settler Colonial Capitalism* (Durham, NC: Duke University Press, 2016); Jaskiran Dhillon, *Prairie Rising: Indigenous Youth, Decolonization, and the Politics of Intervention* (Toronto: University of Toronto Press, 2017); Shiri Pasternak, *Grounded Authority: The Algonquins of Barriere Lake against the State* (Minneapolis: University of Minnesota Press, 2017); Robin Maynard, *Policing Black Lives: State Violence in Canada from Slavery to the Present* (Halifax, Nova Scotia: Fernwood, 2017); and Desmond Cole, *The Skin We're In: A Year of Black Resistance and Power* (Toronto: Doubleday Canada, 2020).

7. The only other use of the phrase *settler memory* I have found is by Mark Rifkin in his article "The Silence of Ely S. Parker: The Emancipation Sublime and the Limits of Settler Memory," *NAIS* 2 (Fall 2014): 1–43. The concept of settler memory is not defined or mobilized in the article as such and only appears in the title. To be clear, I am referring to the concept itself, not criticizing the article, which insightfully engages in the matter of the positioning of Indigeneity in the historical narratives of the U.S. settler nation and has helped shape my thinking on these matters. Rifkin's 2014 *NAIS* article was also the basis for a chapter in his excellent book *Beyond Settler Time: Temporal Sovereignty and Indigenous Self-Determination* (Durham, NC: Duke University Press, 2017).

8. For the history of the Lenape people and the role of the wall in Wall Street in Indigenous-European relations, see Veda Keech, "The Lenape: Original Occupiers of Wall Street," Occupy Wall Street, November 2011, http://occupywallstreet.net/story/lenape-original-occupiers-wall-street; and Joanne Barker, "Social Text: Territory as Analytic: The Dispossession of Lenapehoking and the Subprime Crisis," *Social Text* 36, no. 2 (2018): 27–28.

9. "How Statues Are Falling around the World," *New York Times*, June 24, 2020, updated September 12, 2020, https://www.nytimes.com/2020/06/24/us/confederate-statues-photos.html.

10. For a sample of this debate, see Dave Thompson, "Erasing History? Debate on Heritage, Hate and History Rages around Lee Monument," *Marshall Tribune Courier*, June 30, 2020, https://www.tribunecourier.com/news/erasing-history-debate-on-heritage-hate-and-history-rages-around-lee-monument/article_258d915f-11a0-5e5b-889e-75425c6b0c2b.html; and Dion J. Pierre, "Fighting Racism or Erasing History? Public Support for Leaving Confederate Statues in Place Plummets," *Just the News*, June 20, 2020, https://justthenews.com/nation/culture/anti-racism-and-erasing-history-public-support-leaving-confederate-statues-place.

11. P. J. Brendese, *The Power of Memory in Democratic Politics* (Rochester: University of Rochester Press, 2014), 2.

12. Michael Rothberg, "On the Mbembe Affair: The Specters of Comparison," *Latitude*, May 2020, https://www.goethe.de/prj/lat/en/dis/21864662.html. Rothberg's approach focuses on what he has termed multidirectional memory, a concept he defines and utilizes in his excellent book, *Multidirectional Memory: Remembering the Holocaust in the Age of Decolonization* (Stanford, CA: Stanford University Press, 2009).

13. Layli Long Soldier, "(1) Whereas Statements," in *Whereas* (Minneapolis: Graywolf Press: 2017): 59–85.

14. Christina Sharpe, *In the Wake: On Blackness and Being* (Minneapolis: University of Minnesota Press, 2016), 13–14.

15. Sharpe, *In the Wake*, 9.

16. Sharpe, 18.

17. "In the Wake: A Salon in Honor of Christina Sharpe" (panel discussion, Barnard Center for Research on Women, Barnard College, February 2, 2017), http://bcrw.barnard.edu/event/in-the-wake-a-salon-in-honor-of-christina-sharpe/.

Note on Terminology

1. For an excellent explanation of the history, cultural, and political roots and also the complicated nature of the terms *Indigenous* and *Indigeneity*, see J. Kēhaulani Kauanui, "Indigenous," in *Keywords for American Cultural Studies*, ed. Bruce Burgett and Glenn Hendley, 3rd ed. (New York: New York University Press, 2020), 137–141.

2. On this question of not capitalizing *white* while doing so for *Indigenous* and *Black*, I am persuaded by Joel Olson's argument that whiteness is a political invention and identity that provides benefits and standing that need to be abolished, rather than seeing whiteness as an organically developed and substantial cultural identity, and thus Olson states, "This explains why I do not capitalize white throughout the book, but I do capitalize Black. The two terms are not symmetrical. Black is a cultural identity as well as a political category, and such merits capitalization like American Indian, Chicana, or Irish America." *The Abolition of White Democracy* (Minneapolis: University of Minnesota Press, 2004), xviii–xix.

Introduction

1. Helen Regan, "A Prominent Black Activist Has Been Faking Black Ethnicity, Her Parents Say," *Time*, June 12, 2105, http://time.com/3918660/rachel-dolezal-civil-rights-activist-spokane-naacp/. In terms of Dolezal's claim to Indigenous identity, in an application for a

role with the Office of Police Ombudsman Commission she selected "white, African-American, Native American and two or more races" for her ethnic identity. For this, see A. B. Wilkinson, "What It Means to Become 'BiRachel,'" *Huffington Post*, June 17, 2016, http://www.huffingtonpost.com/a-b-wilkinson/what-it-means-to-become-birachel_b _7591714.html.

2. See Gregory Smithers, "We're a Dolezal Nation, Tonto," *USA Today*, June 17, 2015, https://www.usatoday.com/story/opinion/2015/06/17/race-identity-dolezal-american -indians-column/28801139/; and for the story in which Dolezal speaks of being born in a "Montana tepee" and that her "family hunted with bows and arrows," see Shawntelle Moncey, "A Life to Be Heard," *Easterner*, February 5, 2015, https://theeasterner.org/35006/eagle -life/a-life-to-be-heard/#sthash.1aUk3liU.WbUDBRWQ.dpbs.

3. Along with Smithers, "We're a Dolezal Nation," another effort to address this came from Taté Walker in her blog. See "Honest Injuns*: Policing Native Identity in the Wake of Rachel Dolezal," *Righting Red: Ramblings, Ruminations, and Activism from an Idealistic Lakota Storyteller*, July 1, 2015, https://walkerwrackspurt.wordpress.com/2015/07/01/honest-injuns -policing-native-identity-in-the-wake-of-rachel-dolezal/.

4. For an opinion from the perspective of an enrolled Cherokee citizen, see Rebecca Nagle, "Op-ed: I Am a Cherokee Woman. Elizabeth Warren Is Not," *Think Progress*, November 30, 2017, https://thinkprogress.org/elizabeth-warren-is-not-cherokee-c1ec6c91b696/. For more background, see Garance Franke-Ruta, "Is Elizabeth Warren Native American or What?," *Atlantic*, May 20, 2012, https://www.theatlantic.com/politics/archive/2012/05/is-elizabeth -warren-native-american-or-what/257415/.

5. Kim TallBear, *Native American DNA: Tribal Belonging and the False Promise of Genetic Science* (Minneapolis: University of Minnesota Press, 2013), 46.

6. Manu Vimalassery, Juliana Hu Pegues, and Alyosha Goldstein, "Introduction: On Colonial Unknowing," *Theory & Event* 19, no. 4 (2016).

7. Moon-Kie Jung, *Beneath the Surface of White Supremacy* (Stanford, CA: Stanford University Press, 2015), 143.

8. James Baldwin, "My Dungeon Shook: Letter to My Nephew on the One Hundredth Anniversary of the Emancipation," in *The Fire Next Time* (New York: Vintage International, 1963), 9.

9. George Shulman, *American Prophecy: Race and Redemption in American Political Culture* (Minneapolis: University of Minnesota Press, 2008), 243.

10. Beenash Jafri, "Ongoing Colonial Violence in Settler States," *Lateral* 6, no. 1 (Spring 2017), http://csalateral.org/issue/6-1/forum-alt-humanities-settler-colonialism-ongoing-vio lence-jafri/. Also, on the disavowal of colonial dispossession as a critical feature in the logic and development of U.S. democracy and democratic thought, see Adam Dahl, *Empire of the People: Settler Colonialism and the Foundations of Modern Democratic Thought* (Lawrence: University of Kansas Press, 2018).

11. Justin Leroy, "Black History in Occupied Territory: On the Entanglements of Slavery and Settler Colonialism," *Theory & Event* 19, no. 4 (2016): 8.

12. Leroy is among a number of scholars who draw attention to the need to attend to the mutually constitutive relationship between the dispossession of Indigenous peoples from their lands and the enslavement of African and African-descended peoples and thus also the interrelationship of settler colonialism and white supremacy. I benefit from the insights

of such scholars in formulating this book's analysis. Here are a number of the authors and their works that have influenced my grasp and view on these matters: Jack Forbes, *Africans and Native Americans: The Language of Race and the Evolution of Red-Black Peoples*, 2nd ed. (Chicago: University of Chicago Press, 1993); Aziz Rana, *The Two Faces of American Freedom* (Cambridge, MA: Harvard University Press, 2010); Tiya Miles, *Ties That Bind: The Story of an Afro-Cherokee Family in Slavery and Freedom* (Oakland: University of California Press, 2006); Tiya Miles and Sharron P. Holland, *Crossing Waters, Crossing Worlds: The African Diaspora in Indian Country* (Durham, NC: Duke University Press, 2006); Shona Jackson, *Creole Indigeneity* (Minneapolis: University of Minnesota Press, 2012); Sandra Harvey, "'What's Past Is Prologue': Black Native Refusal and the Colonial Archive," in *Otherwise Worlds: Against Settler Colonialism and Anti-Blackness*, ed. Tiffany King, Jenelle Navarro, and Andrea Smith (Durham, NC: Duke University Press, 2020): 218–235; Oliver Baker, "Democracy, Class, and White Settler Colonialism," *Public* 28, no. 55 (June 2017): 144–153; Manu Karuka, *Empire's Tracks: Indigenous Nations, Chinese Workers, and the Transcontinental Railroad* (Oakland: University of California Press, 2019); Jodi Byrd, *Empire of Transit: Indigenous Critiques of Colonialism* (Minneapolis: University of Minnesota Press, 2011); Gerald Horne, *The Apocalypse of Settler Colonialism: The Roots of Slavery, White Supremacy, and Capitalism in Seventeenth-Century North America and the Caribbean* (New York: Monthly Review Books, 2018); Brenna Bhandar, *The Colonial Lives of Property: Law, Land and Racial Regimes of Ownership* (Durham, NC: Duke University Press, 2018); Tiffany Lethabo King, *Black Shoals: The Offshore Formations of Black and Native Studies* (Durham, NC: Duke University Press, 2019); Mark Rifkin, *Fictions of Land and Flesh: Blackness, Indigeneity, Speculation* (Durham, NC: Duke University Press, 2019); Natsu Taylor Saito, "Race and Decolonization: Whiteness as Property in the American Settler Colonial Project," *Harvard Journal on Racial and Ethnic Justice* (Spring 2015): 31–67; and "Tales of Color and Colonialism: Racial Realism and Settler Colonial Theory," *Florida A&M University Law Review* 10, no. 1 (2014): 3–108. Saito's book *Settler Colonialism, Race, and the Law: Why Structural Racism Persists* (New York: New York University Press, 2020) came out just as I was finishing mine, so I was grateful to have benefited from the earlier iterations of this important work in the aforementioned articles.

13. Frank Wilderson, *Red, White & Black: Cinema and the Structure of U.S. Antagonisms* (Durham, NC: Duke University Press, 2010), 58–59.

14. Wilderson, *Red, White & Black*, 2–3.

15. Wilderson, 7.

16. Wilderson, 23.

17. Wilderson, 26.

18. Shona Jackson, "To Be Anti-Black Is to Be Anti-Indigenous: Reflections on Emancipation," *Stabroek News* (Georgetown, Guyana), July 28, 2014, www.stabroeknews.com/2014/features/07/28/anti-black-anti-indigenousreflections-emancipation/.

19. Patrick Wolfe, *Traces of History: Elementary Structures of Race* (New York: Verso, 2016), 2.

20. Wolfe, *Traces of History*, 10.

21. Wolfe, 5.

22. J. Sakai provided one of the earliest and most comprehensive readings of American whiteness as fundamentally defined by its historical foundations in settler life. However, his

work is not as concerned with the status and role of Indigeneity historically and politically, and he also ends up claiming that "settlerism is a phenomenon of the past, really." See J. Sakai, *Settlers: The Mythology of the White Proletariat from Mayflower to Modern* (Oakland, CA: PM Press, 2014), 431. Originally published in 1983 under the title *Mythology of the White Proletariat: A Short Course in Understanding Babylon.*

23. Aileen Moreton-Robinson, *The White Possessive: Property, Power, and Indigenous Sovereignty* (Minneapolis: University of Minnesota Press, 2015), xix.

24. Moreton-Robinson, *White Possessive*, xx.

25. Moreton-Robinson, 53. See Cheryl Harris, "Whiteness as Property," in *Critical Race Theory: The Key Writings That Formed the Movement*, ed. Kimberlé Crenshaw, Neil Gotanda, Gary Peller, and Kendell Thomas (New York: New Press: 1995), 276–291.

26. Rita Dhamoon, "A Feminist Approach to Decolonizing Anti-racism: Rethinking Transnationalism, Intersectionality, and Settler Colonialism," *Feral Feminisms*, no. 4. (Summer 2015): 32.

27. Jack Turner, *Awakening to Race: Individualism and Social Consciousness in America* (Chicago: University of Chicago Press, 2012), x.

28. Moreton-Robinson, *White Possessive*, 60.

29. Stuart Hall, "Race, Articulation and Societies Structured in Domination," in *Sociological Theories: Race and Colonialism* (Paris: United Nations Educational, Scientific, and Cultural Organization, 1980), 341.

30. Audra Simpson, "The State Is a Man: Theresa Spence, Loretta Saunders and the Gendered Costs of Settler Sovereignty," *Theory & Event* 19, no. 4 (2016) https://muse.jhu.edu/article /633280.

31. Saidiya V. Hartman, *Scenes of Subjection: Terror, Slavery, and Self-Making in Nineteenth Century America* (Oxford: Oxford University Press, 1997), 80–81.

32. For an insightful explanation and analysis of the construction of will, and antiwill, to which Hartman refers, see Robert Nichols, *Theft Is Property! Dispossession and Critical Theory*, (Durham, NC: Duke University Press, 2020), chap. 4.

33. Margaret Jacobs, *White Mother to a Dark Race: Settler Colonialism, Maternalism, and the Removal of Indigenous Children in the American West and Australia, 1880–1940* (Lincoln: University of Nebraska Press, 2009).

34. Charles W. Mills, *Black Rights/White Wrongs: The Critique of Racial Liberalism* (New York: Oxford University Press, 2017), 59. See also the work of Maurice Halbwach, the germinal theorist on the subject, in Maurice Halbwach and L. A. Coser, *On Collective Memory* (Chicago: University of Chicago Press, 1992).

35. Edward Said, "Memory, and Place," *Critical Inquiry* 26, no. 2 (Winter 2000): 185.

36. Saidiya Hartman, *Lose Your Mother: A Journey along the Atlantic Slave Route* (New York: Farrar, Straus and Giroux, 2007), 133.

37. Christina Sharpe, *In the Wake: On Blackness and Being* (Minneapolis: University of Minnesota Press, 2016), 14.

38. Layli Long Soldier, "Layli Long Soldier on Wounded Knee and the Murder of George Floyd," *Literary Hub*, June 3, 2020, https://lithub.com/layli-long-soldier-on-wounded-knee -and-the-murder-of-george-floyd/ (emphasis in original).

39. Mark Rifkin, *Settler Common Sense: Queerness and Everyday Colonialism in the American Renaissance* (Minneapolis: University of Minnesota Press, 2014), 7.

40. Henri Bergson, *Matter and Memory* (1912; repr., Mineola, NY: Dover Philosophical Classics, 2004), 87.

41. Bergson, *Matter and Memory*, 87.

42. Paul Ricoeur, *Memory, History, Forgetting* (Chicago: University of Chicago Press, 2006), 25.

43. Said, "Memory, and Place,"184.

44. Jean M. O'Brien, *Firsting and Lasting: Writing Indians out of Existence in New England* (Minneapolis: University of Minnesota Press, 2010), 55.

45. As an example of a liberal rationalist approach built upon an amnesia framework for the relationship of the present to the past, see Thomas McCarthy, "Vergangenheitsbewalti-gung in the USA: On the Politics of Memory and Slavery," *Political Theory* 30, no. 5 (October 2002): 623–648; and Thomas McCarthy, "Coming to Terms with Our Past, Part II: On the Morality and Politics of Reparations for Slavery," *Political Theory* 32, no. 6 (December 2004): 750–772.

46. Dhamoon, "Feminist Approach," 32.

47. Stefano Harvey and Fred Moten, *The Undercommons: Fugitive Planning and Black Study* (New York: Minor Compositions, 2013), 75.

48. Zoé Samudzi and William C. Anderson, *As Black as Resistance: Finding the Conditions for Liberation* (Chico, CA: AK Press, 2018), 6.

49. Samudzi and Anderson, *Black as Resistance*, 28.

50. For more on these interconnections, see Stephanie Latty and Megan Scribe, with Alena Peters and Anthony Morgan, "Not Enough Human: At the Scenes of Indigenous and Black Dispossession," *Critical Ethnic Studies* 2, no. 2 (Fall 2016): 129–158.

51. Stuart Hall, *The Fateful Triangle: Race, Ethnicity, Nation* (Cambridge, MA: Harvard University Press, 2017), 45–46.

Chapter One

1. Winthrop D. Jordan, *White over Black: American Attitudes toward the Negro, 1550–1812* (Durham, NC: University of North Carolina Press, 2012).

2. Jordan, *White over Black*, viii.

3. Jordan, 229. Jordan does mention Gary B. Nash's work as a "conspicuous exception" in this regard. Nash wrote *Red, White and Black: The Peoples of Early North America* (New York: Prentice Hall, 1974), which came out the same year as *The White Man's Burden*. Jordan thus recommends to his readers Nash's articles, including "Red, White and Black: The Origins of Racism in Colonial America," in *The Great Fear: Race in the Mind of America*, ed. Gary B. Nash and Richard Weiss (New York: Holt, Rinehart, and Winston, 1970): 1–26.

4. Achille Mbembe, "Necropolitics," trans. Libby Meintjes, *Public Culture* 15, no. 1 (2003): 39–40.

5. Shona Jackson, "Movement and Time: A Diasporic Response to Grounded Light," *American Quarterly* 71, no. 2 (June 2019): 346.

6. Ruth Wilson Gilmore, *Golden Gulag: Prisons, Surplus, Crisis, and Opposition in Globalizing California* (Berkeley: University of California Press, 2007), 28.

7. Michelle Alexander, *The New Jim Crow: Mass Incarceration in the Age of Colorblindness* (New York: New Press, 2010), 24.

8. Alexander, *New Jim Crow*, 25.

9. For his detailed history of Bacon's Rebellion, see chap. 13 in Edmund Morgan, *American Slavery, American Freedom: The Ordeal of Colonial Virginia* (New York: W. W. Norton, 1975).

10. Morgan, *American Slavery*, 259.

11. Morgan, 269–270.

12. Morgan, 328.

13. Morgan, 344.

14. Jeffrey B. Perry, introduction to Theodore Allen, *The Invention of the White Race: The Origins of Racial Oppression in Anglo-America*, vol. 2, 2nd ed. (New York: Verso, 2012), x.

15. Barbara Jean Fields, "Slavery, Race and Ideology in the United States of America," *New Left Review*, no. 181 (May/June 1990): 105.

16. Joel Olson, *The Abolition of White Democracy* (Minneapolis: University of Minnesota Press, 2004), 34, 39.

17. Ibram X. Kendi, *Stamped from the Beginning: The Definitive History of Racist Ideas in America* (New York: Nation Books, 2016), 53–54.

18. Asad Haider, *Mistaken Identity: Race and Class in the Age of Trump* (London: Verso, 2018), 55.

19. Morgan, *American Slavery*, 327.

20. Ta-Nehisi Coates, "The Case for Reparations," in *We Were Eight Years in Power: An American Tragedy* (New York: One World, 2017), 181.

21. J. Kēhaulani Kauanui, "Tracing Historical Specificity: Race and the Colonial Politics of (In)Capacity," *American Quarterly* 69, no. 2 (June 2017): 261. In his discussion of Bacon's Rebellion in his 2018 book, Gerald Horne cites Kauanui's intervention as persuading him that left renderings of this historical event limit rather than expand the imaginary for potential political alliances. See Gerald Horne, *The Apocalypse of Settler Colonialism: The Roots of Slavery, White Supremacy, and Capitalism in Seventeenth-Century North America and the Caribbean* (New York: Monthly Review Press, 2018). Also, see Dave Roediger's brief but pointed discussion of Bacon's Rebellion at the end of *Class, Race, and Marxism* (London: Verso, 2017), 183–184; and also from J. Sakai, *Settlers: The Mythology of the White Proletariat from Mayflower to Modern* (Oakland, CA: PM Press, 2014), chap. 2 (originally published in 1983 under the title *Mythology of the White Proletariat: A Short Course in Understanding Babylon*, 25–37). Sakai, however, is concerned with what he deems to be the false assertions of cross-racial class unity that masked white settler bourgeois aims of the likes of Bacon. And while valid, his claim that "there was no Black and White unity" because "those Afrikans who signed up in his army didn't love him, trust him, view him as their leader, or anything of this kind" (36) is premised upon an understanding of coalitions that does not account for how some may be parties to a coalition based upon their own calculus and interests regardless of their trust of a leader. As well, Sakai is not really addressing the role of Bacon's Rebellion in the politics of memory in the contemporary age.

22. James D. Rice, "Bacon's Rebellion in Indian Country," *Journal of American History* 101, no. 3 (December 2014): 730.

23. Kathleen Brown, *Good Wives, Nasty Wenches, and Anxious Patriarchs: Gender, Race and Power in Colonial Virginia* (Chapel Hill: University of North Carolina Press, 1996), 173.

24. Allen, *Invention of the White Race*, 204.

25. Allen, 204–205.

26. Allen, 205.

27. Allen, 257.

28. Rice, "Bacon's Rebellion," 737.

29. Rice, 736, 737.

30. Rice, 736.

31. Michael Omi and Howard Winant, *Racial Formation in the United States: From the 1960s to the 1990s*, 2nd. ed. (London: Routledge, 1994), 55.

32. Brown, *Good Wives*, 169.

33. Brown, 145.

34. Brown, 173.

35. Roxanne Dunbar-Ortiz, *Loaded: A Disarming History of the Second Amendment* (San Francisco: City Lights, 2018), 61.

36. Brown, *Good Wives*, 178.

37. Brown, 174.

38. Brown, 180.

39. Brown, 185.

40. Aileen Moreton-Robinson, "Race and Cultural Entrapment: Critical Indigenous Studies in the Twenty-First Century," in *Critical Indigenous Studies: Engagements in First World Locations*, ed. Aileen Moreton-Robinson (Tucson: University of Arizona Press, 2016), 114.

41. Saidiya Hartman, "The Belly of the World: A Note on Black Women's Labors," *Souls* 18, no. 1 (January–March 2016): 169. For more, see also Gregory D. Smithers, *Slave Breeding: Sex, Violence, and Memory in African American History* (Gainesville: University of Florida Press, 2012).

42. Kauanui, "Tracing Historical Specificity," 262.

43. For a summary of the states with forms of these laws and their specific elements and determinants for a self-defense claim, see "Self Defense and 'Stand Your Ground,'" National Conference of State Legislatures, May 26, 2020, https://www.ncsl.org/research/civil-and-criminal -justice/self-defense-and-stand-your-ground.aspx; and "States That Have Stand Your Ground Laws," FindLaw, June 2, 2020, https://criminal.findlaw.com/criminal-law-basics/states-that -have-stand-your-ground-laws.html. According to FindLaw's list, as of June 2020, at least twenty-four states had some version of a stand-your-ground or castle doctrine law.

44. Cornel West, "Convocation Address to Harvard Divinity School," September 8, 2017, https://hds.harvard.edu/news/2017/09/08/transcript-cornel-wests-2017-convocation -address#.

45. Madison to Marie Joseph Paul Yves Roch Gilbert du Motier, Marquis de Lafayette, November 25, 1820, in *The Writings of James Madison*, ed. Gaillard Hunt (New York: G. P. Putnam's Sons, 1900–1910), https://founders.archives.gov/documents/Madison/04-02-02-0137.

Chapter Two

1. John Hope Franklin, "Mirror for Americans: A Century of Reconstruction History," *American Historical Review* 85, no. 1 (February 1980): 3.

2. It was only the second article by a Black scholar published in the *American Historical Review*, after W. E. B. Du Bois's article on Reconstruction in 1910.

3. Eric Foner, "Why Reconstruction Matters," *New York Times*, March 28, 2015, https://www.nytimes.com/2015/03/29/opinion/sunday/why-reconstruction-matters.html.

4. Ta-Nehisi Coates, "The Case for Reparations," in *We Were Eight Years in Power: An American Tragedy* (New York: One World, 2017), xiii.

5. Reverend Dr. William J. Barber II, with Jonathan Wilson-Hartgrove, *The Third Reconstruction: Moral Mondays, Fusion Politics, and the Rise of a New Justice Movement* (Boston: Beacon Press, 2016), 115. See also this interview with Robin D. G. Kelley, who is theorizing our present moment through a political memory of Reconstruction framework to consider the radical possibilities of contemporary abolitionism: Jeremy Scahill, "Scholar Robin D.G. Kelley on How Today's Abolitionist Movement Can Fundamentally Change the Country," *Intercept*, June 27, 2020, https://theintercept.com/2020/06/27/robin-dg-kelley-intercepted/.

6. Barber, *Third Reconstruction*, 121.

7. Robert Greene, "The Urgency of a Third Reconstruction," *Dissent*, July 9, 2018, https://www.dissentmagazine.org/online_articles/the-urgency-of-a-third-reconstruction.

8. W. Fitzhugh Brundage, introduction to Carole Emberton and Bruce E. Baker, eds., *Remembering Reconstruction: Struggles over the Meaning of America's Most Turbulent Era* (Baton Rouge: Louisiana State Press, 2017), 12. The historical works that do make connections between Reconstruction and the "Conquest of the West" include: Barbara Krauthamer, *Black Slaves, Indian Masters: Slavery, Emancipation, and Citizenship in the Native American South* (Chapel Hill: University of North Carolina Press, 2015); Joseph Genetin-Pilawa, *Crooked Paths to Allotment: The Fight over Federal Indian Policy after the Civil War* (Chapel Hill: University of North Carolina Press, 2014); and Richard Slotkin, *The Fatal Environment: The Myth of the Frontier in the Age of Industrialization, 1800–1890* (Norman: University of Oklahoma Press, 1998).

9. Two major sources for the conceptualization and theorization of *racial capitalism* are Eric Williams, *Capitalism and Slavery* (1944; repr., Chapel Hill: University of North Carolina Press, 1994); and Cedric Robinson, *Black Marxism: The Making of the Black Radical Tradition* (London: Zed Books, 1983). Early in the book, Robinson writes: "As a material force, then, it could be expected that racialism would inevitably permeate the social structures emergent from capitalism. I have used the term 'racial capitalism' to refer to this development and to the subsequent structure as an historical agency," 2–3.

10. Joseph Genetin-Pilawa, "Ely S. Parker and the Paradox of Reconstruction Politics in Indian Country," in *The World the Civil War Made*, ed. Gregory P. Downs and Kate Masur (Chapel Hill: University of North Carolina Press, 2015), 184.

11. Moon-Ho Jung, "*Black Reconstruction* and Empire," *South Atlantic Quarterly* 112, no. 3 (Summer 2013): 465.

12. Vijay Phulwani, "'A Splendid Failure?' *Black Reconstruction* and Du Bois's Tragic Vision of Politics," in *A Political Companion to W.E.B. Du Bois*, ed. Nick Bromell (Lexington: University Press of Kentucky, 2018), 272–273.

13. W. E. B. Du Bois, *Black Reconstruction in America, 1860–1880* (New York: Free Press, 1935), xix.

14. Du Bois, *Black Reconstruction*, 708.

15. See Reginald Stuart, "HBCUs' Mission Rooted in Reconstruction," *Diverse*, February 18, 2016, https://diverseeducation.com/article/81380/; and Matt Stefon, "Historically

Black Colleges and Universities," *Encyclopedia Britannica Online*, accessed August 20, 2020, https://www.britannica.com/topic/historically-black-colleges-and-universities.

16. Du Bois, *Black Reconstruction*, 722.

17. Du Bois, *Black Reconstruction*, 713. Du Bois experienced this dynamic directly when editors removed, as he put it on p. 713, "all my references to Reconstruction" for an article he was asked to write on "the history of the American Negro."

18. For more on the Du Bois/Eastman connection and the UCR as indicative of Black-Indigenous radical connections in the early twentieth century, see Kyle Mays, "Transnational Progressivism: African Americans, Native Americans, and the Universal Races Congress of 1911," *Studies in American Indian Literature* 25, no. 2 (Summer 2013): 241–261.

19. Du Bois, *Black Reconstruction*, 16.

20. Eric Foner, "*Black Reconstruction*: An Introduction," *South Atlantic Quarterly* 112, no. 3 (Summer 2013): 413, 417.

21. For more on the Dawes Act and allotment process and impact, see David Chang, "Enclosures of Land and Sovereignty: The Allotment of American Indian Lands," *Radical History Review* 109 (2010); and David Chang, *The Color of the Land: Race, Nation, and the Politics of Land Ownership in Oklahoma, 1832–1929* (Chapel Hill: University of North Carolina Press, 2010).

22. Sarah Winnemucca, "An Indian Girl's Essay on the Indian Question," *Chicago Tribune*, April 23, 1870. As reprinted in *The Newspaper Warrior: Sarah Winnemucca Hopkin's Campaign for American Indian Rights, 1864–1891*, ed. Cari M. Carpenter and Carolyn Sorisio (Lincoln: University of Nebraska Press, 2015), 39.

23. Layli Long Soldier, "38," in *Whereas* (Minneapolis: Graywolf Press, 2017), 51–52.

24. For more on the Sand Creek Massacre, see Ari Kelman, *A Misplaced Massacre: Struggling over the Memory of Sand Creek* (Cambridge, MA: Harvard University Press, 2015); Gary L. Roberts, *Massacre at Sand Creek: How Methodists Were Involved in an American Tragedy* (Nashville: Abingdon Press, 2015); and Richard Clemmer-Smith, *Report of the John Evans Study Committee*, University of Denver, November 3, 2014, http://portfolio.du.edu/evcomm/page/52699.

25. "Congress Adjourns; Century Afterward, Apology for Wounded Knee Massacre," *New York Times*, October 29, 1990, https://www.nytimes.com/1990/10/29/us/congress-adjourns-century-afterward-apology-for-wounded-knee-massacre.html.

26. Margaret Jacobs, *White Mother to a Dark Race: Settler Colonialism, Maternalism, and the Removal of Indigenous Children in the American West and Australia, 1880–1940* (Lincoln: University of Nebraska Press, 2009), 88–89.

27. Alleen Brown and Nick Estes, "An Untold Number of Indigenous Children Disappeared at U.S. Boarding Schools. Tribal Nations Are Raising the Stakes in Search of Answers," *Intercept*, September 25, 2018, https://theintercept.com/2018/09/25/carlisle-indian-industrial-school-indigenous-children-disappeared/. See also David Wallace Adams, *Education for Extinction: Americans Indians and the Boarding School Experience, 1875–1928* (Lawrence: University Press of Kansas, 1995); Brenda Child, *Boarding School Seasons: American Indian Families, 1900–1940* (Lincoln: University of Nebraska Press, 2000); Jacobs, *White Mother to a Dark Race*; and the section on "Native American Boarding Schools: Family Separation," in Jessica Vasquez-Tokos and Priscilla Yamin, "The Racialization of Privacy: Racial formation as a Family Affair," *Theory and Society*, 2021, https://doi.org/10.1007/s11186-020-09427-9.

28. Du Bois, *Black Reconstruction*, 17.

29. Du Bois, 29.

30. Du Bois, 38.

31. Du Bois, 322.

32. Du Bois, 601.

33. Du Bois, 611.

34. Du Bois, 617.

35. Du Bois, 635.

36. Du Bois, 585.

37. Du Bois, 591.

38. There is a significant historiography on Reconstruction. As a starting point, see Eric Foner, *Reconstruction: America's Unfinished Revolution, 1863–1877* (New York: Harper & Row, 1988); Heather Cox Richardson, *The Death of Reconstruction: Race, Labor, and Politics in the Post-Civil War North, 1865–1901* (Cambridge, MA: Harvard University Press, 2001); Richard M. Valelly, *The Two Reconstructions: The Struggle for Black Enfranchisement* (Chicago: University of Chicago Press, 2004); Thomas J. Brown, ed., *Reconstructions: New Perspectives on the Postbellum United States* (New York: Oxford University Press, 2006); and Allen C. Guelzo, *Reconstruction: A Concise History* (New York: Oxford University Press, 2018).

39. Mishuana Goeman, "Land as Life," in *Native Studies Keywords*, ed. Stephanie Nahelani Teves, Andrea Smith, and Michelle H. Raheja (Tucson: Arizona University Press, 2015), 72.

40. Goeman, "Land as Life," 73, 77.

41. Du Bois, *Black Reconstruction*, 602.

42. "(1865) General William T. Sherman's Special Field Order No. 15," BlackPast, September 29, 2008, https://www.blackpast.org/african-american-history/special-field-orders -no-15/. For more, see Henry Louis Gates Jr., "The Truth behind 'Forty Acres and a Mule,'" *Root*, January 7, 2013, https://www.theroot.com/the-truth-behind-40-acres-and-a-mule -1790894780.

43. Priscilla Yamin, *American Marriage: A Political Institution* (Philadelphia: University of Pennsylvania Press, 2012), 34.

44. Du Bois, *Black Reconstruction*, 673.

45. Du Bois, 35.

46. Du Bois, 43.

47. Hartman, "Comments from the Field," 166

48. Alys Eve Weinbaum, "Gendering the General Strike: W.E.B. Du Bois' *Black Reconstruction* and Black Feminism's 'Propaganda of History,'" *South Atlantic Quarterly* 112, no. 3 (Summer 2013): 444.

49. Alyosha Goldstein, "The Ground Not Given: Colonial Dispositions of Land, Race, and Hunger," *Social Text* 36, no. 2 (June 2018): 85.

50. Robert Nichols, "Theft Is Property! The Recursive Logic of Dispossession," *Political Theory* 46, no. 1 (2018): 22.

51. Nichols, "Theft Is Property!," 14. For the full elaboration of Nichols's vital argument on dispossession, see his book *Theft Is Property: Dispossession and Critical Theory* (Durham, NC: Duke University Press, 2020), especially chap. 1.

52. Brenna Bhandar, *Colonial Lives of Property, Law, Land and Racial Regimes of Ownership* (Durham, NC: Duke University Press, 2018), 193.

53. Du Bois, *Black Reconstruction*, 622.

54. This precise phrasing, "wages of whiteness," is not Du Bois's exact wording but comes from the title and argument of David Roediger's groundbreaking book, which was deeply influenced by Du Bois's work and concept. See David Roediger, *The Wages of Whiteness: Race and the Making of the American Working Class* (New York: Verso, 2007). First published in 1991.

55. Du Bois, *Black Reconstruction*, 700.

56. Du Bois, 700–701.

57. Du Bois, 211–212. For the role of the railroad industry in U.S. imperial expansion, see Manu Karuka, *Empire's Tracks: Indigenous Nations, Chinese Workers, and the Transcontinental Railroad* (Berkeley: University of California Press, 2019).

58. Kerri Leigh Merritt, *Masterless Men: Poor Whites and Slavery in the AnteBellum South* (Cambridge: Cambridge University Press, 2017), 326.

59. Roxanne Dunbar-Ortiz, *An Indigenous Peoples' History of the United States* (Boston: Beacon Press, 2014), 141.

60. Kerri Leigh Merritt, "Land the Roots of African American Poverty," *Aeon*, March 11, 2016, https://aeon.co/ideas/land-and-the-roots-of-african-american-poverty.

61. Du Bois, *Black Reconstruction*, 241.

62. Du Bois, 242.

63. Du Bois, 243.

64. Du Bois, 322.

65. Du Bois, 322.

66. Du Bois, 629.

67. Du Bois, 30.

68. Du Bois, 603.

69. Joanne Barker, "Social Text: Territory as Analytic: The Dispossession of Lenapehoking and the Subprime Crisis," *Social Text* 36, no. 2 (2018): 34.

70. For the perspectives of two Indigenous scholars and writers on the meaning and practices of land relationality, see Leanne Betasamosake Simpson (Michi Saagiig Nishnaabeg), "Land as Pedagogy: Nishnaaabeg Intelligence and Rebellious Transformation," *Decolonization* 3, no. 3 (2014): 1–25; and the concept of *grounded normativity* defined and theorized by Glen Coulthard (Yellowknives Dene) in his book *Red Skin, White Masks: Rejecting the Politics of Colonial Recognition* (Minneapolis: University of Minnesota Press, 2014).

71. For more on *abolition-democracy,* from Du Bois's concept to its modern application, see Du Bois, *Black Reconstruction*, 184–185; Joel Olson, *The Abolition of White Democracy* (Minneapolis: University of Minnesota Press, 2004), chap. 5; Angela Y. Davis, *Abolition Democracy: Beyond Empire, Prisons, and Torture* (New York: Seven Stories Press, 2005); and Allegra M. Mcleod, "Envisioning Abolitionist Democracy," *Harvard Law Review* 132 (April 2019): 1613–1649.

72. Du Bois, *Black Reconstruction*, 603.

73. Treva B. Lindsey, *Colored No More: Reinventing Black Womanhood in Washington D.C.* (Chicago: University of Illinois Press, 2017), 15.

74. Goldstein, "Ground Not Given," 101. In making this argument, Goldstein draws upon Robert Nichols's close and insightful rethinking of the concepts of primitive accumulation,

dispossession, and land theft, in Robert Nichols, "Disaggregating Primitive Accumulation," *Radical Philosophy* 194 (November/December 2015): 18–28.

75. Goldstein, "Ground Not Given," 90.

76. Du Bois, *Black Reconstruction*, 602.

77. Of the more recent, emerging scholarly work and journalistic attention to Black dispossession, see Pete Daniel, *Dispossession: Discrimination against African American Farmers in the Age of Civil Rights* (Chapel Hill: University of North Carolina Press, 2013); Linda Christensen, "Burning Tulsa: The Legacy of Black Dispossession," Zinn Education Project, May 28, 2013, https://www.zinnedproject.org/if-we-knew-our-history/burning-tulsa-the -legacy-of-black-dispossession/; David Love, "From 15 Million Acres to 1 Million: How Black People Lost Their Land," *Atlanta Black Star*, June 30, 2017, https://atlantablackstar .com/2017/06/30/from-15-million-acres-to-1-million-how-black-people-lose-their-land/; Andrew W. Kahrl, "Black People's Land Was Stolen," *New York Times*, June 20, 2019, https:// www.nytimes.com/2019/06/20/opinion/sunday/reparations-hearing.html.

78. Jodi Melamed, "Racial Capitalism," *Critical Ethnic Studies* 1, no. 1 (Spring 2015): 83, 84.

79. For an important examination of the need to address the role of Asian racialization in relationship to and constitutive of the imbrication of settler colonialism and racial capitalism, see Iyko Day, *Alien Capital: Asian Racialization and the Logic of Settler Colonialism* (Chapel Hill: University of North Carolina Press, 2016).

80. For more on this issue of the history, status, and struggles faced by the "freedmen" of the Cherokee and other Indigenous nations that owned slaves, recommended works to see include Tiya Miles, *Ties That Bind: The Story of an Afro-Cherokee Family in Slavery and Freedom* (Oakland: University of California Press, 2006); Circe Sturm, "Blood Politics, Racial Classification, and Cherokee National Identity: The Trials and Tribulations of the Cherokee Freedmen," *American Indian Quarterly* 22, no. 1–2 (Winter/Spring 1998): 230–259; Circe Sturm, *Blood Politics: Race, Culture, and Identity in the Cherokee Nation of Oklahoma* (Berkeley: University of California Press, 2002); the documentary *By Blood*, directed by Marcos Barbery and Sam Russell (Outcast Films, 2015); and Jack Healy, "Black, Native American and Fighting for Recognition in Indian Country," *New York Times*, September 8, 2020, https://www.nytimes.com/2020/09/08/us/enslaved-people-native-americans -oklahoma.html.

81. For more on the buffalo soldiers understood in the context of the long history of African Americans in the West, see Quintard Taylor, *In Search of the Racial Frontier: African Americans in the West: 1528–1990* (New York: W. W. Norton, 1999), chap. 6.

82. Robert N. Clinton, "Treaties with Native Nations: Iconic Historical Realities or Modern Necessity?," in *Nation to Nation: Treaties between the United States and American Indian Nations*, ed. Suzan Shown Harjo (Washington, DC: National Museum of the American Indian, Smithsonian Books, 2014), 23; and on the Oceti Sakowin, see Nick Estes, *Our History Is the Future: Standing Rock versus the Dakota Access Pipeline, and the Long Tradition of Indigenous Resistance* (New York: Verso, 2019), 2–3.

83. Frederick E. Hoxie, ed., *Encyclopedia of North American Indians* (Boston: Houghton Mifflin, 1996), 647.

84. Estes, *Our History*, 109.

85. For more on this, see Estes, *Our History*, 107–110.

86. See Maria Streshinsky, "Saying No to $1 Billion: Why the Impoverished Sioux Nation Won't Take Federal Money," *Atlantic*, March 2011, https://www.theatlantic.com/magazine /archive/2011/03/saying-no-to-1-billion/308380/; "For Great Sioux Nation: Black Hills Can't Be Bought for $1.3 Billion," *PBS NewsHour*, August 24, 2011, https://www.pbs.org /newshour/show/why-the-sioux-are-refusing-1-3-billion; and Brandon Ecoffey, "The Black Hills Are NOT FOR SALE," *Lakota Times*, October 12, 2017, https://www.lakotatimes.com /articles/the-black-hills-are-not-for-sale-2/.

87. General William T. Sherman's Special Field Order No. 15.

88. Adrienne Monteith Petty, "African Americans and the Enduring Quest for Land" (paper presented at the Future of the African American Past conference, Washington, DC, May 19–21, 2016). https://futureafampast.si.edu/sites/default/files/004_Petty%20Adrienne.pdf.

89. Monteith Petty, "African Americans," 8–9.

90. Nik Heynen, "Toward an Abolitionist Ecology," *Abolition* 1, no. 1 (2018): 246.

91. Kendra Field, *Growing Up with the Country: Family, Race, and Nation after the Civil War* (New Haven, CT: Yale University Press, 2018), 22.

92. Field, *Growing Up*, 120.

93. Field, 13.

94. Black/Land Project, accessed July 15, 2019, http://www.blacklandproject.org/.

95. Quoted in Eve Tuck, Allison Guess, and Hannah Sultan, "Not Nowhere: Collaborating on Selfsame Land," *Decolonization*, June 2014, 7.

96. Lindsey, *Colored No More*, 2.

Chapter Three

1. I draw from two versions of this piece, both almost identical, save a word of difference here and there. The textual version is James Baldwin, "The White Problem," in *The Cross of Redemption: Uncollected Writings*, ed. Randall Keenan (New York: Vintage International, 2011), 93. A recording of his speech can be located at James Baldwin, "Free and Brave: James Baldwin Talks about American History from the Negro View," 1963, recorded by Lorenz Graham, Second Baptist Church, Los Angeles, broadcast on KPFA, May 10, 1963.

2. Baldwin, "White Problem," 93.

3. James Baldwin and Audre Lorde, "Revolutionary Hope: A Conversation between James Baldwin and Audre Lorde," *Culture*, accessed June 20, 2020, http://theculture .forharriet.com/2014/03/revolutionary-hope-conversation-between.html. First published in *Essence* magazine, 1984.

4. James Baldwin, "Here Be Dragons," in *The Price of the Ticket: Collected Nonfiction: 1948–1985* (New York: St. Martin's/Marek, 1985), 678.

5. Jesmyn Ward, "Introduction," in *The Fire This Time: A New Generation Speaks about Race*, ed. Jesmyn Ward (New York: Scribner, 2016), 7–8, 9.

6. Eddie Glaude, *Begin Again: James Baldwin's America and Its Urgent Lessons for Our Own* (New York: Penguin, 2020), 19.

7. Susan McWilliams, introduction to *A Political Companion to James Baldwin*, ed. Susan McWilliams (Lexington: University Press of Kentucky, 2017), 1, 2.

8. James Baldwin, debate with William F. Buckley Jr., Cambridge University, 1965, YouTube video, https://www.youtube.com/watch?v=oFeoS41xe7w. For a transcript, see "The

American Dream and the American Negro," *New York Times*, March 7, 1965, https://www .nytimes.com/images/blogs/papercuts/baldwin-and-buckley.pdf. For an insightful history and analysis of this debate between Baldwin and Buckley, see Nicholas Buccola, *The Fire Is upon Us: James Baldwin, William Buckley Jr., and the Debate over Race in America* (Princeton, NJ: Princeton University Press, 2019).

9. Baldwin describes two such incidents, one when he was thirteen in midtown Manhattan and a cop said to him, "Why don't you niggers stay uptown where you belong?" and another when he was ten, and two cops harassed him, mocked him, beat him up, and left him flat on "his back in an empty Harlem lot," in "Down at the Cross: Letter from a Region in My Mind," in *The Fire Next Time* (New York: Vintage Press, 1963), 19, 20.

10. Kyle Mays, "Indigenous Genocide and Black Liberation: A Short Critique of I Am Not Your Negro—with Love," *Indian Country Today*, February 24, 2017, https://indiancountry medianetwork.com/news/opinions/indigenous-genocide-black-liberation-short-critique -not-negro-love/.

11. "James Baldwin Interviewed, John Hall/1970," in *Conversations with James Baldwin*, ed. Fred L. Standley and Louis H. Pratt (Jackson: University Press of Mississippi, 1989), 99–100. First published in *Transatlantic Review*, Autumn–Winter 1970–1971, 37–38.

12. Baldwin engaged in the same rhetorical move during a 1969 appearance, along with Betty Shabazz, before a House select subcommittee concerning a House of Representatives bill to "establish a national commission on 'Negro History and Culture.'" During questioning by Congressman William Hathaway on how to address racial inequality and injustice, Baldwin stated: "Yes. Let me get a job, allow me the right to protect my women, my house, my children. That is all the Negro wants: his autonomy. Nobody hates you. The time is gone for that. I simply want to live my life." James Baldwin, "The Nigger We Invent," in Keenan, *Cross of Redemption*, 116.

13. Dwight McBride, "Can the Queen Speak? Racial Essentialism, Sexuality, and the Problem of Authority," *Callaloo* 22, no. 2 (March 1998): 376.

14. McBride, "Can the Queen Speak?," 378.

15. McBride, 377.

16. Brittney Cooper, *Beyond Respectability: The Intellectual Thought of Race Women* (Urbana: University of Illinois Press, 2017), 121.

17. Marlon Ross, "Baldwin's Sissy Heroics," *African American Review* 46, no. 4 (Winter 2013): 633.

18. Ross, "Baldwin's Sissy Heroics," 636.

19. James Baldwin, *No Name in the Street* (New York: Vintage International, 1972), 61.

20. Baldwin, *No Name in the Street*, 61.

21. Baldwin, 63, 62.

22. Ross, "Baldwin's Sissy Heroics," 647.

23. Scott Lauria Morgensen, *Spaces between Us: Queer Settler Colonialism and Indigenous Decolonization* (Minneapolis: University of Minnesota Press, 2011), 31.

24. Maile Arvin, Eve Tuck, and Angie Morrill, "Decolonizing Feminism: Challenging Connections between Settler Colonialism and Heteropatriarchy," *Feminist Formations* 25, no. 1 (Spring 2013): 14–15.

25. Lee Maracle, *I am Woman: A Native Perspective on Sociology and Feminism* (Richmond, BC: Press Gang, 1996), 93.

26. Joanne Barker, introduction to *Critically Sovereign: Indigenous Gender, Sexuality, and Feminist Studies*, ed. Joanne Barker (Durham, NC: Duke University Press, 2017), 3.

27. Baldwin and Lorde, "Revolutionary Hope."

28. James Baldwin, "A Talk to Teachers" (speech, October 16, 1963, as "The Negro Child—His Self-Image"). Originally published in the *Saturday Review*, December 21, 1963, and reprinted in Baldwin, *Price of the Ticket*, 330.

29. Baldwin, "Down at the Cross," 84–85.

30. Eve Tuck and K. Wayne Yang, "Decolonization Is Not a Metaphor," *Decolonization* 1, no. 1 (2012): 22–23.

31. James Baldwin, "The International War Crimes Tribunal: Reader's Forum, *Freedomways*," in Keenan, *Cross of Redemption*, 248. Originally written in 1967.

32. Baldwin, "On Language, Race, and the Black Writer," in Keenan, *Cross of Redemption*, 141.

33. James Baldwin, "On Being White . . . and Other Lies," in Keenan, *Cross of Redemption*, 167–168.

34. Baldwin, "On Being White," 170.

35. Lisa Beard, "James Baldwin on Violence and Disavowal," in McWilliams, *Political Companion to James Baldwin*, 343.

36. Baldwin, "Down at the Cross," 104.

37. Baldwin, 23.

38. Vine Deloria Jr., *Custer Died for Your Sins: An Indian Manifesto* (Norman: University of Oklahoma Press, 1968), 189.

39. Vine Deloria Jr.'s work is the centerpiece for my argument in "Between Civil Rights and Decolonization: The Claim for Postcolonial Nationhood," in *The Third Space of Sovereignty: The Postcolonial Politics of U.S.-Indigenous Relations* (Minneapolis: University of Minnesota Press, 2007), 123–169. For a more recent, comprehensive, and insightful elaboration and analysis of Deloria's work in the context of the politics of his time period, see David Martínez, *Life of the Indigenous Mind: Vine Deloria Jr. and the Birth of the Red Power Movement* (Omaha: University of Nebraska Press, 2019).

40. Moon-Kie Jung, *Beneath the Surface of White Supremacy* (Stanford, CA: Stanford University Press, 2015), 180.

41. Jung, *Beneath the Surface*, 182.

42. Lawrie Balfour, *James Baldwin and the Promise of American Democracy* (Ithaca, NY: Cornell University Press, 2001), 138.

43. Balfour, *James Baldwin*, 112.

44. Jack Turner, *Awakening to Race: Individual and Social Consciousness in America* (Chicago: University of Chicago Press, 2012), 98.

45. Turner, *Awakening to Race*, 117.

46. Deloria, *Custer Died*, 194.

47. Baldwin, "White Problem," 91–92.

48. Mishuana Goeman, "Ongoing Storms and Struggles: Gendered Violence and Resource Exploitation," in Barker, *Critically Sovereign*, 113.

49. James Baldwin, "My Dungeon Shook: Letter to My Nephew on the One Hundredth Anniversary of the Emancipation," in *Fire Next Time*, 6.

50. James Baldwin, "Theater: The Negro In and Out," in Keenan, *Cross of Redemption*, 27.

51. George Shulman, *American Prophecy: Race and Redemption in American Political Culture* (Minneapolis: University of Minnesota Press, 2008), 134.

52. Baldwin, "My Dungeon Shook," 92.

53. Deloria, *Custer Died*, 195.

54. James Baldwin, "The White Man's Guilt," in *Collected Essays*, ed. Toni Morrison (New York: Library of America, 1998), 722–723.

55. "James Baldwin: How to Cool It: The Landmark 1968 Q&A on race in America," August 2, 2017, *Esquire*, https://www.esquire.com/news-politics/a23960/james-baldwin-cool-it/. First published in July 1968.

56. Shulman, *American Prophecy*, 148.

57. James Baldwin, "Stranger in the Village," in *Notes of a Native Son* (1954; repr., Boston: Beacon Street Books, 2012), 167.

58. Deloria, *Custer Died*, 174–175.

59. Baldwin, debate with Buckley, 1965.

60. Baldwin, "White Man's Guilt," 723.

61. James Baldwin, interview by Frank Shantz, 1973, transcript, "John Brown's Body: James Baldwin and Frank Shantz in Conversation," *Transition* 81/82 (2000): 258.

62. P. J. Brendese, "The Race of a More Perfect Union: James Baldwin, Segregated Memory, and the Presidential Race," in McWilliams, *Political Companion to James Baldwin*, 50.

63. Brendese, "Race of a More Perfect Union," 50, 51.

64. Brendese, 76.

65. Baldwin, "John Brown's Body," 258–259. By "had," it seems likely that Baldwin meant "kept," as in kept the promises of the treaty.

66. Baldwin, "White Man's Guilt," 409.

67. For a political history of this particular period in Indigenous radical politics, see Paul Chaat Smith and Robert Warrior, *Like a Hurricane: The Indian Movement from Alcatraz to Wounded Knee* (New York: New Press, 1996).

68. Deloria, *Custer Died*, 51.

69. "Are We on the Edge of Civil War? David Frost/1970," in Standley and Pratt, *Conversations with James Baldwin*, 95–96. Originally published in *The Americans* (New York: Stein and Day, 1970).

70. Baldwin and Lorde, "Revolutionary Hope."

71. Maracle, *I Am Woman*, 138, 139.

72. "James Baldwin, an Interview. Wolfgang Binder/1980," in Standley and Pratt, *Conversations with James Baldwin*, 192–193.

73. Lawrie Balfour, personal communication. Thanks to Lawrie Balfour for calling attention to the exceptionalist tone of Baldwin's remarks here.

74. For the concept of *chain of equivalence*, see Ernesto Laclau, *On Populist Reason* (London: Verso, 2005).

75. "Baldwin, an Interview," 200.

Chapter Four

1. Erik Stegman and Victoria Phillips, *Missing the Point: The Real Impact of Native Mascots and Team Names on American Indian and Alaska Native Youth* (Washington, DC: Center for

American Progress, 2014), http://www.americanprogress.org/events/2014/07/14/93821 /missing-the-point-the-real-impact-of-native-mascots-and-team-names-on-american-indian -and-alaska-native-youth/.

2. Stegman and Phillips, *Missing the Point*.

3. In this chapter, I will most often refer to the Washington NFL name as the "team name"—and in fact since the announcement in July 2020 that the team would no longer use their R-word name the team is now officially called the "Washington football team." However, when I do mention the name, I write it as the "Redsk*ns" to mark the denigrating nature of the word. The only times in the chapter that I do not mark it with an * is when I am directly quoting someone. I do this because, for example, I do not want to convey that people such as Washington team owner Dan Snyder deem the word to be denigrating, and inserting the asterisk-marked form may give that impression.

4. David Waldstein and Michael S. Schmidt, "Cleveland's Baseball Team Will Drop Its Indian Team Name," *New York Times*, December 13, 2020, https://www.nytimes.com/2020 /12/13/sports/baseball/cleveland-indians-baseball-name-change.html?smid=fb-share &fbclid=IwAR1CRSvQisvyl7je7WettlNABqPGmqRh34ngATv30i-Yzhx4D74YeP06BUU.

5. Just as a snapshot of the political work these four women have done: Suzan Shown Harjo has engaged in movement organizing and legal cases for decades on this and many other matters of concern to Indigenous peoples and sued the NFL over the team's name in Pro-Football, Inc. v. Suzan Shown Harjo et al. (2005), https://www.greenamerica.org/investing -can-change-world/something-means-justice-interview-suzan-shown-harjo. In a case building out of and with the Harjo case, Amanda Blackhorse was the lead plaintiff in Blackhorse v. Pro-Football, Inc. (2015), which challenged the trademark status of the Washington team name. For more, see https://acluva.org/en/cases/pro-football-inc-v-blackhorse; https:// www.scotusblog.com/case-files/cases/pro-football-inc-v-blackhorse/; also listen to an interview with Blackhorse on the *Red Nation Power Hour* at https://soundcloud.com/there dnationpod/teaser-red-power-hour-launch-w. Jacqueline Keeler is an activist and radical journalist who cofounded the organization Eradicating Offensive Native Mascotry, which also coined the hashtag #NotYourMascot. Keeler writes on the misrepresentation of this issue in the wider political culture. See, for example, https://www.thenation.com/article /archive/on-the-shameful-and-skewed-redskins-poll/. Jody TallBear successfully sued the U.S. Department of Energy for damages for the display of the Washington football team's name in the workplace; see https://www.nativesunnews.today/articles/tallbear-wins-lawsuit -against-department-of-energy/; and https://www.indianz.com/News/2020/05/12/native-sun -news-today-it-was-all-about-t.asp.

6. For a map listing the hundreds of examples of mascots at the high school, college, and professional level in the United States, with details of their status, see the Native American Mascot Database, accessed February 28, 2019, https://nativeamericanmascotdatabase.com/. For another source of the many examples of mascotry across the United States, see MascotDB, https://www.mascotdb.com/lists/native-american-related-mascots. Thanks to Ellen Staurowsky, professor of sports management at Drexel University, for recommending this resource.

7. For more on racial liberalism, especially concerning its function in cultural contexts and the emergence of liberal multiculturalism, see Jodi Melamed, *Represent and Destroy: Rationalizing Violence in the New Racial Capitalism* (Minneapolis: University of Minnesota Press,

2011), especially chap. 1 and chap. 2. For a political theory and intellectual history perspective, see Charles Mills, *Black Rights, White Wrongs: A Critique of Racial Liberalism* (Oxford: Oxford University Press, 2017).

8. Ives Goddard, "I Am a Red-Skin: The Adoption of a Native American Expression (1769–1826)," *Native American Studies* 19, no. 2 (2005): 1.

9. *Winona Daily Republican*, September 23, 1863, Thursday evening ed. See Colette Routel, "Minnesota Bounties on Dakota Men during the U.S.-Dakota War" (Legal Studies Research Papers, paper no, 2013-01, William Mitchell College of Law, Saint Paul, MN, October 1863).

10. Gordon J. Hylton, "Before the Redskins Were the Redskins: The Use of Native American Team Names in the Formative Era of American Sports, 1857–1933," *North Dakota Law Review* 86 (2010): 895.

11. Theodore Roosevelt, "The Struggle for Self-Determination: First Annual Message, 1901," December 3, 1901, Digital History, ID 720, accessed January 4, 2015, http://www.digitalhistory.uh.edu/disp_textbook.cfm?smtid=3&psid=720.

12. See Russell Thornton, *American Indian Holocaust and Survival: A Population History since 1492* (Norman: University of Oklahoma Press, 1987).

13. For more, see Gary C. Stein, "The Indian Citizenship Act of 1924," *New Mexico Historical Review* 72, no. 3 (1972): 252–274; and Kevin Bruyneel, "Challenging American Boundaries: Indigenous People and the 'Gift' of U.S. Citizenship," *Studies in American Political Development* 18, no. 1 (2004): 30–43.

14. For a documentary that places the Indian team name and mascot issue into rigorous and insightful historical and political context, see *More than a Word*, directed by John Little and Kenn Little (Northampton, MA: Media Education Foundation, 2017).

15. C. Richard King, *Redskins: Insult and Brand* (Lincoln: University of Nebraska, 2016), 24.

16. Jennifer Guiliano, "Gendered Discourse: Higher Education, Mascots, and Race," in *The Native American Mascot Controversy: A Handbook*, ed. C. Richard King (Lanham, MD: Scarecrow Press, 2010), 41–45; and Jennifer Guiliano, *Indian Spectacle: College Mascots and the Anxiety of Modern America* (New Brunswick, NJ: Rutgers University Press, 2015).

17. Hylton, "Before the Redskins," 888; and Linda M. Waggoner, "On Trial: The Washington R*dskins' Wily Mascot: Coach William 'Lone Star' Dietz," *Montana: The Magazine of Western History* (Spring 2013): 1.

18. Hylton, "Before the Redskins," 888–889.

19. Hylton, 902.

20. Alex Park, "That Time Nazis Marched to 'Keep Redskins White,'" *Mother Jones*, November 7, 2013, https://www.motherjones.com/politics/2013/11/nazis-desegregating-washington-nfl-football-team/.

21. Thomas Smith, *Showdown: JFK and the Integration of the Washington Redskins* (Boston: Beacon Press, 2011).

22. See "Indigenous Tribes of Washington, D.C.," American Library Association, http://www.ala.org/aboutala/indigenous-tribes-washington-dc. Major credit for work on this overview goes to Donavan Begay (Diné).

23. Theresa Vargas and Annys Shin, "President Obama Says, 'I'd Think about Changing' Name of Washington Redskins," *Washington Post*, October 5, 2013, http://www.washingtonpost.com/local/president-obama-says-id-think-about-changing-name-of-washington-redskins/2013/10/05/e170b914-2b70-11e3-8ade-a1f23cda135e_story.html.

24. Roy Hallbritter, "The 'N-Word' and the 'R-Word,'" *Huffington Post*, February 28, 2014, http://www.huffingtonpost.com/ray-halbritter/the-n-word-and-the-r-word_b_4877660.html.

25. U.S. Senate, "Letter to NFL Commissioner Roger Goodell," Washington, DC, May 21, 2014.

26. Dan Steinberg, "AP Finds Support for Redskins Name," *Washington Post*, May 3, 2013, http://www.washingtonpost.com/blogs/dc-sports-bog/wp/2013/05/03/ap-poll-finds-support-for-redskins-name-redskins-com-rejoices/.

27. Robert Nichols, "Contract and Usurpation: Enfranchisement and Racial Governance in Settler-Colonial Contexts," in *Theorizing Native Studies*, ed. Audra Simpson and Andrea Smith (Durham, NC: Duke University Press, 2014), 103.

28. Nichols, "Contract and Usurpation," 113.

29. To view this image, see Regina F. Graham, "Racism of Sports Logos Put into Context by American Indian Group," CBS Cleveland, October 8, 2013, http://cleveland.cbslocal.com/2013/10/08/racism-of-sports-logos-put-into-context-by-american-indian-group/.

30. Jordan Baston, "Indians to Stop Using Wahoo Logo Starting in '19," MLB Advanced Media, January 29, 2018, https://www.mlb.com/news/indians-to-stop-using-chief-wahoo-logo/c-265489544.

31. "Cleveland Team Name FAQs," MLB Advanced Media, accessed December 30, 2020, https://www.mlb.com/indians/fans/cleteamname/faqs. My thanks to Professor Laurel Davis-Delano for sharing this information and link to the ever-so-valuable "Scholars of Native Stereotypes" email listserv that Davis-Delano established and manages.

32. For more on this dynamic as it concerns the commodification and consumption of stereotypical Indigenous identities in the U.S. marketplace, see Jason Edward Black, "The 'Mascotting' of Native America: Construction, Commodity, and Assimilation," *American Indian Quarterly* 26, no. 4 (Fall 2012): 613.

33. Dan Snyder, "Letter from Washington Redskins Owner Dan Snyder to Fans," *Washington Post*, October 9, 2013, http://www.washingtonpost.com/local/letter-from-washington-redskins-owner-dan-snyder-to-fans/2013/10/09/e7670ba0-30fe-11e3-8627-c5d7de0a046b_story.html.

34. Jean M. O'Brien, *Firsting and Lasting: Writing Indians out of Existence in New England* (Minneapolis: University of Minnesota Press, 2010), xxii–xxiii.

35. O'Brien, *Firsting and Lasting*, 57.

36. Roger Goodell, "Letter to Congressman Cole and Congresswoman McCollum," *Indian Country Today*, June 5, 2013, http://indiancountrytodaymedianetwork.com/2013/06/11/nfl-commissioner-tells-congress-redskins-positive-name-149843.

37. Dan Steinberg, "Daniel Snyder: 'A Redskin Is a Football Player. A Redskin Is Our Fans,'" *Washington Post*, August 5, 2014, http://www.washingtonpost.com/blogs/dc-sports-bog/wp/2014/08/05/daniel-snyder-a-redskin-is-a-football-player-a-redskin-is-our-fans/.

38. Redskinsfacts, archived January 4, 2019, https://webarchive.loc.gov/all/20190104031016/http://www.redskinsfacts.com/ (emphasis in original).

39. Philip J. Deloria, *Playing Indian* (New Haven, CT: Yale University Press, 1998), 191.

40. Stephanie Fryberg, Hazel Rose Markus, Daphna Oyserman, and Joseph M. Stone, "Of Warrior Chiefs and Indian Princesses: The Psychological Consequences of American Indian Mascots," *Basic and Applied Social Psychology* 30, no. 3 (2008): 216.

41. Eric Lott, *Love and Theft: Blackface Minstrelsy and the American Working Class* (Oxford: Oxford University Press, 1993).

42. While blackface minstrelsy is not publicly defended in the way in which we see with Indian mascotry, a 2019 Pew survey found that 34 percent of respondents and 39 percent of white people feel it is "always or sometimes acceptable" to wear blackface for a Halloween costume. See Anna Brown, "About a Third of Americans Say Blackface in a Halloween Costume Is Acceptable at Least Sometimes," Pew Research Center, February 11, 2019, http://www.pewresearch.org/fact-tank/2019/02/11/about-a-third-of-americans-say-blackface-in-a-halloween-costume-is-acceptable-at-least-sometimes/.

43. For an insightful discussion of the relationship between redface and blackface, listen to an interview with Jacqueline Keeler, "The Unbearable Whiteness of Being in Black- and Red-Face, with Monthly Co-host Jacqueline Keeler," *Wednesday Talk Radio*, KBOO, February 13, 2019, https://kboo.fm/media/71166-unbearable-whiteness-being-black-and-red-face-monthly-co-host-jacqueline-keeler.

44. Chris Burke, "NFL Competition Committee Passes on N-word Rule, Considers Extra Point Changes," *Sports Illustrated*, March 19, 2014, http://www.si.com/nfl/audibles/2014/03/19/nfl-competition-committee-passes-on-n-word-rule-considers-extra-point-changes.

45. Simon Moya-Smith, "NFL May Throw Flag on N-word, but What about the 'R-word'?," Comedy Central, February 26, 2014, http://www.cnn.com/2014/02/25/opinion/moya-smith-nfl-flag-r-word/.

46. King, *Redskins*, 82.

47. M. H. Mazetti, "Behind the Hunt for Bin Laden," *New York Times*, May 2, 2011, http://www.nytimes.com/2011/05/03/world/asia/03intel.html?hp&_r=0.

48. Barack Obama, "Perfecting Our Union: The President of the United States Reflects on What Abraham Lincoln Means to Him, and to America," *Atlantic*, December 2011.

49. Barack Obama, "Presidential Proclamation—150th Anniversary of the Emancipation Proclamation," Office of the Press Secretary, White House, December 31, 2012, http://www.whitehouse.gov/the-press-office/2012/12/31/presidential-proclamation-150th-anniversary-emancipation-proclamation.

50. David Martinez, "Remembering the Thirty-Eight: Abraham Lincoln, the Dakota, and the U.S. War on Barbarism," *Wicazo Sa Review* 28, no. 2 (Fall 2013): 6.

51. Obama, "Presidential Proclamation."

52. Layli Long Soldier, "38," in *Whereas* (Minneapolis: Graywolf Press, 2017), 49. For an excellent analysis of the absence and presence of Indigeneity in the movie *Lincoln*, see Mark Rifkin's "The Silence of Ely S. Parker: The Emancipation Sublime and the Limits of Settler Memory," *NAIS* 2 (Fall 2014): 1–43.

53. For more on the meaning and impact of bin Laden's death for the nation, as a "temporary feeling of relief," see Elisabeth R. Anker, *Orgies of Feeling: Melodrama and the Politics of Freedom* (Durham, NC: Duke University Press, 2014), 250–251. For the link between settler colonial anti-Indian violence and U.S. imperial violence and actions, in the bin Laden example and beyond, see Nikhil Pal Singh, *Race and America's Long War* (Berkeley: University of California Press), 16.

54. Winona LaDuke, "Native American Activist Winona LaDuke on Use of 'Geronimo' as Code for Osama bin Laden: The Continuation of the Wars against Indigenous People," *Democracy Now*, interview by Amy Goodman, May 6, 2011.

55. N. Tucker, "American Indians Object to 'Geronimo' as Code for Bin Laden Raid," *Washington Post*, May 3, 2011, http://www.washingtonpost.com/lifestyle/style/american -indians-object-to-geronimo-as-code-name-for-bin-laden-raid/2011/05/03/AF2FZIjF _story.html.

Chapter Five

1. For the transcript and video with these quotations, see Tim Haines, "President Trump to Naval Academy Graduates: Cynics and Critics Are Trying to Tear Down America," *RealClearPolitics*, May 25, 2018, https://www.realclearpolitics.com/video/2018/05/25/president _trump_to_naval_academy_graduates_cynics_and_critics_are_trying_to_tear_down _america.html.

2. Samuel Sinyangwe, Twitter, May 25, 2018, https://twitter.com/samswey/status/1000 139766250209280?ref_src=twsrc%5Etfw%7Ctwcamp%5Etweetembed&ref_url=https%3A% 2F%2Fd-23232008591874474248.ampproject.net%2F1907301630320%2Fframe.html; see also Greg Evans, "People Have Noticed Something Worrying about Trump's 'Tamed a Continent' Speech," *Indy100*, May 25, 2018, https://www.indy100.com/article/donald-trump-us -president-ancestors-native-americans-speech-tamed-continent-8371421.

3. Glenn Thrush, "Full Transcript: President Trump's National Convention Speech," *New York Times*, August 28, 2020, https://www.nytimes.com/2020/08/28/us/politics/trump-rnc -speech-transcript.html.

4. For more on the complex and at times even multiracial assemblage comprising contemporary white nationalism and the movements of the New Right, see Daniel Martinez HoSang and Joseph E. Lowndes, *Producers, Parasites, Patriots: Race and the New Right-Wing Politics of Precarity* (Minneapolis: University of Minnesota Press, 2019).

5. Adam Sewer, "The Cruelty Is the Point," *Atlantic*, October 3, 2018, https://www .theatlantic.com/ideas/archive/2018/10/the-cruelty-is-the-point/572104/.

6. For the structural background and role of the police that can help explain the difference in their response at the Capitol from their approaches to other movements, such as those of Black Lives Matter and Indigenous peoples, see Debra Thompson, "The Insurrection in Washington Shows Police Decide Who to Protect and Serve," *Globe and Mail*, January 8, 2021, https://www.theglobeandmail.com/opinion/article-the-insurrection-in-washington-sh ows-police-decide-who-to-protect-and/?fbclid=IwAR0SftwlgO02ZE4kdz-75RlCUUOB _1NgcYLcoQ-iYSlUF3bqqRJzgHFyLs8; see also the interview with Alex Vitale, author of *The End of Policing* (New York: Verso, 2017); Leah Donnella and Alex Vitale, "How the Storming of the Capitol Was—and Wasn't—about Police," *Code Switch*, January 7, 2021, https:// www.npr.org/sections/codeswitch/2021/01/07/613802462/how-the-storming-of-the -capitol-was-and-wasnt-about-police. Also, for one example of the treatment by police and state forces of Indigenous activists at Standing Rock in comparison to that of the settler insurrectionists at the Capitol, see Dalton Walker, "Use of Force: Capitol vs. Standing Rock," *Indian Country Today*, January 6, 2021, https://indiancountrytoday.com/news/use-of-force -capitol-vs-standing-rock-etPN-ehSKoCf3skTv6tWrQ.

7. Cristina Beltrán, *Cruelty as Citizenship: How Migrant Suffering Sustains White Democracy* (Minneapolis: University of Minnesota Press, 2020), 41–42.

8. Leigh Patel, "Trump and Settler Colonialism," *CTheory: Consequence* 2, December 1, 2017, http://ctheory.net/ctheory_wp/trump-and-settler-colonialism/.

9. Rita Dhamoon, "A Feminist Approach to Decolonizing Anti-racism: Rethinking Transnationalism, Intersectionality, and Settler Colonialism," *Feral Feminisms*, no. 4 (Summer 2015): 32.

10. I thank Mark Rifkin for his clarification on the precise form of the stanza.

11. Jodi Dean, "Trump, Candidate of Truth," *I Cite*, August 10, 2015, https://jdeanicite .typepad.com/i_cite/2015/08/index.html.

12. John Breech, "Donald Trump Says the Washington Redskins Should Keep Their Name," CBS Sports, October 5, 2015, https://www.cbssports.com/nfl/news/donald-trump-says -the-washington-redskins-should-keep-their-name/.

13. Max Greenwood, "Trump Hangs Portrait of Andrew Jackson in Oval Office," *Hill*, January 25, 2017, http://thehill.com/homenews/administration/316115-trump-hangs-portrait -of-andrew-jackson-in-oval-office.

14. Joseph Lowndes, "Trump and the Populist Presidency," in *Populism in Global Perspective: A Performative and Discursive Approach*, ed. Benjamin Moffitt, Pierre Ostiguy, and Francisco Panizza (New York: Routledge, 2020): 122.

15. "Slavery: Understanding the Other Families at the Hermitage," *Hermitage*, accessed March 15, 2019, https://thehermitage.com/learn/mansion-grounds/slavery/.

16. For more on Jackson and his view of and relationship toward Indigenous peoples, see Michael Paul Rogin's fundamental work, *Father and Children: Andrew Jackson and the Subjugation of the Indian* (1975; repr. New Brunswick, NJ: Transaction, 1991).

17. Adrienne Keene, "How I Feel as a Native Woman When Trump Idolizes Andrew Jackson," *Teen Vogue*, April 19, 2017, https://www.teenvogue.com/story/andrew-jackson -native-woman-idolize-donald-trump.

18. For more on Jackson's role in the Trail of Tears and his connection to Trump, see Bruce Johansen, "Commentary: Donald Trump, Andrew Jackson, Lebensraum, and Manifest Destiny," *American Indian Culture and Research Journal* 4, no. 4 (2017): 115–122.

19. Keene, "How I Feel." Also, for more on the connections between Trump and Jackson as analyzed from the perspective of an Indigenous scholar, see Cutcha Risling Baldy (Hoopa Valley Tribe), "Andrew Jackson (AKA Donald Trump) Is President Once Again . . . Now What?," *Sometimes Writer-Blogger* (blog), November 11, 2016, https://www.cutcharislingbaldy .com/blog/andrew-jackson-aka-donald-trump-is-president-once-again-now-what-or-i-cant -guarantee-that-this-blog-entry-wont-just-devolve-into-a-bunch-of-angry-face-emojis.

20. Juliet Elperin and Brady Dennis, "Trump Administration to Approve Final Permit for Dakota Access Pipeline," *Washington Post*, February 7, 2017, https://www.washingtonpost .com/news/energy-environment/wp/2017/02/07/trump-administration-to-approve-final -permit-for-dakota-access-pipeline/?utm_term=.4389ba2abe35.

21. Nick Estes, *Our History Is the Future* (London: Verso, 2019), 64. Also, while the Trump administration did approve the pipeline, this should not be simply read as indicating that the Standing Rock/NoDAPL movement failed. For a complex and insightful sense of the historical context and political implications and impact of the movement, see Elizabeth Ellis, "Centering Sovereignty: How Standing Rock Changed the Conversation," in *Standing with Standing Rock: Voices from the #NoDAPL Movement*, ed. Nick Estes and Jaskiran Dhillon (Minneapolis: University of Minnesota Press, 2019): 172–197.

22. Adam Vaughn, "How Keystone XL, the Pipeline Rejected by Obama, Went Ahead under Trump," *Guardian*, March 24, 2017, https://www.theguardian.com/environment/2017/mar/24/keystone-xl-pipeline-approval-timeline-obama-trump.

23. Adam Wernick, "Judge Halts Keystone XL Pipeline, Citing 'Complete Disregard' for Climate," Public Radio International, December 12, 2018, https://www.pri.org/stories/2018-12-12/judge-halts-keystone-xl-pipeline-citing-complete-disregard-climate; and Nicholas Kusnetz, "Trump Aims to Speed Pipeline Projects by Limiting State Environmental Reviews," *Inside Climate News*, April 11, 2019, https://insideclimatenews.org/news/11042019/trump-pipeline-executive-order-environmental-review-keystone-xl-clean-water-act-states-rights.

24. John Dougherty, "Trump's Dismemberment of Bears Ears National Monument: Perspective from Indigenous Scholars," *Revelator*, December 5, 2017, https://therevelator.org/trump-bears-ears-indigenous-scholars/. For the importance and meaning of Bears Ears, see the excellent collection by Jacqueline Keeler, ed., *Edge of Morning: Native Voices Speak for the Bears Ears* (Salt Lake City: Torrey House Press, 2017).

25. "Secretary of Interior Orders Mashpee Wampanoag Reservation 'Disestablished,' Tribe Says," *WBUR News*, March 28, 2020, https://www.wbur.org/news/2020/03/28/mashpee-wampanoag-reservation-secretary-interior-land-trust.

26. "Mashpee Wampanoag Tribe Threatened with Land Disestablishment, Tribal Leaders Step in to Address Ongoing Land Issues and Threats to Sovereignty," Mashpee Wampanoag Tribe, March 30, 2020, https://mashpeewampanoagtribe-nsn.gov/news/2020/3/30/mashpee-wampanoag-tribe-threatened-with-land-disestablishment-tribal-leaders-step-in-to-address-ongoing-land-issues-and-threats-to-sovereignty. For more on the history of this decision and the court cases that undergird it, see "Secretary of Interior Orders Mashpee Wampanoag"; and Rory Taylor, "Trump Administration Revokes Reservation Status for Mashpee Wampanoag Tribe amid Coronavirus Crisis," *Vox*, April 2, 2020, https://www.vox.com/identities/2020/4/2/21204113/mashpee-wampanoag-tribe-trump-reservation-native-land.

27. See Levi Rickert, "House Passes Bill to Protect Mashpee Wampanoag Reservation," *Native News Online*, July 25, 2020, https://nativenewsonline.net/currents/house-passes-bill-to-protect-mashpee-wampanoag-reservation; and Ryan Spencer, "Trump Administration Appeals Court Decision That Favored Mashpee Wampanoag Tribe," *Mashpee Enterprise*, August 1, 2020, https://www.capenews.net/mashpee/news/trump-administration-appeals-court-decision-that-favored-mashpee-wampanoag-tribe/article_10c970c4-35f8-5706-9399-501eba4ac3dd.html.

28. Carl Prine, "Miramar Marine Museum Marks 75th Anniversary of Navajo Code," *San Diego Tribune*, August 27, 2017, https://www.sandiegouniontribune.com/military/sd-me-code-talker-20170827-story.html.

29. "The Bronco Buster," White House Historical Association, accessed July 20, 2020, https://www.whitehousehistory.org/photos/the-bronco-buster.

30. As quoted in Hermann Hagedorn, *Roosevelt in the Bad Lands* (New York: Roosevelt Memorial Association, 1921), 355.

31. Majerle Lister, "'The Only Way to Save the Land Is to Give It Back': A Critique of Settler Conservatism," Red Nation, July 23, 2018, https://therednation.org/2018/07/23/the-only-way-to-save-the-land-is-to-give-it-back-a-critique-of-settler-conservationism/; on the role

of Indigenous dispossession in creating national parks, see Dina Gilio-Whitaker, *As Long as Grass Grows: The Indigenous Fight for Environmental Justice, from Colonization to Standing Rock* (Boston: Beacon Press, 2019), 92–95.

32. For video of Trump's testimony, see "'They Don't Look Like Indians to Me': Donald Trump on Native American Casinos in 1993," *Washington Post*, July 1, 2016. The "They don't look like Indians to me" comment occurs at the 4:00 mark and the taxes comment at 5:10, https://www.washingtonpost.com/video/politics/they-dont-look-like-indians-to-me-donald -trump-on-native-american-casinos-in-1993/2016/07/01/20736038-3fd4-11e6-9e16 -4cf01a41decb_video.html?utm_term=.0315dd1200cb.

33. Dan Diamond, "Trump Challenges Native Americans' Historical Standing," *Politico*, April 22, 2018, https://www.politico.com/story/2018/04/22/trump-native-americans -historical-standing-492794; also, the Trump administration's effort here runs into conflict with the unanimous Supreme Court decision in Morton v. Mancari, 417 U.S. 535 (1974), a case concerning the BIA's policy preference of hiring Native people. In *Mancari*, the court determined that this was not racial discrimination because the BIA policy concerned a person's status as a citizen of their sovereign Native nation, not as part of a "race."

34. Courtney Parker, "'Paper Genocide': Trump's Political Maneuvers Could Rob Native America of Tribal Sovereignty, Culture, Health Care," Global Research: Centre for Research on Globalization, May 10, 2018, https://www.globalresearch.ca/paper-genocide-trumps -political-maneuvers-could-rob-native-america-of-tribal-sovereignty-culture-health-care /5639945.

35. Jodi Byrd, *The Transit of Empire: Indigenous Critiques of Colonialism* (Minneapolis: University of Minnesota Press, 2011), 202–203.

36. For the letter from ten U.S. senators protesting this Health and Human Services decision, see "Letter to Secretary Alex Azar," *Politico*, April 27, 2018, https://www.politico.com /f/?id=00000163-092f-da04-a1fb-1dffcc1d0001. For the Trump administration's modification of the policy in early 2019, see Rachana Pradhan, "Trump Exempts Most Tribes from Medicaid Work Rules," *Politico*, January 18, 2019, https://www.politico.com/story/2019/01 /18/trump-medicaid-work-rules-1099559.

37. For more on the history, context, and contemporary implications of the cases concerning the Indian Child Welfare Act, see Matthew L. M. Fletcher and Wenona T. Singel, "Indian Children and the Federal-Tribal Trust Relationship," *Nebraska Law Review* 95, no. 2 (2007): 896–964; Alleen Brown, "How a Right-Wing Attack on Protections for Native American Children Could Upend Indian Law," *Intercept*, June 17, 2019, https://theintercept .com/2019/06/17/indian-child-welfare-act-goldwater-institute-legal-battle/; and Rebecca Nagle, "Episode 8: The Next Battleground," *This Land*, podcast, July 22, 2019, https:// crooked.com/podcast/this-land-episode-8-the-next-battleground/.

38. For the full video of the gathering, with transcript, see "Full Replay: Navajo Code Talker Delivered a Beautiful Speech before President Trump Stole Show," *RealClearPolitics*, November 28, 2017, https://www.realclearpolitics.com/video/2017/11/28/full_replay _navajo_code_talker_delivered_a_beautiful_speech_before_president_trump_stole _show.html.

39. John Haltiwanger, "Who Are the Navajo Code Talkers? Trump Insults World War II Heroes with 'Pocahontas' Joke," *Newsweek*, November 27, 2017, https://www.newsweek .com/who-are-navajo-code-talkers-trump-insults-wwii-heroes-pocahontas-joke-723821;

Felicia Fonseca and Laurie Kellman, "Families of Navajo Code Talkers Decry Trump's Use of 'Pocahontas,'" *PBS Newshour*, November 28, 2017, https://www.pbs.org/newshour/politics /families-of-navajo-code-talkers-decry-trumps-use-of-pocahontas.

40. Darren R. Reid, *Native American Racism in the Age of Donald Trump: History and Contemporary Perspectives* (Cham, Switzerland: Palgrave Macmillan, 2020), 34.

41. "Donald Trump Repeatedly Calls Elizabeth Warren 'Pocahontas'—Video," *Guardian*, June 11, 2016, https://www.theguardian.com/us-news/video/2016/jun/11/donald-trump -repeatedly-elizabeth-warren-pocahontas-us-election-presidential-video.

42. Honor Sachs, "How Pocahontas—the Myth and the Slur—Props Up White Supremacy," *Washington Post*, October 16, 2018, https://www.washingtonpost.com/outlook/2018 /10/16/how-pocahontas-myth-slur-props-up-white-supremacy/?utm_term=.bfeada32aa8e.

43. Rebecca Nagle, "Op-ed: I Am a Cherokee Woman. Elizabeth Warren Is Not," *Think-Progress*, November 30, 2017, https://thinkprogress.org/elizabeth-warren-is-not-cherokee -c1ec6c91b696/?utm_campaign=trueAnthem:+Trending+Content&utm_content=5a20 a28b04d30173e0560243&utm_medium=trueAnthem&utm_source=twitter.

44. Ellen Gorsevski, "Native America Persists: Pocahontas versus Trump," *Journal of Multicultural Discourses* 13, no. 2 (2018): 170. See also Vincent Shilling, "The True Story of Pocahontas: Historical Myths versus Sad Reality," *Indian Country Today*, September 8, 2017, https://newsmaven.io/indiancountrytoday/archive/the-true-story-of-pocahontas -historical-myths-versus-sad-reality-WRzmVMu47E6GuzoLudQ3QQ/.

45. Gorsevski, "Native America Persists," 164, 170.

46. For the audio and transcript of his comments, see "US Election: Full Transcript of Donald Trump's Obscene Videotape," BBC, October 9, 2016, https://www.bbc.com/news /election-us-2016-37595321.

47. Isabel Altamirano-Jiménez, "Trump, NAFTA, and Indigenous Resistance in Turtle Island," Suppl., *Theory & Event* 20, no. 1 (January 2017): 3.

48. For more, please see the political work and documentation around this matter organized by the Coalition to Stop Violence against Indigenous Women, www.csvanw.org/mmiw/; see also the Red Nation's statement on the annual May 5 day of remembrance of missing and murdered Indigenous women, accessed July 30, 2020, https://therednation.org/2019 /05/05/statement-on-may-5-mmiw-remembrance-day/.

49. Chris Finley, "Decolonizing the Queer Native Body (and Recovering the Native Bull-Dyke): Bringing 'Sexy Back' and out of Native Studies' Closet," in *Queer Indigenous Studies: Critical Interventions in Theory, Politics, and Literature*, ed. Qwo-Li Driskill et al. (Tucson: University of Arizona Press, 2011), 35. See also Rayna Green, "The Pocahontas Perplex: The Image of Indian Women in American Culture," *Massachusetts Review* 16, no. 4 (1975): 698–715.

50. Joanne Barker, "Looking for Warrior Woman (beyond Pocahontas)," in *This Bridge We Call Home: Radical Visions for Transformation*, ed. Gloria E. Anzaldúa and Analouise Keating (London: Routledge, 2002), 316–317.

51. Sarah Deer, *The Beginning and End of Rape: Confronting Sexual Violence in Native America* (Minneapolis: University of Minnesota Press, 2015), 78. See also *CBC News*, accessed July 30, 2019, https://www.cbc.ca/news/politics/resource-development-mmiwg-1.5164568.

52. Kirsty Kirkup, "Safety Concerns for Indigenous Women in Resource Development: MMIWG Inquiry," *CBC News*, June 6, 2009, https://www.cbc.ca/news/politics/resource

-development-mmiwg-1.5164568. See the full report of the inquiry here, accessed July 30, 2019: https://www.mmiwg-ffada.ca/final-report/.

53. For an excellent study of Indigenous people's migrant and border experiences, especially those migrating from Latin and South America to the United States, see Shannon Speed, *Incarcerated Stories* (Durham, NC: University of North Carolina Press, 2019).

54. Greg Grandin, *The End of the Myth: From the Frontier to the Border Wall in the Mind of America* (New York: Metropolitan Books, 2019), 275.

55. For videos of the students surrounding and mocking Phillips and of a student saying, "Land gets stolen. That's how it works," see Jacqueline Keeler, "'Land Gets Stolen. That's How It Works,'" *Sierra*, January 23, 2019, https://www.sierraclub.org/sierra/land-gets-stolen-s -how-it-works-native-covington-catholic-lincoln-memorial.

56. Alyosha Goldstein, "Stolen Land, Standing Ground, and the Viral Spectacle of White Entitlement: 'Land Gets Stolen, That's How It Works,'" Public Seminar, April 4, 2019, http:// www.publicseminar.org/2019/04/stolen-land-standing-ground-and-the-viral-spectacle-of -white-entitlement/?fbclid=IwAR2v3fTf8lyFfEZsqDRk5dN4WrNcAz9a54xHVZcFUs7y5 _Q-UyVxtQNhGKg.

57. For the interview with Nathan Phillips, see "The MAGA Hat–Wearing Teens Who Taunted a Native American Elder Could Be Expelled," *3ChicsPolitico*, January 19, 2019, https:// 3chicspolitico.com/2019/01/19/the-maga-hat-wearing-teens-who-taunted-a-native-american -elder-could-be-expelled/.

58. Alyssa Mt. Pleasant and David Chang, "The Horror of Trump's Wounded Knee Tweet," *Politico*, January 17, 2019, https://www.politico.com/magazine/story/2019/01/17/the -horror-of-trumps-wounded-knee-tweet-224024.

59. Mt. Pleasant and Chang, "Horror of Trump's Tweet."

60. Dan Desai Martin, "Trump Admits Cruelty Was Always the Point of Family Separa- tions," *SoCalDaily Media*, October 15, 2018, https://socaldailymedia.com/family-separation -trump-admits-cruelty-was-point/.

61. Christina Leza, "For Native Americans, United States-Mexico Border Is an 'Imaginary Line,'" *Indian Country Today*, March 21, 2019, https://newsmaven.io/indiancountrytoday /opinion/for-native-americans-united-states-mexico-border-is-an-imaginary-line-e4cMG bo0GUuarEjHt8amZg/.

62. Altamirano-Jiménez, "Trump, NAFTA," 5–6. For more on the Tohono O'odham and other Indigenous nations' political struggle over the border, see Eileen Luna-Firebaugh, "The Border Crossed Us: Border Crossing Issues of the Indigenous Peoples of America," *Wicazo Sa Review* 17, no. 1 (Spring 2002): 159–181.

63. Margo Tamez, "On Indigenous Resistance to the U.S.-Mexico Border Wall," in *Speaking of Indigenous Politics: Conversations with Activists, Scholars, and Tribal Leaders*, ed. J. Kēhaulani Kauanui (Minneapolis: University of Minnesota Press, 2018), 293.

64. Tamez, "On Indigenous Resistance," 298.

65. Tamez, 302.

66. India Reed Bowers, Margo Tamez (Lipan Apache), Michael Paul Hill (San Carlos Apache), and Lorraine Garcia (Chihene Nde), "Letter to Committee on the Elimination of Racial Discrimination (CERD), Re: Follow Up, Urgent Action/Early Warning, U.S.A. Ex- ecutive Order to Further Construct US-Mexico Border Wall," Apache Ndé Nneé Working Group, April 30, 2017, http://iosde.org/uploads/3/5/1/9/35199981/apache_nde_nnee

_working_group_endorsement_of_tamez_letter_to_cerd__4-2017_.pdf (emphasis in original).

67. Aaron Miguel Cantú, "Down in the Valley: How Trump's Border Wall Perpetuates the Legacy of Colonialism in the Rio Grande," *Intercept*, March 31, 2019, https://theintercept .com/2019/03/31/border-wall-rio-grande-valley/.

68. For evidence regarding Crusius's repeated use of the language of invasion and the *great replacement* theory—that nonwhite people will replace white people in the United States—and its direct link to Trump and his supporters, especially in the right-wing media, see Jeremy W. Peters, Michael M. Grynbaum, Keith Collins, Rich Harris, and Rumsey Taylor, "How the El Paso Killer Echoed the Incendiary Words of Conservative Media Stars," *New York Times*, August 11, 2019, https://www.nytimes.com/interactive/2019/08/11/business /media/el-paso-killer-conservative-media.html.

69. The Patrick Crusius manifesto is reprinted/excerpted in "Parts of the Manifesto from the White Supremacist El Paso Terrorist Shows Anti-Mexican, Anti-immigrant Radicalization," *Latino Rebels*, August 3, 2019, https://www.latinorebels.com/2019/08/03/mani festoelpasoterrorist/.

70. HoSang and Lowndes, *Producers, Parasites, Patriots*, 130, 133.

71. HoSang and Lowndes, 132.

72. HoSang and Lowndes, 148.

73. For reporting on the groups that were identified as part of the invasion of the Capitol building, see Sabrina Tavernise and Matthew Rosenberg, "These Are the Rioters Who Stormed the Nation's Capitol," *New York Times*, January 8, 2021, https://www.nytimes.com /2021/01/07/us/names-of-rioters-capitol.html.

74. "President Donald J. Trump Keeps His Promise to Open U.S. Embassy in Jerusalem, Israel," White House, May 14, 2018, https://www.whitehouse.gov/briefings-statements /president-donald-j-trump-keeps-promise-open-u-s-embassy-jerusalem-israel/.

75. For example, as Noura Erakat notes: "In 1981, Israel unilaterally annexed the Golan Heights. The Ronald Reagan administration rebuked Israel's annexation and declared it 'null and void,' not least because it violates the international principle prohibiting the acquisition of territory by force." Noura Erakat, "Trump's Golan Heights Tweet Disregards History, Law and Ethics," *Truthout*, March 24, 2019, https://truthout.org/articles/trumps -golan-heights-tweet-disregards-history-law-and-ethics/.

76. See "Immigration and Customs Enforcement (ICE) and Deadly Exchange: The US-Israel Military Relationship and the U.S.-Mexico Border," Deadly Exchange, accessed December 20, 2020, https://deadlyexchange.org/immigration-and-customs-enforcement-ice -and-deadly-exchange/; and "Trump: Is a Border Wall Effective? Ask Israel," *CBN News*, December 17, 2018, https://www1.cbn.com/cbnnews/us/2018/december/trump-is-a-border -wall-effective-ask-israel.

77. For more on the work of the Red Nation, see, accessed May 2, 2019, https://thered nation.org/.

78. Emily Crane, "White Nationalists Storm Washington D.C. Bookstore Chanting 'This Is Our Land' to Protest Launch of Book on Politics of Racial Resentment," *Daily Mail*, April 28, 2019, https://www.dailymail.co.uk/news/article-6969935/White-nationalists-storm -Washington-DC-book-launch.html.

Conclusion

1. Erica Chenoweth and Jeremy Pressman, "This Is What We Learned by Counting the Women's Marches," *Washington Post*, February 7, 2017, https://www.washingtonpost.com /news/monkey-cage/wp/2017/02/07/this-is-what-we-learned-by-counting-the-womens -marches/?utm_term=.0c4e008f3f62.

2. Tim Wallace and Alicia Parlapiano, "Crowd Scientists Say Women's March in Washington Had 3 Times as Many People as Trump's Inauguration," *New York Times*, January 22, 2017, https://www.nytimes.com/interactive/2017/01/22/us/politics/womens-march-trump -crowd-estimates.html; and Nancy Benac, "Survey: DC Women's March Drew Many First-Time Protestors," *APNEWS*, January 26, 2017, https://apnews.com/712f88ea46aa40babae9 9702514b3344.

3. "Angela Davis: Trump Is a Wake-Up Call to Americans," *Newsmax*, February 27, 2017, http://www.newsmax.com/US/Angela-Davis-Trump-Wake-Up-Call-Americans/2017/02 /27/id/775833/. To be clear, Davis is making an observation about the country, not herself. Davis, of course, does not need a wake-up call regarding the past and present of oppression and authoritarianism in the United States.

4. Jonathan Rosa and Yarimar Bonilla, "Deprovincializing Trump, Decolonizing Diversity, and Unsettling Anthropology," *American Ethnologist* 44, no. 2 (May 2017): 201.

5. LaDonna Brave Bull Allard, "Why the Founder of Standing Rock Sioux Camp Can't Forget the Whitestone Massacre," *Yes! Magazine*, September 3, 2016, http://www.yesmagazine .org/people-power/why-the-founder-of-standing-rock-sioux-camp-cant-forget-the -whitestone-massacre-20160903.

6. Mishuana R. Goeman, "Disrupting a Settler-Colonial Grammar of Place," in *Theorizing Native Studies*, ed. Audra Simpson and Andrea Smith (Durham, NC: Duke University Press, 2014), 245.

7. Sameer Rao, "Mass. Mayor to Bobby Jindal: 'Come and Get Me,'" *Colorlines*, August 4, 2015, https://www.colorlines.com/articles/mass-mayor-bobby-jindal-come-and-get-me.

8. Paul Garland, "Removing the College Involvement 'Research Asterisk': Identifying and Rethinking Predictors of American Indian College Student Involvement" (PhD diss., University of Maryland, 2010), 1, https://drum.lib.umd.edu/bitstream/handle/1903/10781 /Garland_umd_0117E_11416.pdf?sequence=1&isAllowed=y; see also Paul Garland, "Review of the Book *Serving Native American Students: New Directions for Student Services*," *Journal of College Student Development* 48, (2007): 612–614.

9. Eve Tuck and K. Wayne Yang, "Decolonization Is Not a Metaphor," *Decolonization* 1, no. 1 (2012): 22, 23.

10. Roxanne Dunbar-Ortiz persuasively argues that the idea of the United States as a "nation of immigrants" is a "convenient myth developed as a response to the 1960s movements against colonialism, neocolonialism, and white supremacy." See her essay "Stop Saying This Is a Nation of Immigrants!," *MROnline*, May 29, 2006, https://mronline.org/2006/05 /29/stop-saying-this-is-a-nation-of-immigrants/.

11. Hillary Clinton, "Full Text: Hillary Clinton's DNC Speech," *Politico*, July 28, 2016, http://www.politico.com/story/2016/07/full-text-hillary-clintons-dnc-speech-226410.

12. In the weeks prior to the Democratic National Convention, on July 5, 2016, Alton Sterling was killed by police in Baton Rouge, Louisiana, and on July 6, 2016, Philando Castile

was killed by police in a suburb of Saint Paul, Minnesota. The shooting and death of both men were recorded on video and became the source of increased BLM demonstrations in these locales and nationwide in the following weeks.

13. The 2016 Democratic National Convention in Philadelphia lasted from July 25 to 28. On July 25, 2016, "the U.S. Army Corps of Engineers approved three easements for water crossings for the Dakota pipeline at Sakakawea, the Mississippi River, and the ancestral site for the Standing Rock Sioux tribe, Lake Oahe." Two days later, lawyers for the Standing Rock Nation filed injunctions against the Army Corp of Engineers. See "#NoDAPL: Full Timeline of Dakota Access Pipeline Protest," *TrueNews*, December 1, 2016, http://www.trunews .com/article/nodapl-full-timeline-of-dakota-access-pipeline-protest.

14. Kim TallBear, "Statement on Elizabeth Warren's DNA test," Twitter, October 15, 2018, https://twitter.com/kimtallbear/status/1052017467021651969?lang=en.

15. Jacqueline Keeler, "The Story of America: Warren's Family Stories in an America Built on Trumpian Triumphalism," *TiyospayeNow*, February 11, 2019, http://tiyospayenow .blogspot.com/2019/05/the-story-of-america-warrens-family.html.

16. Rebecca Nagle, "Op-ed: I Am a Cherokee Woman. Elizabeth Warren Is Not," *Think-Progress*, November 30, 2017, https://thinkprogress.org/elizabeth-warren-is-not-cherokee -c1ec6c91b696/?utm_campaign=trueAnthem:+Trending+Content&utm_content =5a20a28b04d30173e0560243&utm_medium=trueAnthem&utm_source=twitter.

17. For a valuable resource of materials that directly concern or provide historical, political, and theoretical context to the Warren case, and thus others like it, see Adrienne Keene, Rebecca Nagle, and Joseph Pierce, *Critical Ethnic Studies* (blog), "Syllabus: Elizabeth Warren, Cherokee Citizenship, and DNA Testing," December 19, 2018, http://www.criticaleth- nicstudiesjournal.org/blog/2018/12/19/syllabus-elizabeth-warren-cherokee-citizenship -and-dna-testing.

18. For full text, see S. Res. 14, 1st Sess., April 30, 2009, https://www.congress.gov/bill /111th-congress/senate-joint-resolution/14/text. The resolution was signed into law on December 19, 2009, as Section 8113 in the FY 2010 Defense Appropriations Act, H.R. 3326, Public Law No. 111–118. For a critique of the lack of public attention to the resolution, see Lisa Balk King, "A Tree Fell in the Forest: The U.S. Apologized to Native Americans and No One Heard a Sound," *Indian Country Today*, December 3, 2011, http://indiancountry todaymedianetwork.com/ict_sbc/a-tree-fell-in-the-forest-the-u-s-apologized-to-native -americans-and-no-one-heard-a-sound.

19. Layli Long Soldier, "(1) Whereas Statements," in *Whereas* (Minneapolis: Graywolf Press, 2017), 79.

20. Layli Long Soldier, "38," in *Whereas*, 53.

21. Long Soldier, "(1) Whereas Statements," 79.

22. Layli Long Soldier, "(3) Disclaimer," in *Whereas*, 101.

23. Long Soldier, "(1) Whereas Statements," 71.

24. Long Soldier, 74.

25. Long Soldier, "38," 53.

26. Long Soldier, 49.

27. Christina Sharpe, *In the Wake: On Blackness and Being* (Minneapolis: University of Minnesota Press, 2016), 18.

28. Kelly Hayes, "Where Movements Meet: Black Lives Matter Organizers Visit #NoDAPL," *Truthout*, September 2, 2016, http://www.truth-out.org/news/item/37468-where-movements -meet-black-lives-matter-organizers-visit-nodapl.

29. One such example that refuses this dichotomy is the Black/Land Project, accessed August 1, 2019, http://www.blacklandproject.org/, which "gathers and analyzes stories about the relationship between Black people, land and place." The project's stated mission includes: "We identify and amplify conversations happening inside Black communities (including African-Americans, Caribbean-Americans and African immigrants) about the relationship between Black people, land, and place in order to share their powerful traditions of resourcefulness, resilience and regeneration." This project does not reproduce governmental nor capitalistic/commodified relationships of people to land and life but rather tells stories that would fit into a relationality framework. The organizers of the Black/Land Project have also worked with Indigenous scholars and activists in studies of Black and Indigenous land relationships, encounters, contestations, and collaborations. For more see Eve Tuck, Mistinguette Smith, Allison M. Guess, Tavia Benjamin, and Brian K. Jones, "Geo-theorizing Black/Land," *Departures in Qualitative Research* 3, no. 1 (Spring 2014): 52–74.

30. Black Lives Matter, "Black Lives Matter Stands in Solidarity with Water Protectors at Standing Rock," Official #BlackLivesMatter Organization, September 2016, http://black livesmatter.com/solidarity-with-standing-rock/.

31. Zoé Samudzi and William C. Anderson, *As Black as Resistance: Finding the Conditions for Liberation* (Chico, CA: AK Press, 2018), 6.

32. Samudzi and Anderson, *Black as Resistance*, 13.

33. Samudzi and Anderson, 31.

34. Samudzi and Anderson, 114–115.

35. Samudzi and Anderson, 53.

36. Samudzi and Anderson, 56.

37. Cedric Robinson, *Black Marxism: The Making of the Black Radical Tradition* (London: Zed Books, 1983), 183, 196.

38. Cedric Robinson, *Black Movements in America* (New York: Routledge, 1997), 20.

39. Robinson, *Black Movements in America*, 53.

40. Samudzi and Anderson, *Black as Resistance*, 104.

41. To be clear, these lessons include those regarding moments when there was no collaboration but rather conflict and the perpetuation or acceptance of the oppression of one group by the other. Yael Ben-zvi notes this dynamic in nineteenth-century clashes between "Indigenous peoples' acceptance of settlers' perception of slaves as property and African Americans' acceptance of settler's perception of Indigenous peoples as vanishing savages." Yael Ben-zvi, *Native Land Talk: Indigenous and Arrivant Rights Theories* (Hanover, NH: Dartmouth College Press, 2018), 209.

42. Kyle Mays, "Song 'Let's Meet by the Water' Invites Support at Indigenous Water Ceremony in Flint," *Indian Country Today*, April 14, 2016, https://indiancountrymedianetwork .com/news/native-news/song-lets-meet-by-the-water-invites-support-at-indigenous-water -ceremony-in-flint/.

43. Matt Agorist, "Police Are Killing Native Americans at Higher Rate than Any Race, and Nobody Is Talking About It," Free Thought Project, August 2, 2015, http://thefree

thoughtproject.com/police-killing-native-americans-higher-rate-race-talking/. For more on the police abuse, surveillance, and incarceration of Indigenous people, see Lakota People's Law Project, *Native Lives Matter*, February 2015, https://s3-us-west-1.amazonaws.com/lakota -peoples-law/uploads/Native-Lives-Matter-PDF.pdf.

44. Leanne Betasamosake Simpson, "An Indigenous View of #BlackLivesMatter," *Yes! Magazine*, December 5, 2014, http://www.yesmagazine.org/peace-justice/indigenous-view -black-lives-matter-leanne-simpson.

45. Leanne Betasamosake Simpson, "Caribous and Ghosts," in *The Accident of Being Lost: Songs and Stories* (Toronto: House of Anansi Press, 2017), 34.

46. Julia Craven, "Black Lives Matter Toronto Stands by Pride Parade Shutdown," *Huffington Post*, July 6, 2016, https://www.huffpost.com/entry/black-lives-matter-toronto-pride _n_577c15aee4b0a629c1ab0ab4.

47. Simpson, "Caribous and Ghosts," 34.

48. See Ontario Institute for Studies in Education, "We Are All Treaty People," University of Toronto, accessed December 20, 2020, https://www.oise.utoronto.ca/abed101/we -are-all-treaty-people/.

49. Tara Williamson, "We Are All Treaty People," *Decolonization: Indigeneity, Education, and Society* (blog), December 24, 2012, https://decolonization.wordpress.com/2012/12/24 /we-are-all-treaty-people/.

50. "No One Is Illegal," *Rabble.ca*, accessed December 20, 2020, http://rabble.ca/toolkit /rabblepedia/no-one-illegal.

51. "About Us—Read More about Our Vision Here," No One Is Illegal-Vancouver Coast Salish Territories, https://noii-van.resist.ca/about-us/. For a link to the organizations in four cities (Montreal, Ottawa, Toronto, and Vancouver) in Canada, see, accessed December 20, 2020, http://www.nooneisillegal.org/.

52. Harsha Walia and Andrew Dilts, "Dismantle and Transform: On Abolition, Decolonization, and Insurgent Politics," *Abolition*, no. 1 (2018): 19. See also Harsha Walia, *Undoing Border Imperialism* (Chico, CA: AK Press, 2013).

53. See "CAN Statement of Solidarity with Migrant Caravan and Call to Action," Campus Action Network, November 29, 2018, http://campusantifascistnetwork.com/.

54. For this history, see Afua Cooper, *The Hanging of Angelique: The Untold Story of Canadian Slavery and the Burning of Old Montreal* (Athens: University of Georgia Press, 2007); and Kyle G. Brown, "Canada's Slavery Secret: The Whitewashing of 200 Years of Enslavement," *CBC News*, February 18, 2019, https://www.cbc.ca/radio/ideas/canada-s-slavery-secret -the-whitewashing-of-200-years-of-enslavement-1.4726313.

55. *Reclaiming Power and Place: The Final Report of the National Inquiry into Missing and Murdered Indigenous Women and Girls*, National Inquiry into Missing and Murdered Indigenous Women and Girls, 2019, https://www.mmiwg-ffada.ca/final-report/?fbclid=IwAR1g WPMLt-6mp8kpJZnyRWesirIysrp7UsxDNuPjwH2igxUhjy4L2OhTP20; and Jorge Barrera, "Canada Aimed to 'Destroy Indigenous People': The MMIWG Inquiry's Case for Genocide," *CBC News*, June 3, 2019, https://www.cbc.ca/news/indigenous/genocide-case -inquiry-1.5160941.

56. See "Black Women and Sexual Violence," National Organization for Women, accessed December 20, 2020, https://now.org/wp-content/uploads/2018/02/Black-Women -and-Sexual-Violence-6.pdf; Maya Finoh and Jasmine Sankofa, "The Legal System Has

Failed Black Girls, Women, and Non-binary Survivors of Violence," American Civil Liberties Union, January 28, 2019, https://www.aclu.org/blog/racial-justice/race-and-criminal-justice/legal-system-has-failed-black-girls-women-and-non; see also Treva B. Lindsey. "Ain't Nobody Got Time for That: Anti-Black Girl Violence in the Era of #SayHerName," *Urban Education* 53, no. 2 (2018): 162–175.

57. National Organization for Women, "Black Women and Sexual Violence."

58. Sharpe, *In the Wake*, 90.

59. Sharpe, 97.

60. Sharpe, 101.

61. For a concrete "Land Back" study and steps for the return of jurisdiction over territories to Indigenous peoples, see *Land Back: A Yellowhead Institute Red Paper* (Toronto: Yellowhead Institute, 2019), https://redpaper.yellowheadinstitute.org/wp-content/uploads/2019/10/red-paper-report-final.pdf.

62. The Red Nation collective devised the Red Deal to radically expand upon the idea of the Green New Deal, with an aim of directly opposing and conceiving of a world beyond capitalism and colonialism, in particular. See The Red Nation, *The Red Deal: Indigenous Action to Save Our Earth* (Brooklyn, NY: Common Notions, 2021).

63. Layli Long Soldier, "Epigraph," in *Whereas*, 5.

Index